MONSTER BOOK OF BASIC DECLARER PLAY

Dave Huggett

and

Stephen Cashmore

B.T. Batsford • London

First published 2003

ISBN 0 7134 8882 4

A CIP catalogue record for this book is available from the British Library.

Typeset in the U.K. by Ruth Edmondson
Printed in the U.K. by Creative Print & Design, Ebbw Vale,Wales

for the publishers

B T Batsford, The Chrysalis Building, Bramley Road, London W10 6SP

An imprint of Chrysalis Books Group plc

Distributed in the United States and Canada by Sterling Publishing Co., 387 Park Avenue South, New York, NY 10016, USA

Editor: Elena Jeronimidis

INTRODUCTION

An enormous number of books have been written on declarer play but none of them, it seems to the present authors, have been designed specifically to give practice for beginners. There are textbooks which lay out various techniques, giving examples, and sometimes posing questions for the reader – but the questions are few and far between. There are books consisting entirely of declarer-play problems – but all are for experienced if not expert players.

This book is different.

If you are an experienced player, put it down. If you have been playing for more than about a year and a half, put it down. This book is written for *beginners*. It consists of 240 deals where very basic techniques will bring home the contract. It gives beginners the chance to practise counting up tricks and losers, planning the order in which to play the cards, and working out where extra tricks are to come from. In fact, it gives beginners the chance to practise looking at a printed hand and work out how it should be played – in itself an important stepping stone on the way to more advanced treatises.

The book is divided into three sections:

- Section 1 contains 80 no-trump deals, and is headed by an introduction explaining how to approach planning the play of a no-trump contract. Alongside the solution to each deal is a table showing Top Tricks Available (TTA). The play of the hand usually revolves around working out how to bridge the gap between top tricks available and the number of tricks required for the contract.

- Section 2 contains 80 deals to be played in suit contracts, also headed by an introduction on how to plan the play. This time, the table alongside each solution shows the number of losers rather than the number of top tricks available (TLT – Total Losing Tricks). The play of the hand usually revolves around how to reduce the number of potential losers down to the number allowed by the level of the contract.

- Section 3 contains the remaining 80 deals, a mixture of contracts. By this time the reader should be completely familiar with the idea of totalling top tricks available, or potential losers, so the tables are not included. However, the deals are slightly more difficult and the extra space released is utilised by making the explanations as clear as possible!

So, if you are a beginner, why should you bother to work through this book? There are four reasons. One, you will learn how to focus on the main problems of playing contracts – keeping track of winners and losers, and being in the right hand at the right time. Two, you will gain confidence and not panic when confronted with playing a hand at the table. Three, you will gain experience of how to read a bridge book, so that you can move on to more advanced topics. Four – last but by no means least – since you have obviously been bitten by the bridge bug, you will enjoy it!

Dave Huggett and Stephen Cashmore
2003

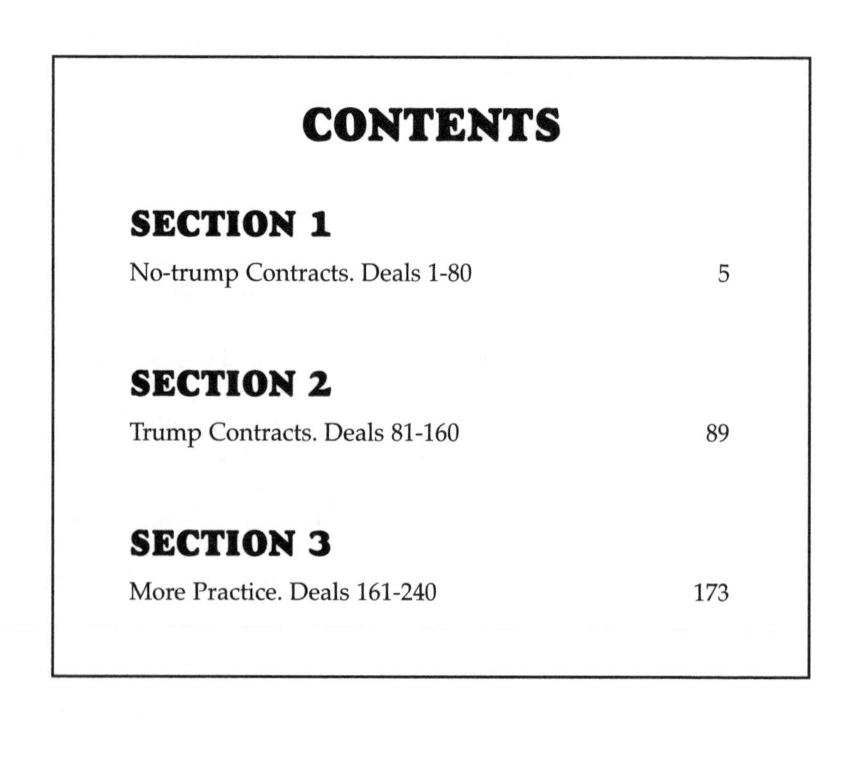

CONTENTS

SECTION 1
NO-TRUMP CONTRACTS

NO-TRUMP CONTRACTS

In this section you are invited to take the helm in a variety of no-trump contracts. In every case you should count up how many tricks you can take immediately and, if you fall short, figure out where you can make up that shortfall. This is the normal way to plan no-trump contracts, and you will find when you turn to the solutions page that each answer has a small box alongside it showing 'Top Tricks Available'.

If the number of top tricks available (TTA) is enough for your contract, then there is very little to think about, other than making sure that you are in the right place to cash your top tricks. For example:

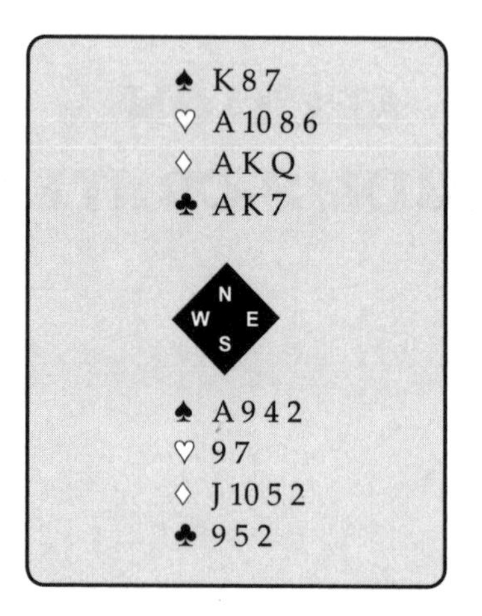

On this deal you are in a contract of 3NT and the opening lead is ♠Q. You count up your top tricks – two spades, one heart, four diamonds and two clubs. That makes nine, so all should be well. You win with ♠A, cross over to dummy with, say, ♣A and play off all dummy's beautiful top cards. That comes to eight tricks and ◇J in your own hand should be the ninth . . . only you have no way across to your own hand! That's right, you should have won the first trick with ♠K in dummy. Now you can cash all dummy's winners, then cross to ♠A to make the contract with ◇J.

Of course, sometimes the number of top tricks falls short of the number required for the contract. In that case you have to cast around for a source of extra tricks. If that means you have to lose the lead at some stage, then it is usually better to lose it early rather than later. If you don't . . .

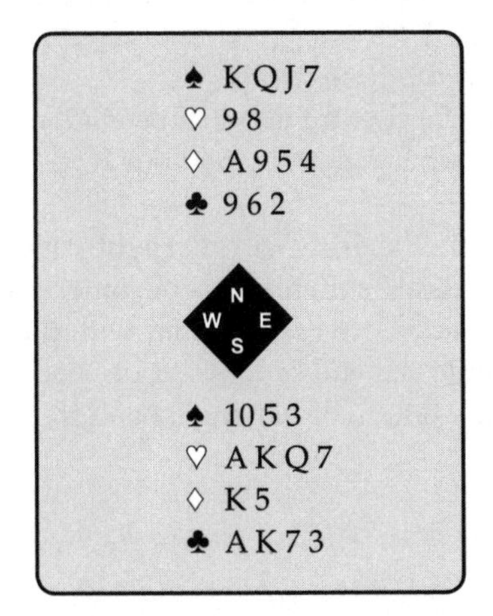

You are in 3NT again and the opening lead is ♡5. TTA = three hearts, two diamonds and two clubs, a total of seven. Where are the extra two tricks coming from? Spades, of course. Once the defence has taken ♠A you can capture three spade tricks, more than enough for the contract.

So you confidently win the top three hearts, the top diamonds and the top clubs, then lead a spade to 'knock out' ♠A. All would be well if the defenders continued spades but, alas, they now cash two hearts, two diamonds and a club. You end up with seven tricks – the same top tricks you started with. Disaster! What went wrong?

What went wrong is the way you cashed all the top tricks first. By doing that, you removed all your 'stoppers' in hearts, diamonds and clubs. You allowed the defenders' cards in those suits to become winners. See the difference if you play to knock out ♠A immediately. You win Trick 1 with a top heart, and immediately play spades. A defender wins with ♠A and . . . and what? You still have top hearts, top diamonds and top clubs. Not to mention top spades. You have all four suits 'stopped'. The defence has nowhere to go and you end up making ten tricks in comfort.

The deals in this section will take you through counting up tricks, working out where extra tricks will come from, communication between declarer and dummy's hands, knocking out stoppers, finessing and counting how many cards have gone in a suit. It sounds a lot, doesn't it? But all of these techniques arise from a simple three-step process which you should apply in all no-trump contracts:

- count your top tricks available
- work out where extra tricks (if needed) can come from
- decide on what order to play your cards

As you work through, the deals will get slightly more difficult. But not by much. All the deals are suitable for a beginner – for someone who is learning the game and is not very familiar with playing the cards. But by the time you get to the end of this section, you should be perfectly comfortable with the notion of playing a hand in no-trumps.

Good luck!

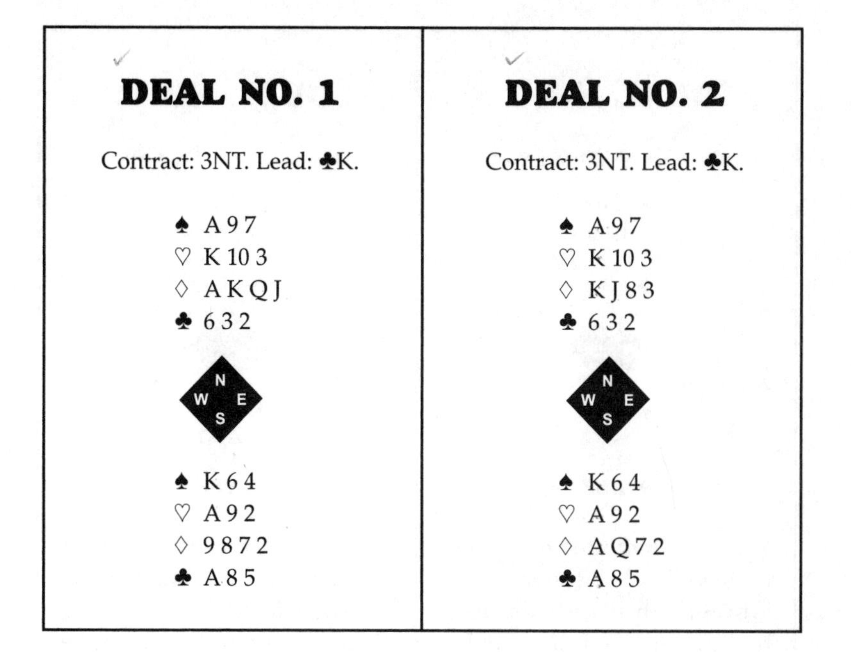

DEAL NO. 1

Contract: 3NT. Lead: ♣K.

♠ A 9 7
♡ K 10 3
♢ A K Q J
♣ 6 3 2

N
W E
S

♠ K 6 4
♡ A 9 2
♢ 9 8 7 2
♣ A 8 5

DEAL NO. 2

Contract: 3NT. Lead: ♣K.

♠ A 9 7
♡ K 10 3
♢ K J 8 3
♣ 6 3 2

N
W E
S

♠ K 6 4
♡ A 9 2
♢ A Q 7 2
♣ A 8 5

DEAL NO. 1

Contract: 3NT. Lead: ♣K.

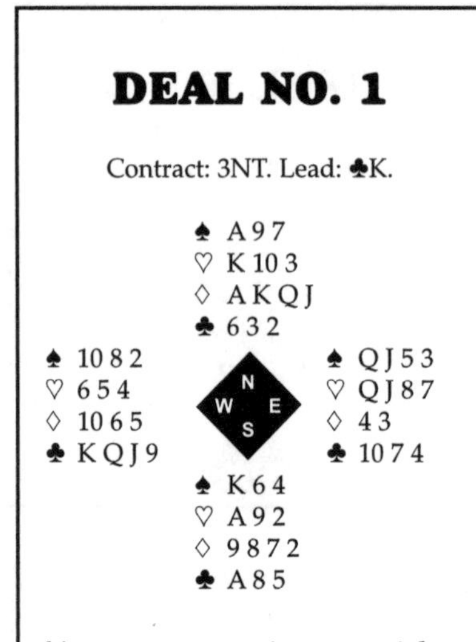

You can count nine top tricks, so there should be no problem. Win ♣A, then cash the four top diamonds followed by ♡A-K and ♠A-K. Now nothing should go wrong and it does not matter in which order you decide to cash your tricks.

♠	2
♡	2
♢	4
♣	1
TTA	9

DEAL NO. 2

Contract: 3NT. Lead: ♣K.

This is really the same as *Deal 1* but here the diamond honours are shared between North and South. Win ♣A, then cash the four top diamonds followed by ♡A-K and ♠A-K. Nothing should go wrong provided that you do not accidentally play two diamond honours on the same trick.

♠	2
♡	2
♢	4
♣	1
TTA	9

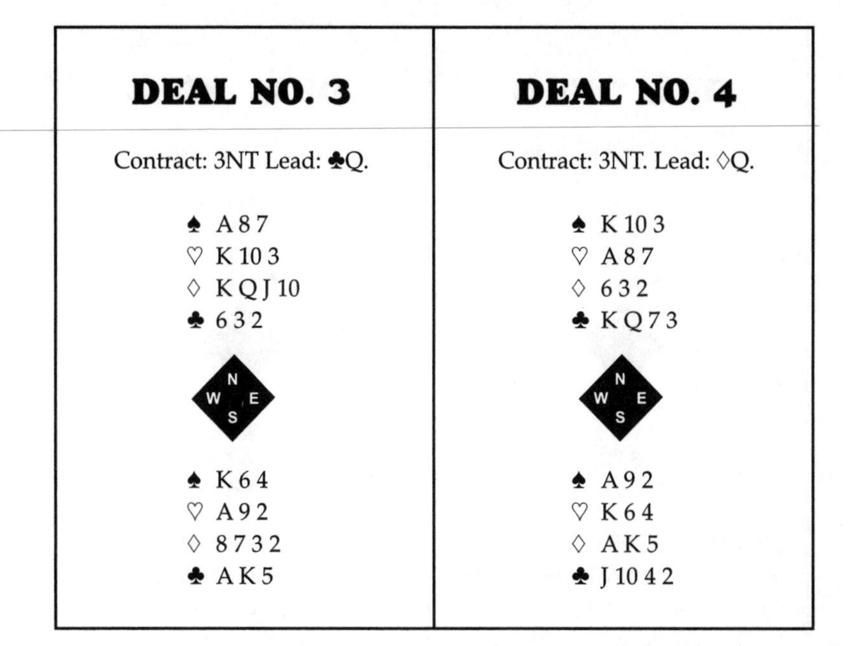
DEAL NO. 3
Contract: 3NT Lead: ♣Q.
♠ A 8 7
♡ K 10 3
♢ K Q J 10
♣ 6 3 2
N
W E
S
♠ K 6 4
♡ A 9 2
♢ 8 7 3 2
♣ A K 5
DEAL NO. 4
Contract: 3NT. Lead: ♢Q.
♠ K 10 3
♡ A 8 7
♢ 6 3 2
♣ K Q 7 3
N
W E
S
♠ A 9 2
♡ K 6 4
♢ A K 5
♣ J 10 4 2

DEAL NO. 3

This time TTA only amounts to 6, but the diamond suit should provide the extra three tricks you need. Win ♣A and then play a diamond straight away to dislodge the defenders' ace. Once ◇A has gone, you have three diamond tricks and the A-K of the other three suits. It would be a mistake to play the aces and kings first, because that means you can no longer stop those suits and when the defenders win ◇A they would be able to cash tricks to put you down.

♠	2
♡	2
◇	0
♣	2
TTA	6

DEAL NO. 4

Again TTA = 6, and this time it is the clubs which come to the rescue. Win ◇A and play clubs straight away to force out the defenders' ace. You can either play ♣J from hand, or lead a low club towards ♣K-Q in dummy. It does not matter which honour you decide to play first, as long as you do not accidentally play two honours on the same trick. As with *Deal 3*, it would be a mistake to play the A-K combinations first.

♠	2
♡	2
◇	2
♣	0
TTA	6

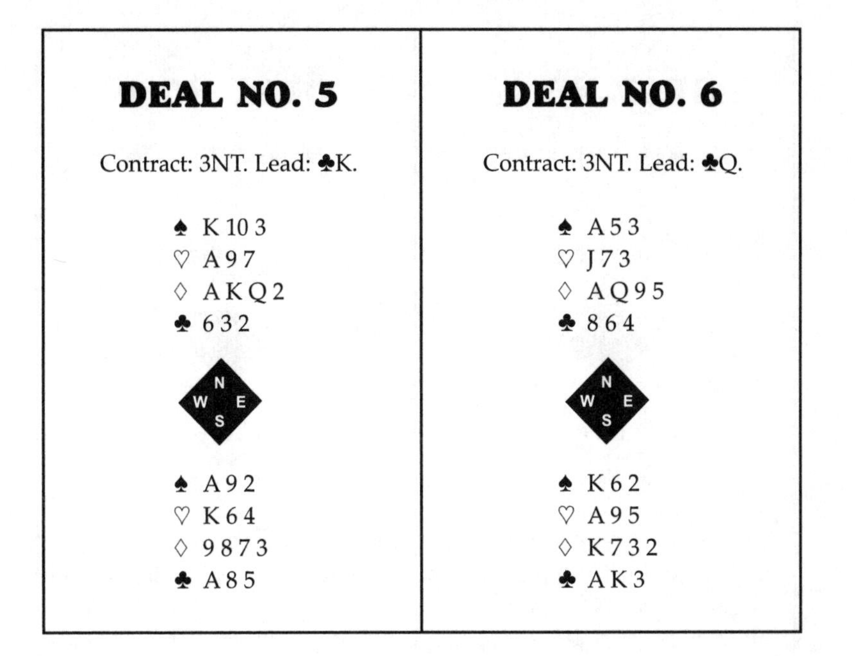
DEAL NO. 5
Contract: 3NT. Lead: ♣K.
♠ K 10 3
♡ A 9 7
♢ A K Q 2
♣ 6 3 2
N
W E
S
♠ A 9 2
♡ K 6 4
♢ 9 8 7 3
♣ A 8 5
DEAL NO. 6
Contract: 3NT. Lead: ♣Q.
♠ A 5 3
♡ J 7 3
♢ A Q 9 5
♣ 8 6 4
N
W E
S
♠ K 6 2
♡ A 9 5
♢ K 7 3 2
♣ A K 3

DEAL NO. 5

Contract: 3NT. Lead: ♣K.

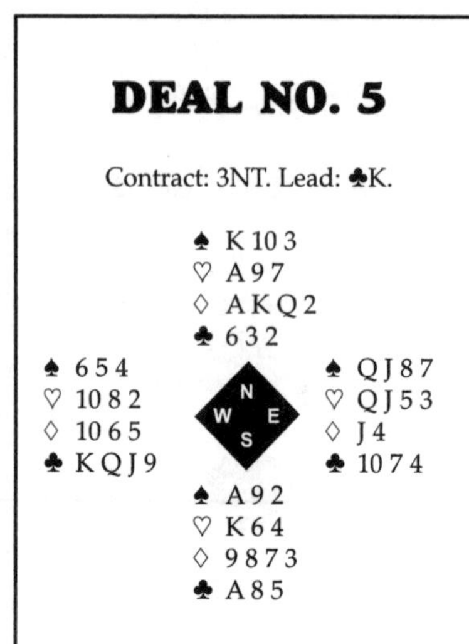

TTA leaves you one trick short of your contract, but diamonds ought to provide that vital ninth trick. Win ♣A and cash ◇A-K-Q immediately. There is a greater than 60% chance that this will draw all the opponents' diamonds so that you can win a fourth round with ◇9 while they have to discard. The four diamond tricks and top cards in the other suits are enough for the contract.

♠	2
♡	2
◇	3
♣	1
TTA	8

DEAL NO. 6

Contract: 3NT. Lead: ♣Q.

North: ♠ A 5 3 ♡ J 7 3 ◇ A Q 9 5 ♣ 8 6 4

West: ♠ Q 10 7 ♡ 10 4 ◇ 8 6 4 ♣ Q J 10 7 2

East: ♠ J 9 8 4 ♡ K Q 8 6 2 ◇ J 10 ♣ 9 5

South: ♠ K 6 2 ♡ A 9 5 ◇ K 7 3 2 ♣ A K 3

Again you have only eight top tricks and again diamonds should provide the ninth. This is essentially the same as *Deal 5* except that ◇A-K-Q are not all in one hand. Just cash ◇A-K-Q, in any order: provided the defenders' diamonds split 3-2, ◇9 will again be that vital game-going trick.

♠	2
♡	1
◇	3
♣	2
TTA	8

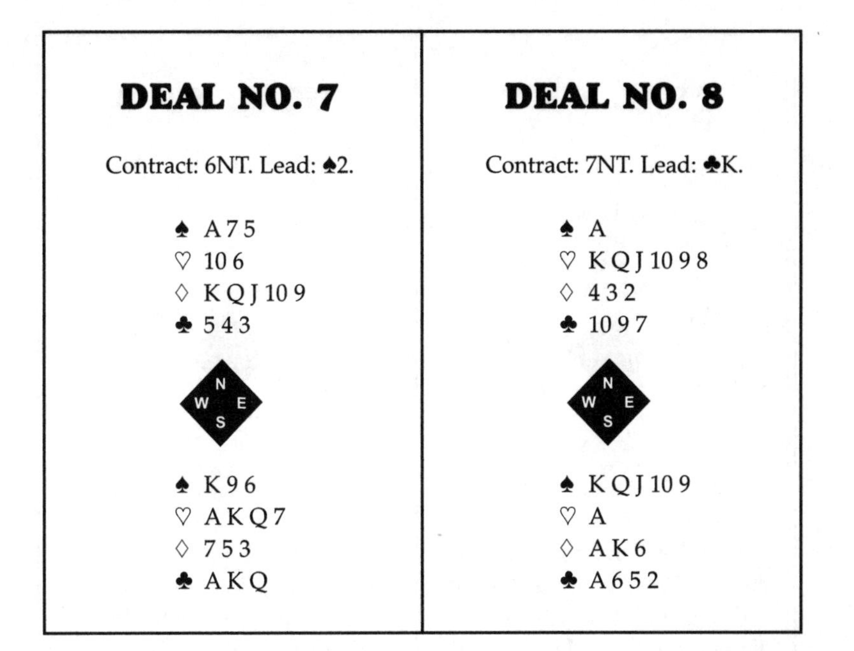
DEAL NO. 7
Contract: 6NT. Lead: ♠2.
♠ A 7 5
♡ 10 6
◊ K Q J 10 9
♣ 5 4 3
N
W E
S
♠ K 9 6
♡ A K Q 7
◊ 7 5 3
♣ A K Q
DEAL NO. 8
Contract: 7NT. Lead: ♣K.
♠ A
♡ K Q J 10 9 8
◊ 4 3 2
♣ 10 9 7
N
W E
S
♠ K Q J 10 9
♡ A
◊ A K 6
♣ A 6 5 2

DEAL NO. 7

Contract: 6NT. Lead: ♠2.

Win with ♠K in hand and play diamonds. As soon as ♢A has been forced out you have four diamond tricks and eight more top cards in the other suits. Avoid the trap of winning Trick 1 with ♠A. If you do that, an astute defender might be able to withhold ♢A until the third round . . . you will find that you have ♢10-9 waiting in dummy but, with ♠A gone, no way to get to them.

♠	2
♡	3
♢	0
♣	3
TTA	8

DEAL NO. 8

Contract: 7NT. Lead: ♣K.

There are plenty of tricks (TTA = 14!), but you must be careful to take them in the right order. Win with ♣A, then cash ♡A. Cross to dummy with ♠A and cash the other five heart tricks, on which you discard your four small cards and one of your winners! Then play a diamond back to hand to cash the remaining spades for your contract. You will find that if you mistakenly play ♠A before ♡A you will be obliged to come back to hand for the next trick and dummy's hearts will go to waste.

♠	5
♡	6
♢	2
♣	1
TTA	14

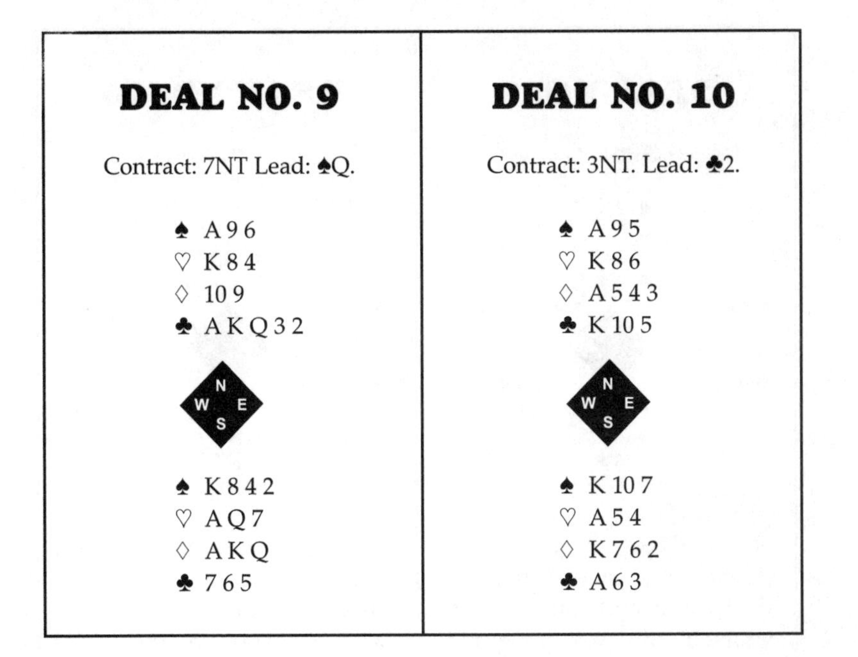

DEAL NO. 9

Contract: 7NT Lead: ♠Q.

♠ A 9 6
♡ K 8 4
♢ 10 9
♣ A K Q 3 2

N / W E / S

♠ K 8 4 2
♡ A Q 7
♢ A K Q
♣ 7 6 5

DEAL NO. 10

Contract: 3NT. Lead: ♣2.

♠ A 9 5
♡ K 8 6
♢ A 5 4 3
♣ K 10 5

N / W E / S

♠ K 10 7
♡ A 5 4
♢ K 7 6 2
♣ A 6 3

DEAL NO. 9

Contract: 7NT Lead: ♠Q.

Somebody – your partner, no doubt – has pressed hard in the bidding and you now find yourself in a 34-point grand slam with TTA = 11. Don't panic! If you look closely you will see that the smallest cards in the pack – ♣2 and ♣3 – will provide the needed extra tricks, provided the defenders' clubs break 3-2 (which they are odds-on to do). Just cash all your top tricks including ♣A-K-Q and finish off with ♣3-2!

♠	2
♡	3
◇	3
♣	3
TTA	11

DEAL NO. 10

Contract: 3NT. Lead: ♣2.

North: ♠ A 9 5 ♡ K 8 6 ◇ A 5 4 3 ♣ K 10 5

West: ♠ 6 4 2 ♡ Q 7 3 ◇ 10 9 8 ♣ Q 9 7 2

East: ♠ Q J 8 3 ♡ J 10 9 2 ◇ Q J ♣ J 8 4

South: ♠ K 10 7 ♡ A 5 4 ◇ K 7 6 2 ♣ A 6 3

TTA leaves you a trick short but you should be able to gain an extra diamond trick. Win with either ♣K or ♣A, then cash ◇A and ◇K, and *give up a diamond.* Provided the defenders' diamonds break 3-2, you now have an established diamond winner and, when you regain the lead at the next trick, that fourth diamond will be your ninth trick. As usual, it would be a mistake to cash all the A-K combinations first – you need those as stoppers for when the defence wins its diamond trick.

♠	2
♡	2
◇	2
♣	2
TTA	8

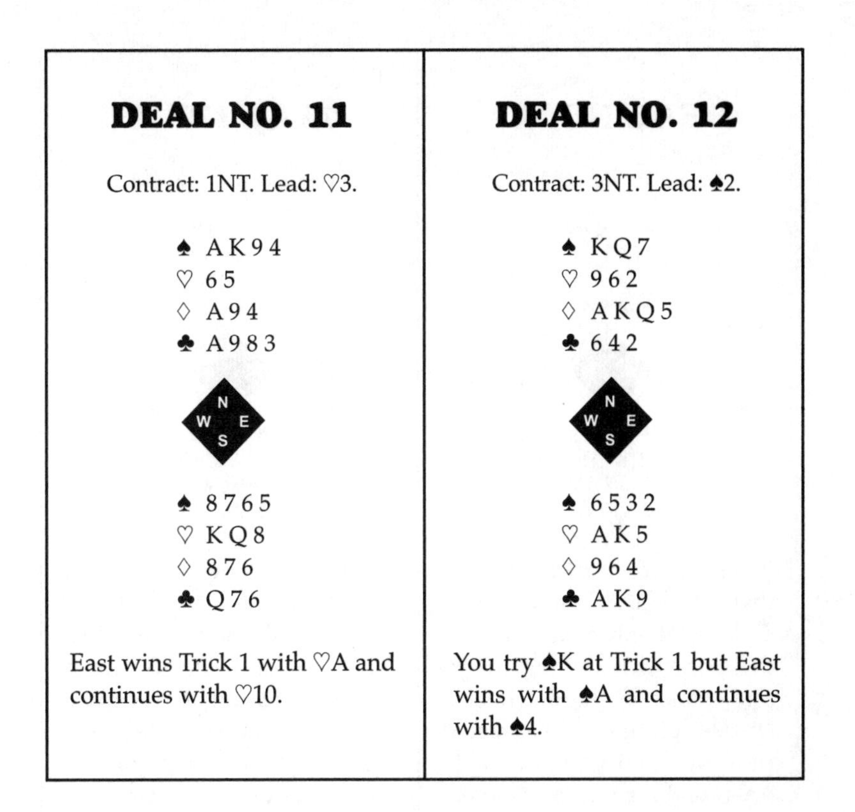

DEAL NO. 11

Contract: 1NT. Lead: ♡3.

♠ A K 9 4
♡ 6 5
♢ A 9 4
♣ A 9 8 3

♠ 8 7 6 5
♡ K Q 8
♢ 8 7 6
♣ Q 7 6

East wins Trick 1 with ♡A and continues with ♡10.

DEAL NO. 12

Contract: 3NT. Lead: ♠2.

♠ K Q 7
♡ 9 6 2
♢ A K Q 5
♣ 6 4 2

♠ 6 5 3 2
♡ A K 5
♢ 9 6 4
♣ A K 9

You try ♠K at Trick 1 but East wins with ♠A and continues with ♠4.

DEAL NO. 11

Contract: 1NT. Lead: ♡3.

You have two heart tricks now that ♡A is out of the way, but TTA is still only 6. So where is the extra trick coming from? The chance of the defenders' spades splitting 3-2 is greater than 60%, so you can cash ♠A-K and give up a spade on the next round. This is quite safe, as all the other suits are still stopped. When you regain the lead, you can cash a fourth spade to bring TTA up to 7.

♠	2
♡	2
◇	1
♣	1
TTA	6

DEAL NO. 12

Contract: 3NT. Lead: ♠J.

North: ♠ K Q 7 ♡ 9 6 2 ◇ A K Q 5 ♣ 6 4 2

West: ♠ J 10 9 8 ♡ Q 8 4 ◇ 10 7 2 ♣ 10 8 5

East: ♠ A 4 ♡ J 10 7 3 ◇ J 8 3 ♣ Q J 7 3

South: ♠ 6 5 3 2 ♡ A K 5 ◇ 9 6 4 ♣ A K 9

With ♠K losing to ♠A, you only have one spade trick and TTA is only 8 in total. This time it is harder to see where the extra trick might come from. Your best hope is that the defenders' diamonds split 3-3, in which case you can cash ◇A-K-Q to set up dummy's ◇5 as a winner. The chance of the diamonds splitting 3-3 is only about 36%, but you really don't have much else to try for on this deal.

♠	1
♡	2
◇	3
♣	2
TTA	8

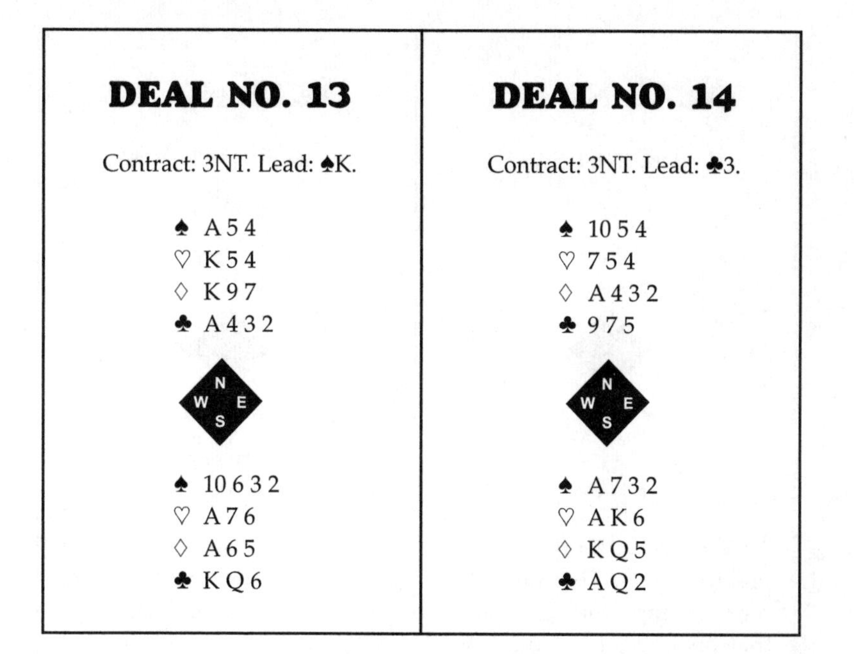

DEAL NO. 13

Contract: 3NT. Lead: ♠K.

♠ A 5 4
♡ K 5 4
♢ K 9 7
♣ A 4 3 2

♠ 10 6 3 2
♡ A 7 6
♢ A 6 5
♣ K Q 6

DEAL NO. 14

Contract: 3NT. Lead: ♣3.

♠ 10 5 4
♡ 7 5 4
♢ A 4 3 2
♣ 9 7 5

♠ A 7 3 2
♡ A K 6
♢ K Q 5
♣ A Q 2

DEAL NO. 13

Contract: 3NT. Lead: ♠K.

This is very similar to the previous deal. This time you have to hope that it is clubs that break 3-3 but, somehow, this chance is easy to overlook when the top honours are split between the declarer and dummy hands. On this deal you can cash ♣A-K-Q in any order and, if the suit does break 3-3, dummy's last little club will provide your ninth trick.

♠	1
♡	2
♢	2
♣	3
TTA	8

DEAL NO. 14

Contract: 3NT. Lead: ♣3.

As soon as you see the club lead, you know you have two club tricks (either East plays low, in which case you win ♣Q immediately, or he plays ♣K, in which case you win ♣A and still have ♣Q for later). So TTA = 8. You must try to win four diamonds by cashing ♢K, ♢Q and ♢A *in that order,* hoping they break 3-3. Do not make the mistake of winning the first (or second) diamond with ♢A. You will have to take the next two diamonds in hand and, even if ♢4 has become a winner, you have no way of reaching it.

♠	1
♡	2
♢	3
♣	2
TTA	8

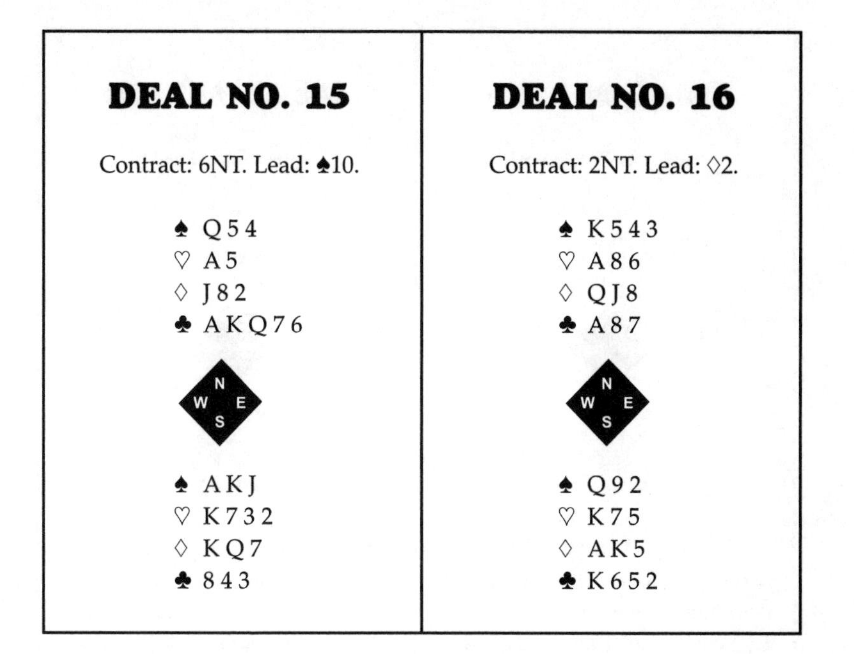

DEAL NO. 15

Contract: 6NT. Lead: ♠10.

North:
♠ Q 5 4
♡ A 5
♢ J 8 2
♣ A K Q 7 6

South:
♠ A K J
♡ K 7 3 2
♢ K Q 7
♣ 8 4 3

DEAL NO. 16

Contract: 2NT. Lead: ♢2.

North:
♠ K 5 4 3
♡ A 8 6
♢ Q J 8
♣ A 8 7

South:
♠ Q 9 2
♡ K 7 5
♢ A K 5
♣ K 6 5 2

DEAL NO. 15

Contract: 6NT. Lead: ♠10.

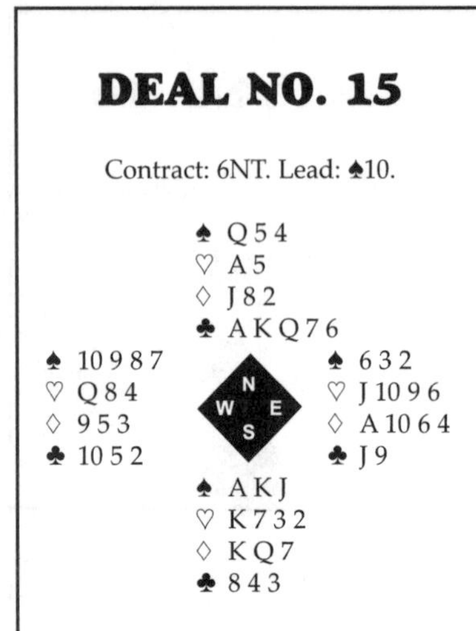

Win with ♠A, and then play a diamond to drive out the opponents' ace. Once you have two diamond tricks in the bag, play out the top clubs. So long as the defenders' clubs are divided 3-2, the ♣A-K-Q will draw them all, so that dummy's ♣7-6 become winners too. You gain two extra diamond tricks and two extra club tricks which, added to the TTA of 8, gives you 12 in all.

♠	3
♡	2
◇	0
♣	3
TTA	8

DEAL NO. 16

Contract: 2NT. Lead: ◇2.

TTA leaves you a trick short again, but the combined ♠K-Q enables you to make up the deficit. Win with ◇A and play a low spade towards dummy's ♠K straight away. If West plays ♠A, you will make both ♠K and ♠Q (and nine tricks in all). If ♠K wins, you have your eighth trick immediately. And if East wins ♠A over dummy's ♠K, your ♠Q becomes your eighth trick instead.

♠	0
♡	2
◇	3
♣	2
TTA	7

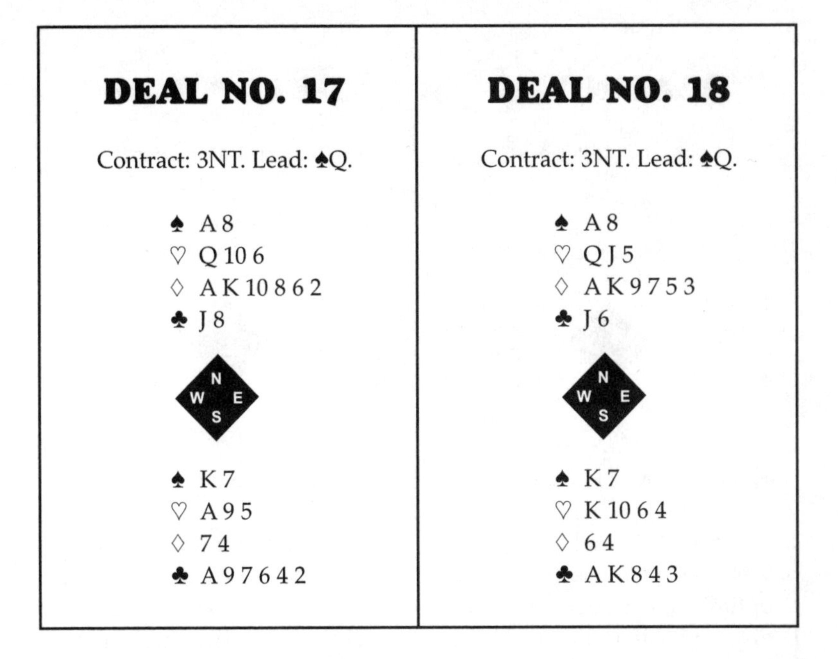
DEAL NO. 17
Contract: 3NT. Lead: ♠Q.
♠ A 8
♡ Q 10 6
◇ A K 10 8 6 2
♣ J 8
N
W E
S
♠ K 7
♡ A 9 5
◇ 7 4
♣ A 9 7 6 4 2
DEAL NO. 18
Contract: 3NT. Lead: ♠Q.
♠ A 8
♡ Q J 5
◇ A K 9 7 5 3
♣ J 6
N
W E
S
♠ K 7
♡ K 10 6 4
◇ 6 4
♣ A K 8 4 3

DEAL NO. 17

Contract: 3NT. Lead: ♠Q.

TTA is only 6, well short of the 9 needed to make this rather optimistic contract. But don't give up! All is not lost. You have eight diamonds between declarer and dummy, so the defenders have five and you must hope they divide 3-2 (which is, in fact, their most likely division). Win ♠K (not ♠A because you will need that as an entry to the diamonds), cash ◊A-K and then give up a diamond. If things go according to plan, you will make all of dummy's remaining diamonds (◊10-8-6) to bring home the contract.

♠	2
♡	1
◊	2
♣	1
TTA	6

DEAL NO. 18

Contract: 3NT. Lead: ♠Q.

North: ♠ A 8 ♡ Q J 5 ◊ A K 9 7 5 3 ♣ J 6

West: ♠ Q J 10 6 2 ♡ 9 ◊ J 10 8 2 ♣ Q 9 2

East: ♠ 9 5 4 3 ♡ A 8 7 3 2 ◊ Q ♣ 10 7 5

South: ♠ K 7 ♡ K 10 6 4 ◊ 6 4 ♣ A K 8 4 3

At first glance this is similar to the previous deal, where you set up three extra diamond tricks to bring the TTA of 6 up to 9. However, you can see that the diamonds don't break 3-2 this time, so that plan is doomed to failure. Did you spot the sure-fire plan? Just knock out ♡A and now your remaining three heart honours will enable you to make the contract.

♠	2
♡	0
◊	2
♣	2
TTA	6

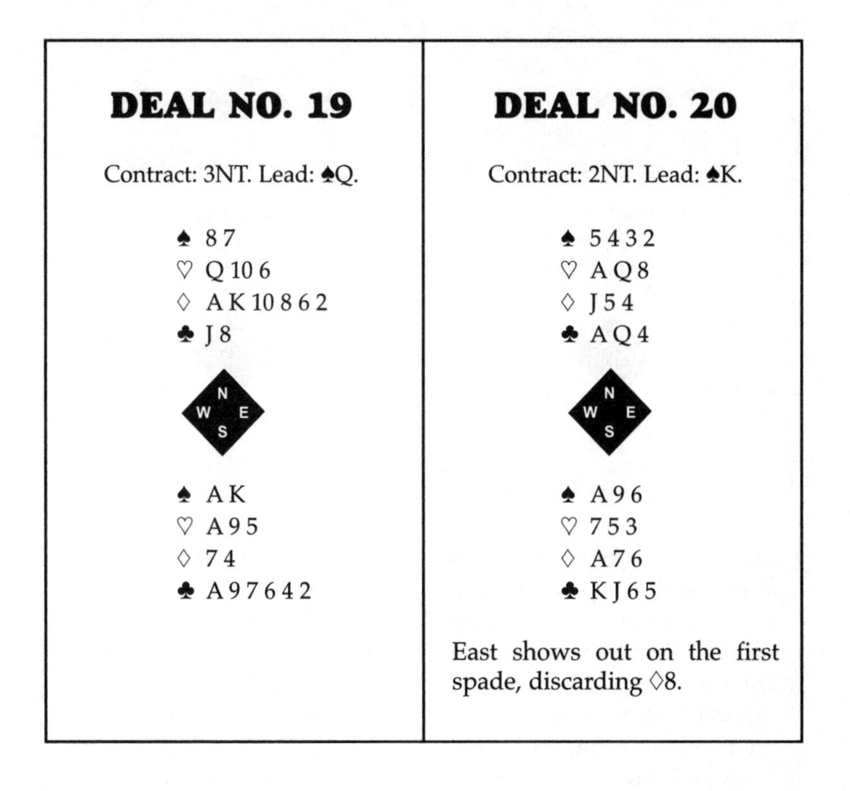

DEAL NO. 19

Contract: 3NT. Lead: ♠Q.

♠ 8 7
♡ Q 10 6
◊ A K 10 8 6 2
♣ J 8

♠ A K
♡ A 9 5
◊ 7 4
♣ A 9 7 6 4 2

DEAL NO. 20

Contract: 2NT. Lead: ♠K.

♠ 5 4 3 2
♡ A Q 8
◊ J 5 4
♣ A Q 4

♠ A 9 6
♡ 7 5 3
◊ A 7 6
♣ K J 6 5

East shows out on the first spade, discarding ◊8.

DEAL NO. 19

Contract: 3NT. Lead: ♠Q.

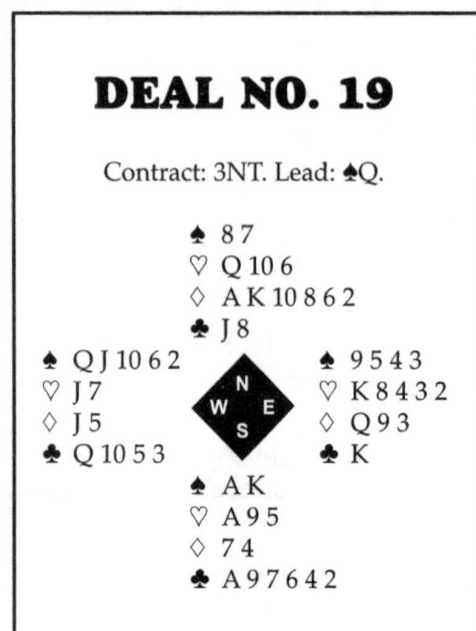

This is an apparent repeat of *Deal 17* where you set up three extra diamond tricks and retained ♠A in dummy as an entry to them. On this deal you still have to set up the diamonds to bring TTA from 6 up to 9, but – alas – ♠A is inconveniently in the South hand and there is no apparent entry to dummy. Do you see the solution? Instead of playing ◇A-K and giving up a diamond, give up the diamond first. Then you still have ◇7 in hand, and can happily cross to dummy's ◇A and cash ◇K and the remaining diamonds.

♠	2
♡	1
◇	2
♣	1
TTA	6

DEAL NO. 20

Contract: 2NT. Lead: ♠K.

TTA leaves you one trick short and this time there is no long suit to come to the rescue. The best chance of an eighth trick lies in ♡Q. Win with ♠A and play a heart intending to 'finesse' ♡Q if West plays low. If West holds ♡K, your finesse will work and you will make the contract. If East has it, you will be one down – but at least you will have tried the legitimate 50% chance of success.

♠	1
♡	1
◇	1
♣	4
TTA	7

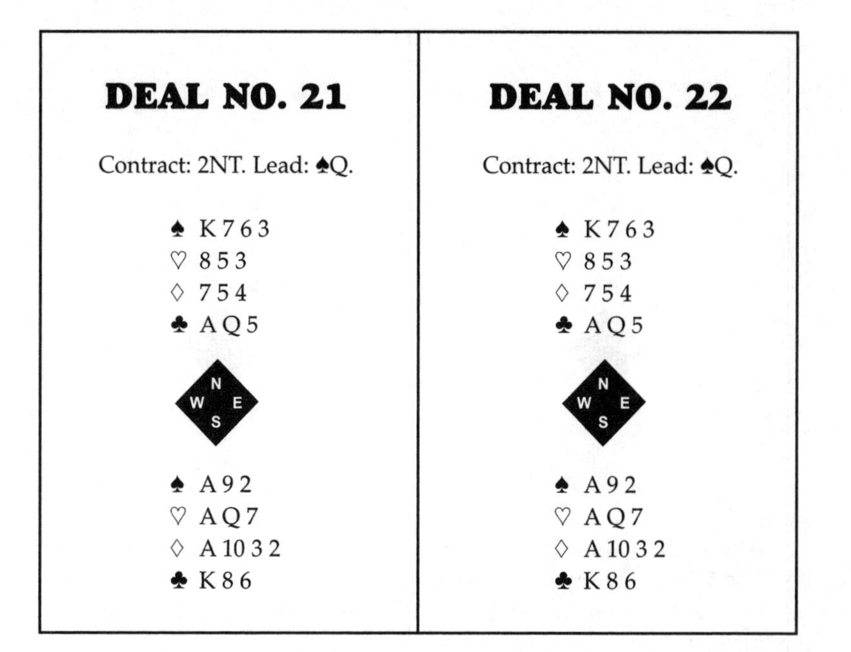

DEAL NO. 21
Contract: 2NT. Lead: ♠Q.
♠ K 7 6 3
♡ 8 5 3
◇ 7 5 4
♣ A Q 5
N
W E
S
♠ A 9 2
♡ A Q 7
◇ A 10 3 2
♣ K 8 6
DEAL NO. 22
Contract: 2NT. Lead: ♠Q.
♠ K 7 6 3
♡ 8 5 3
◇ 7 5 4
♣ A Q 5
N
W E
S
♠ A 9 2
♡ A Q 7
◇ A 10 3 2
♣ K 8 6

DEAL NO. 21

Contract: 2NT. Lead: ♠Q.

Almost the same as *Deal 20*. The TTA is the same, but now you have two spade stoppers instead of one. Can you see the difference that makes? It means you can afford to lose the lead because, after winning ♠A, you still have the spades stopped. Your best chance of an eighth trick is still ♡Q, but now you can afford to play off ♡A first, just in case West holds ♡K singleton. It's unlikely, but it costs nothing to try! If ♡K does not fall, you go back to dummy and play a small heart towards ♡Q. If East has ♡K, you will still make the contract.

♠	2
♡	1
◊	1
♣	3
TTA	7

DEAL NO. 22

Contract: 2NT. Lead: ♠Q.

North: ♠ K 7 6 3 ♡ Q 5 3 ◊ 7 5 4 ♣ A Q 5

West: ♠ Q J 10 8 5 ♡ K 2 ◊ Q J 8 6 ♣ 10 9

East: ♠ 4 ♡ J 10 9 6 4 ◊ K 9 ♣ J 7 4 3 2

South: ♠ A 9 2 ♡ A 8 7 ◊ A 10 3 2 ♣ K 8 6

Yet again ♡Q represents your best chance of finding an eighth trick – but how do you go about it? Do not make the mistake of leading ♡Q for a 'finesse'. If East puts ♡K on, you will win ♡A and only one heart trick. If West wins with ♡K, you still have ♡A but that too is only one trick. Instead, cash ♡A (in case ♡K is singleton somewhere), then play a low card from hand towards ♡Q. If West holds ♡K, your ♡Q will score and you will make the contract.

♠	2
♡	1
◊	1
♣	3
TTA	7

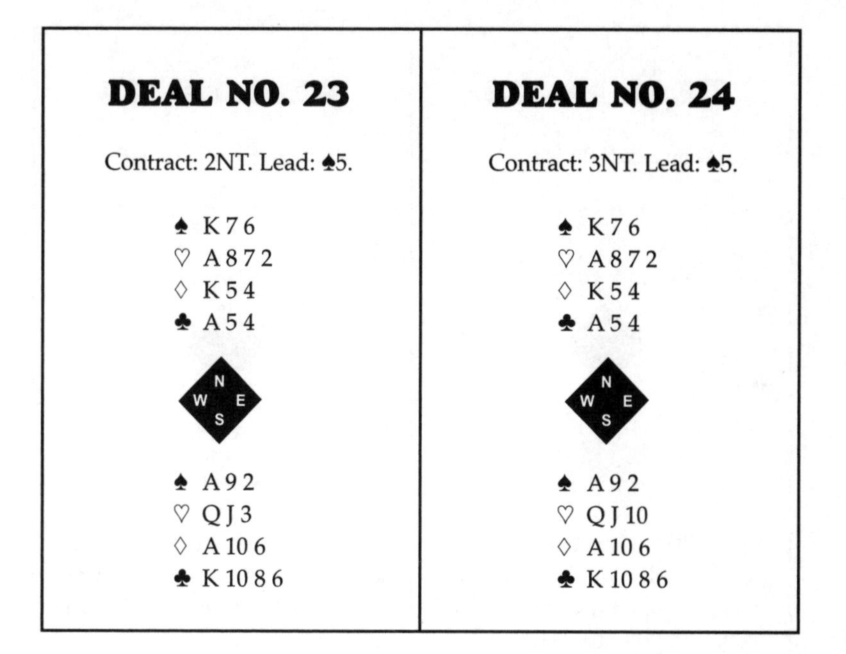

DEAL NO. 23

Contract: 2NT. Lead: ♠5.

♠ K 7 6
♡ A 8 7 2
◊ K 5 4
♣ A 5 4

♠ A 9 2
♡ Q J 3
◊ A 10 6
♣ K 10 8 6

DEAL NO. 24

Contract: 3NT. Lead: ♠5.

♠ K 7 6
♡ A 8 7 2
◊ K 5 4
♣ A 5 4

♠ A 9 2
♡ Q J 10
◊ A 10 6
♣ K 10 8 6

DEAL NO. 23

Contract: 2NT. Lead: ♠5.

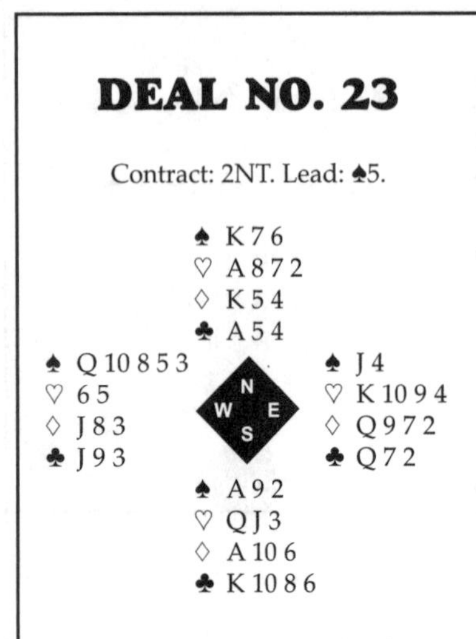

You will often meet the heart position shown in this deal. Because you now have ♡J to back up ♡Q, the contract is guaranteed. You can guarantee another heart trick to bring your TTA up to the required 8. Win the spade lead and either lead ♡Q for a finesse, or cash ♡A and then lead another heart to knock out ♡K. It does not matter when the defence takes its ♡K. You must make two heart tricks.

♠	2
♡	1
♢	2
♣	2
TTA	7

DEAL NO. 24

Contract: 3NT. Lead: ♠5.

North: ♠ K 7 6 ♡ A 8 7 2 ♢ K 5 4 ♣ A 5 4

West: ♠ Q 10 8 5 3 ♡ 6 5 ♢ J 8 3 ♣ J 9 3

East: ♠ J 4 ♡ K 9 4 3 ♢ Q 9 7 2 ♣ Q 7 2

South: ♠ A 9 2 ♡ Q J 10 ♢ A 10 6 ♣ K 10 8 6

This time your hearts are such that you must make three heart tricks, bringing TTA up to 9. Simply lead ♡Q. If West plays ♡K you can win ♡A and still make ♡J and ♡10. If East is able to win ♡K you are still safe because spades are still stopped and you can take ♡A, ♡J and ♡10. In short, you make the contract whether or not the heart finesse succeeds.

♠	2
♡	1
♢	2
♣	2
TTA	7

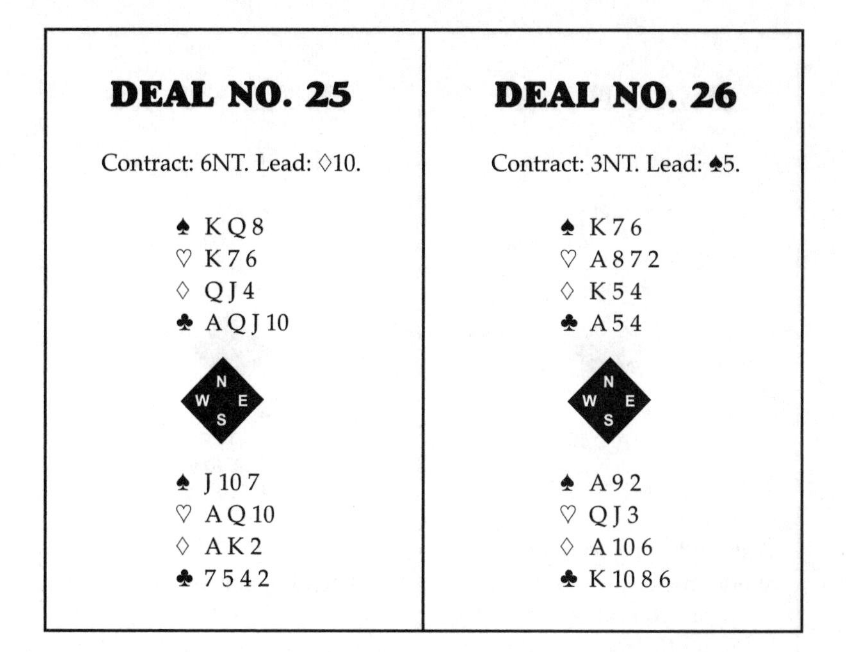
DEAL NO. 25
Contract: 6NT. Lead: ♢10.
♠ K Q 8
♡ K 7 6
♢ Q J 4
♣ A Q J 10
N
W E
S
♠ J 10 7
♡ A Q 10
♢ A K 2
♣ 7 5 4 2
DEAL NO. 26
Contract: 3NT. Lead: ♠5.
♠ K 7 6
♡ A 8 7 2
♢ K 5 4
♣ A 5 4
N
W E
S
♠ A 9 2
♡ Q J 3
♢ A 10 6
♣ K 10 8 6

DEAL NO. 25

Contract: 6NT. Lead: ♢10.

North: ♠ K Q 8 ♡ K 7 6 ♢ Q J 4 ♣ A Q J 10

West: ♠ A 9 ♡ J 5 4 ♢ 10 9 8 7 ♣ K 9 8 3

East: ♠ 6 5 4 3 2 ♡ 9 8 3 2 ♢ 6 5 3 ♣ 6

South: ♠ J 10 7 ♡ A Q 10 ♢ A K 2 ♣ 7 5 4 2

Although TTA is only 7, two spade tricks are available as soon as you knock out ♠A, bringing the total up to 9. The remaining three tricks will have to come from (you hope) successfully finessing against ♣K. Win with ♢Q and knock out ♠A. Then finesse ♣10, come back to hand in diamonds or hearts in order to finesse ♣J, and finally return to your hand again to finesse ♣Q. You will need three finesses if West has four clubs but, as long as he holds ♣K, he cannot prevent you from making the contract.

♠	0
♡	3
♢	3
♣	1
TTA	7

DEAL NO. 26

Contract: 3NT. Lead: ♠5.

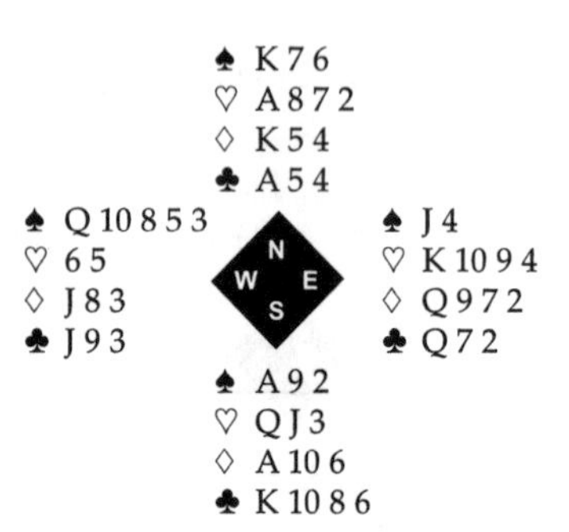

North: ♠ K 7 6 ♡ A 8 7 2 ♢ K 5 4 ♣ A 5 4

West: ♠ Q 10 8 5 3 ♡ 6 5 ♢ J 8 3 ♣ J 9 3

East: ♠ J 4 ♡ K 10 9 4 ♢ Q 9 7 2 ♣ Q 7 2

South: ♠ A 9 2 ♡ Q J 3 ♢ A 10 6 ♣ K 10 8 6

The eagle-eyed among you will realise that this deal is a replica of *Deal 23,* except that the contract is now 3NT. This means that you must make three heart tricks – two is not enough. Leading ♡Q for a finesse is therefore not the best option because, wherever ♡K is, that route leads to only two certain heart tricks. You would make three only if the hearts broke 3-3 (a 36% chance). Better to lead a low heart from dummy, hoping East has ♡K (a 50% chance). If he has, you can make all three of ♡J, ♡Q and ♡A – and the contract.

♠	2
♡	1
♢	2
♣	2
TTA	7

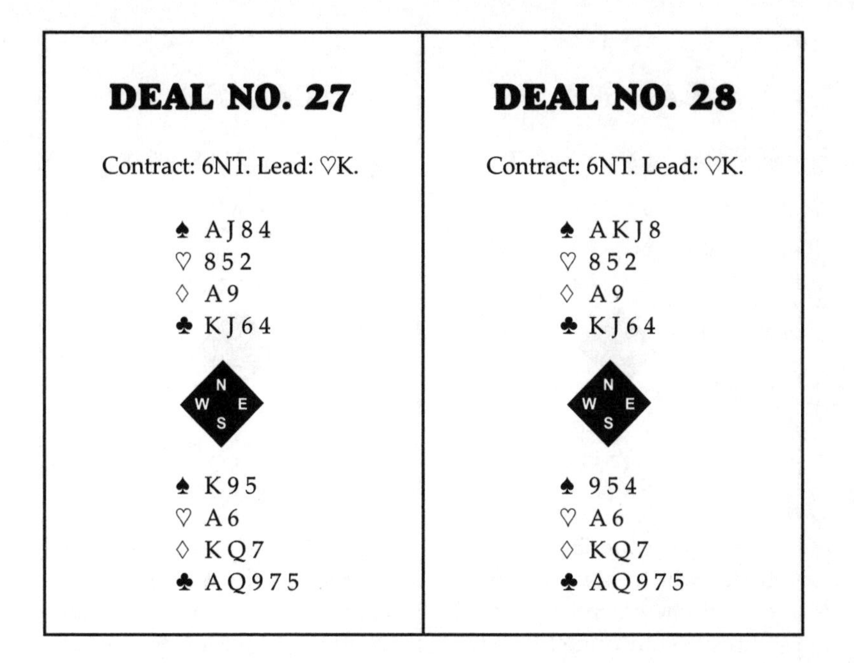

DEAL NO. 27

Contract: 6NT. Lead: ♡K.

♠ AJ84
♡ 852
♢ A9
♣ KJ64

♠ K95
♡ A6
♢ KQ7
♣ AQ975

DEAL NO. 28

Contract: 6NT. Lead: ♡K.

♠ AKJ8
♡ 852
♢ A9
♣ KJ64

♠ 954
♡ A6
♢ KQ7
♣ AQ975

DEAL NO. 27

Contract: 6NT. Lead: ♡K.

North: ♠ A J 8 4 ♡ 8 5 2 ◇ A 9 ♣ K J 6 4

West: ♠ Q 7 2 ♡ K Q J 4 3 ◇ 8 ♣ 10 8 3 2

East: ♠ 10 6 3 ♡ 10 9 7 ◇ J 10 6 5 4 3 2 ♣ —

South: ♠ K 9 5 ♡ A 6 ◇ K Q 7 ♣ A Q 9 7 5

TTA = 11, counting five club tricks which must be yours even if one defender holds all four outstanding clubs. The twelfth trick can only come from a successful finesse of ♠J. So win ♡A, cash your minor suit winners and ♠K, cross your fingers, and play a spade to dummy's ♠J. If it is your lucky day this 50% shot will come off and you will make your contract.

♠	2
♡	1
◇	3
♣	5
TTA	11

DEAL NO. 28

Contract: 6NT. Lead: ♡K.

North: ♠ A K J 8 ♡ 8 5 2 ◇ A 9 ♣ K J 6 4

West: ♠ 10 7 6 3 2 ♡ K Q J 4 ◇ 8 5 ♣ 10 8

East: ♠ Q ♡ 10 9 7 3 ◇ J 10 6 4 3 2 ♣ 3 2

South: ♠ 9 5 4 ♡ A 6 ◇ K Q 7 ♣ A Q 9 7 5

Again TTA is 11 and again ♠J represents the only realistic chance of a twelfth trick. So you plan to finesse ♠J, just as you did on the previous deal – but don't forget to cash ♠A first! It's just possible that East holds ♠Q singleton, after all. Somehow it is easy to forget to play a top honour first when they are in the same hand, unlike the previous deal when South held ♠K and North ♠A.

♠	2
♡	1
◇	3
♣	5
TTA	11

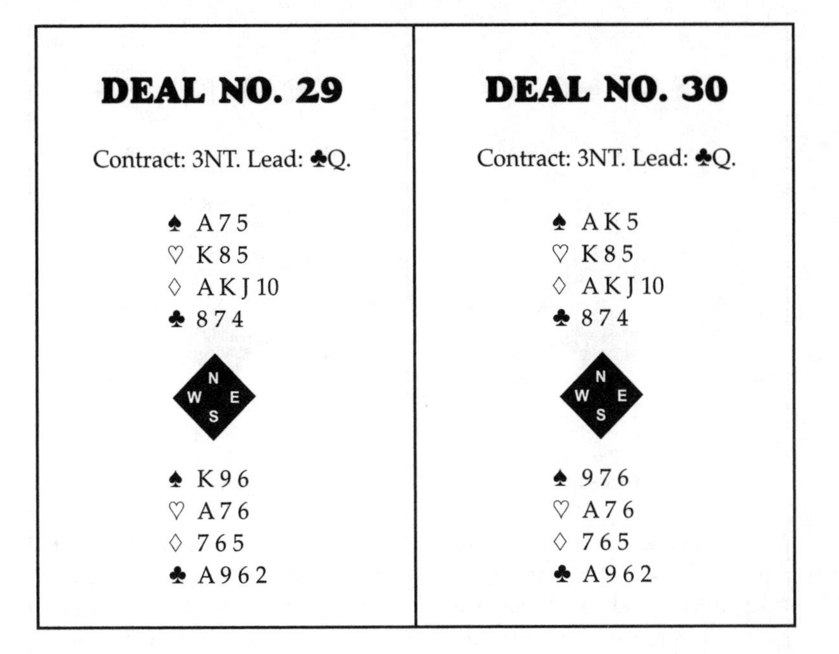
DEAL NO. 29
Contract: 3NT. Lead: ♣Q.
♠ A 7 5
♡ K 8 5
♢ A K J 10
♣ 8 7 4
N
W E
S
♠ K 9 6
♡ A 7 6
♢ 7 6 5
♣ A 9 6 2
DEAL NO. 30
Contract: 3NT. Lead: ♣Q.
♠ A K 5
♡ K 8 5
♢ A K J 10
♣ 8 7 4
N
W E
S
♠ 9 7 6
♡ A 7 6
♢ 7 6 5
♣ A 9 6 2

DEAL NO. 29

Contract: 3NT. Lead: ♣Q.

TTA leaves you two tricks short but, if West holds ◇Q, dummy's ◇J-10 will make up the difference. Win ♣A and then cross to ◇A just in case East has ◇Q singleton. When nothing exciting happens, come back to ♠K and take a diamond finesse with ◇10. If that proves successful, come back to your hand with ♡A to take a second diamond finesse, and then cash your remaining top cards to chalk up your contract.

♠	2
♡	2
◇	2
♣	1
TTA	7

DEAL NO. 30

Contract: 3NT. Lead: ♣Q.

North: ♠ A K 5 ♡ K 8 5 ◇ A K J 10 ♣ 8 7 4

West: ♠ J 8 ♡ J 9 2 ◇ Q 4 3 2 ♣ Q J 10 5

East: ♠ Q 10 4 3 2 ♡ Q 10 4 3 ◇ 9 8 ♣ K 3

South: ♠ 9 7 6 ♡ A 7 6 ◇ 7 6 5 ♣ A 9 6 2

This is the same as *Deal 29* except that ♠K has mysteriously moved into the North hand. Do you see what difference that makes to the play? Let's say you win ♣A, cash ◇A, cross back to ♡A to take a successful diamond finesse and then . . . oh, dear! Because ♠K has emigrated, there is no second entry to South. You cannot take another diamond finesse, therefore, and will eventually lose to ◇Q. The remedy is to win ♣A, take an immediate diamond finesse and use ♡A as your entry to the second diamond finesse and success.

♠	2
♡	2
◇	2
♣	1
TTA	7

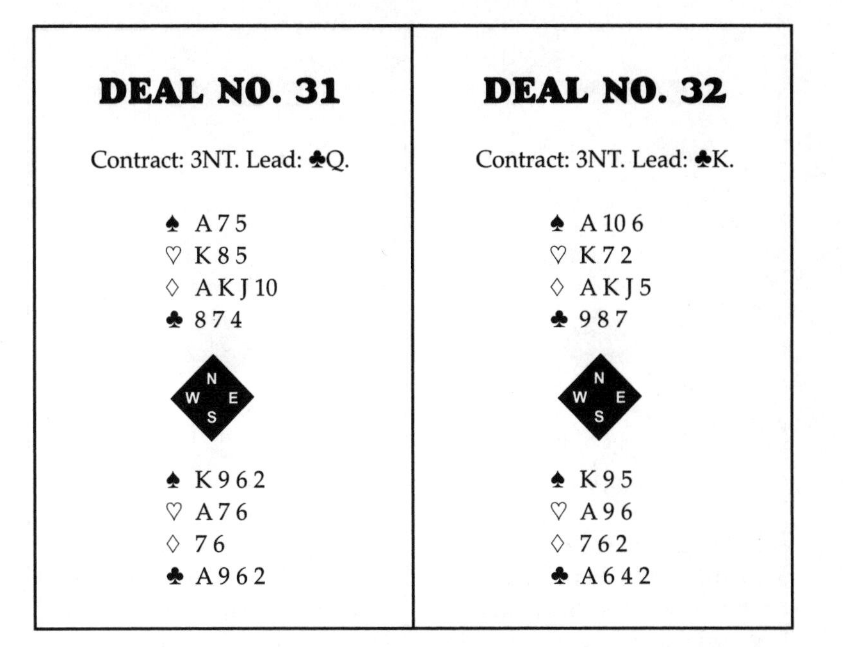

DEAL NO. 31
Contract: 3NT. Lead: ♣Q.
♠ A 7 5
♡ K 8 5
◊ A K J 10
♣ 8 7 4
N
W E
S
♠ K 9 6 2
♡ A 7 6
◊ 7 6
♣ A 9 6 2
DEAL NO. 32
Contract: 3NT. Lead: ♣K.
♠ A 10 6
♡ K 7 2
◊ A K J 5
♣ 9 8 7
N
W E
S
♠ K 9 5
♡ A 9 6
◊ 7 6 2
♣ A 6 4 2

DEAL NO. 31

Contract: 3NT. Lead: ♣Q.

For this deal, ♠K has returned to the South hand, but now one of South's diamonds has vanished. Again, do you see what difference that makes to your plan to win four diamond tricks? You cannot now cash a top diamond, take a diamond finesse and then take another diamond finesse, because you don't have enough diamonds to manage that. No, you have to win ♣A and take a diamond finesse immediately, return to hand with ♠K and use South's last diamond for the second finesse. You must play in the same way as *Deal 30*, but for a different reason.

♠	2
♡	2
◇	2
♣	1
TTA	7

DEAL NO. 32

Contract: 3NT. Lead: ♣K.

Yet again you are looking to the diamonds to bring your TTA from 7 up to 9. You have to hope that West has ◇Q so that dummy's ◇J is a trick. And you have to hope that the outstanding diamonds are 3-3, so that dummy's ◇5 is also a winner. Finesse ◇J, cash ◇A-K and hopefully cash ◇5 for the contract. You can cash a top diamond in case someone has singleton ◇Q, if you want to, but it would not help because that would mean that the other defender has ◇10-9-8-4-3 and dummy's ◇5 will never win a trick.

♠	2
♡	2
◇	2
♣	1
TTA	7

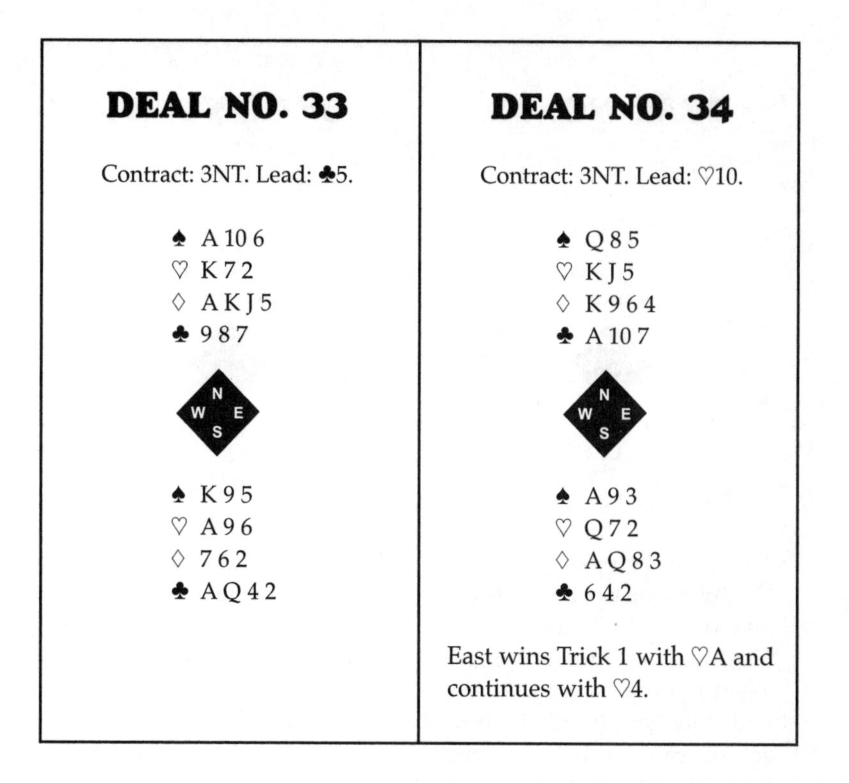

DEAL NO. 33

Contract: 3NT. Lead: ♣5.

North:
♠ A 10 6
♡ K 7 2
♢ A K J 5
♣ 9 8 7

South:
♠ K 9 5
♡ A 9 6
♢ 7 6 2
♣ A Q 4 2

DEAL NO. 34

Contract: 3NT. Lead: ♡10.

North:
♠ Q 8 5
♡ K J 5
♢ K 9 6 4
♣ A 10 7

South:
♠ A 9 3
♡ Q 7 2
♢ A Q 8 3
♣ 6 4 2

East wins Trick 1 with ♡A and continues with ♡4.

DEAL NO. 33

Contract: 3NT. Lead: ♣5.

This time the opening lead is helpful as you can immediately add two clubs tricks to your TTA, making a total of eight. What's more, spades, hearts and clubs are all still stopped, so you can afford to lose the lead. So, rather than finesse ◇J straight away, cash ◇A-K first, in case East has ◇Q-x doubleton. If ◇Q doesn't fall, you can still come back to hand and lead a diamond towards ◇J, making the contract if West holds ◇Q, or if diamonds are 3-3.

♠	2
♡	2
◇	2
♣	2
TTA	8

DEAL NO. 34

Contract: 3NT. Lead: ♡10.

North:
♠ Q 8 5
♡ K J 5
◇ K 9 6 4
♣ A 10 7

West:
♠ K 10
♡ 10 9 8 6 3
◇ 10 7 2
♣ J 9 3

East:
♠ J 7 6 4 2
♡ A 4
◇ J 5
♣ K Q 8 5

South:
♠ A 9 3
♡ Q 7 2
◇ A Q 8 3
♣ 6 4 2

TTA is only 5. Where are four extra tricks coming from? Well, now that ♡A is gone you will make two heart tricks. So long as East-West's diamonds break 3-2, that suit should provide an extra trick too. There is nothing to be gained from the clubs, so the only chance for the ninth trick lies in ♠Q. Do not lead ♠Q for a 'finesse'. That only works if you have ♠J (and preferably ♠10) to back it up. Lead a low spade from hand, hoping that West has ♠K, in which case you cannot be prevented from making dummy's ♠Q.

♠	1
♡	0
◇	3
♣	1
TTA	5

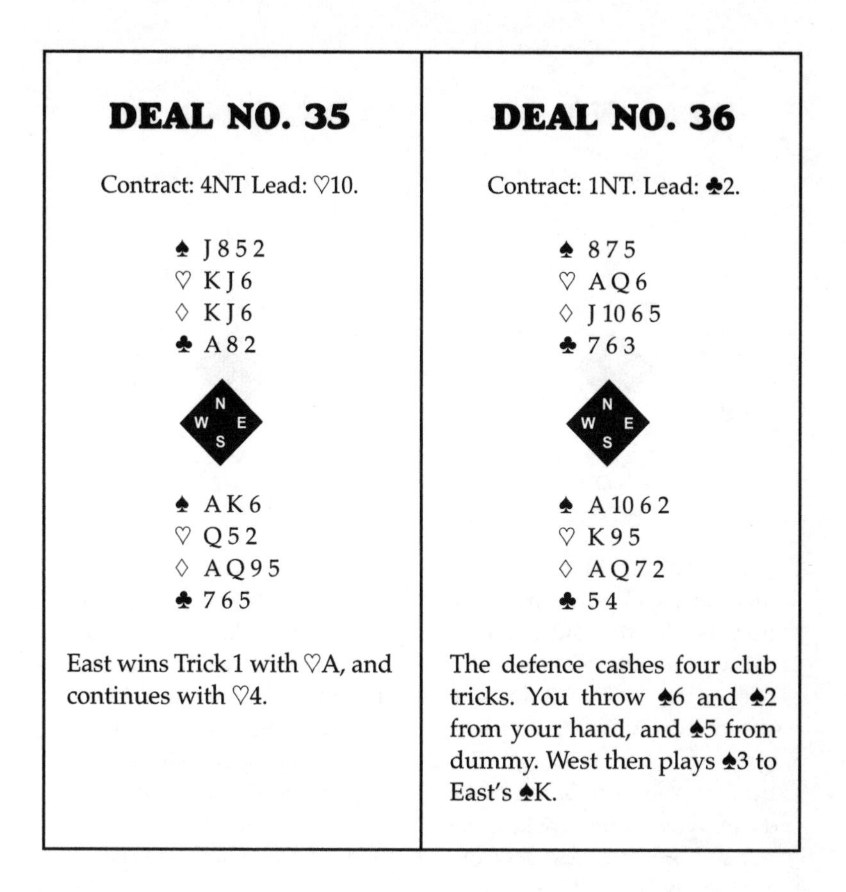

DEAL NO. 35

Contract: 4NT Lead: ♡10.

♠ J 8 5 2
♡ K J 6
♢ K J 6
♣ A 8 2

♠ A K 6
♡ Q 5 2
♢ A Q 9 5
♣ 7 6 5

East wins Trick 1 with ♡A, and continues with ♡4.

DEAL NO. 36

Contract: 1NT. Lead: ♣2.

♠ 8 7 5
♡ A Q 6
♢ J 10 6 5
♣ 7 6 3

♠ A 10 6 2
♡ K 9 5
♢ A Q 7 2
♣ 5 4

The defence cashes four club tricks. You throw ♠6 and ♠2 from your hand, and ♠5 from dummy. West then plays ♠3 to East's ♠K.

DEAL NO. 35

Contract: 4NT Lead: ♡10.

You have misbid to a rather inelegant 4NT and are lucky that the defence did not kick off with a club lead or find a club switch at Trick 2. Luckily you can count two heart tricks after trick one, bringing TTA up to 9. You must try to make ♠J for your tenth trick. Cash ♠A and ♠K, and lead ♠6 from the South hand, hoping that either (a) somebody holds ♠Q doubleton, or (b) West has that card and cannot stop you from making ♠J on the table, or (c) spades break 3-3.

♠	2
♡	0
◇	4
♣	1
TTA	7

DEAL NO. 36

Contract: 1NT. Lead: ♣2.

TTA leaves you two tricks short and the only source of extra tricks is the diamond suit. What's more, you have to take the extra tricks without losing the lead, otherwise the defence will surely cash some spades to put you down. So win with ♠A, cross to dummy's ♡A, and lead ◇J for a finesse against East's hoped-for ◇K. If this wins, not only will you make your contract, but you will probably end up with an overtrick as well!

♠	1
♡	3
◇	1
♣	0
TTA	5

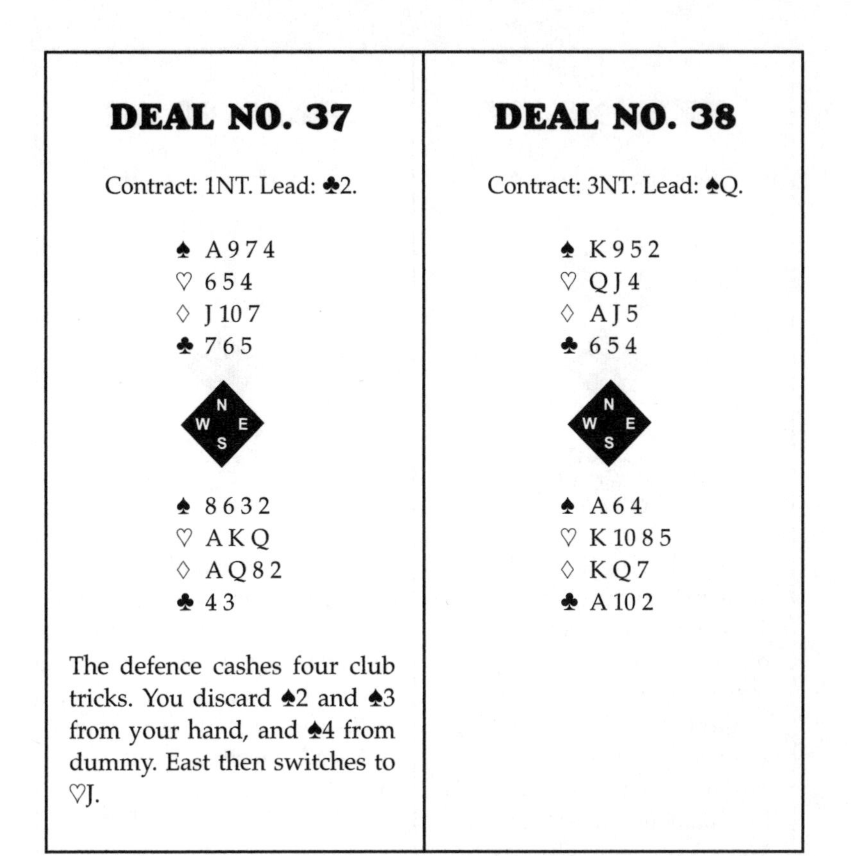
DEAL NO. 37
Contract: 1NT. Lead: ♣2.
♠ A 9 7 4
♡ 6 5 4
◊ J 10 7
♣ 7 6 5
N
W E
S
♠ 8 6 3 2
♡ A K Q
◊ A Q 8 2
♣ 4 3
The defence cashes four club tricks. You discard ♠2 and ♠3 from your hand, and ♠4 from dummy. East then switches to ♡J.
DEAL NO. 38
Contract: 3NT. Lead: ♠Q.
♠ K 9 5 2
♡ Q J 4
◊ A J 5
♣ 6 5 4
N
W E
S
♠ A 6 4
♡ K 10 8 5
◊ K Q 7
♣ A 10 2

DEAL NO. 37

Contract: 1NT. Lead: ♣2.

On the last deal the defence switched unerringly to spades. There you had to hope that the diamond finesse was right to make your contract. This time the defence has slipped up, switching instead to a heart. You must win ♡A and play a low diamond towards dummy. You do not care who has ◊K. You don't need the finesse to take three diamond tricks. In fact, taking the finesse would be a costly mistake because you would have to cross to ♠A in order to take it and, if West holds ◊K, the defence will cash two spades when the diamond finesse loses.

♠	1
♡	3
◊	1
♣	0
TTA	5

DEAL NO. 38

Contract: 3NT. Lead: ♠Q.

North: ♠ K 9 5 2 ♡ Q J 4 ◊ A J 5 ♣ 6 5 4

West: ♠ Q J 10 8 7 ♡ 7 6 ◊ 10 6 ♣ Q 9 8 7

East: ♠ 3 ♡ A 9 3 2 ◊ 9 8 4 3 2 ♣ K J 3

South: ♠ A 6 4 ♡ K 10 8 5 ◊ K Q 7 ♣ A 10 2

By now this should seem a straightforward deal. Although TTA is only 6, three easy tricks are available in hearts as soon as ♡A has been knocked out. It is just a matter of winning the lead – in either hand – and knocking out ♡A.

♠	2
♡	0
◊	3
♣	1
TTA	6

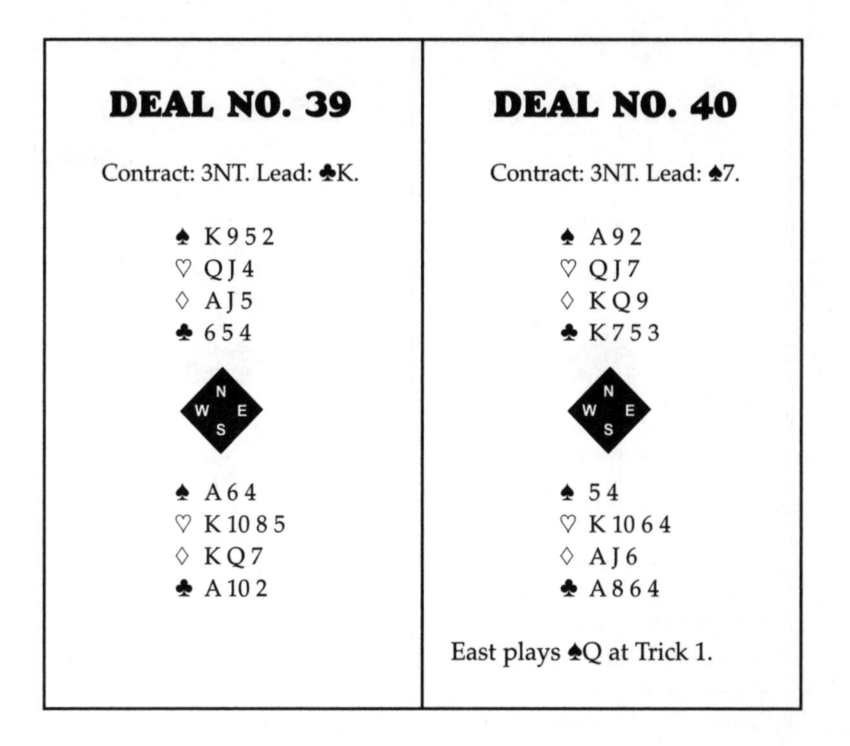

DEAL NO. 39

Contract: 3NT. Lead: ♣K.

♠ K 9 5 2
♡ Q J 4
♢ A J 5
♣ 6 5 4

N / W E / S

♠ A 6 4
♡ K 10 8 5
♢ K Q 7
♣ A 10 2

DEAL NO. 40

Contract: 3NT. Lead: ♠7.

♠ A 9 2
♡ Q J 7
♢ K Q 9
♣ K 7 5 3

N / W E / S

♠ 5 4
♡ K 10 6 4
♢ A J 6
♣ A 8 6 4

East plays ♠Q at Trick 1.

DEAL NO. 39

Contract: 3NT. Lead: ♣K.

Again TTA = 6 and you have to knock out ♡A to gain three extra tricks. Unfortunately, the defence have attacked in clubs. If you win the first club to play hearts, and West started with a five-card suit, they will surely cash four clubs to defeat you. Try 'holding up' ♣A at Trick 1, winning it instead at Trick 2. When you play hearts, luckily it is East who has ♡A and he is now out of clubs. If West held ♡A you were always going to be defeated. Alternatively, if East held a third club, then West only had four, and you were always safe.

♠	2
♡	0
◊	3
♣	1
TTA	6

DEAL NO. 40

Contract: 3NT. Lead: ♠7.

Again you have to knock out ♡A to bring TTA from 6 up to 9 and, again, the defence have attacked your weak spot. Do the arithmetic. If West has five spades, then East must have three. Therefore, win the third spade trick and hope that it is East who holds ♡A (a 50% chance). By playing in this way, you will exhaust East of spades and West will never be able to get in to cash his winners – unless the spades were 4-4 originally, in which case you were never in any danger.

♠	1
♡	0
◊	3
♣	2
TTA	6

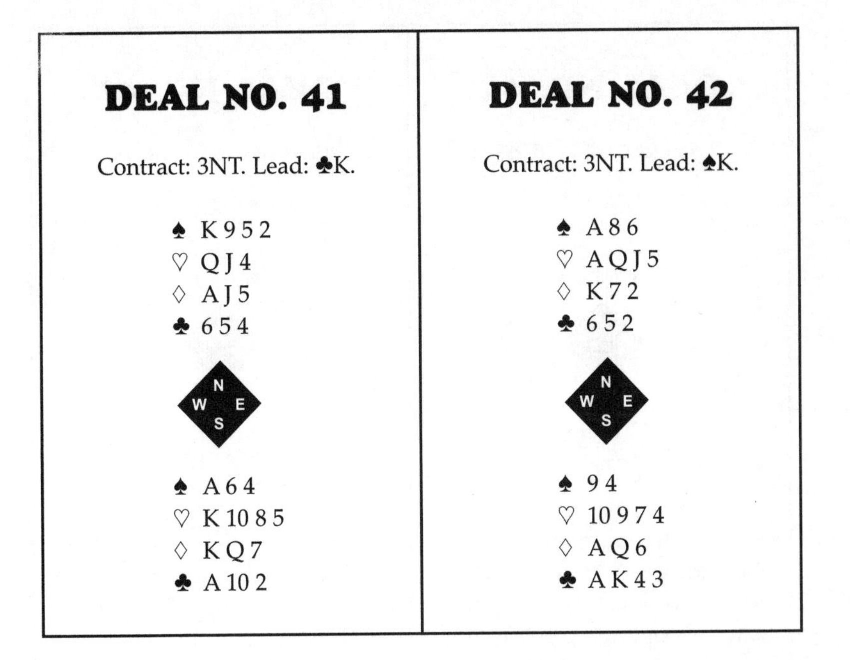

DEAL NO. 41

Contract: 3NT. Lead: ♣K.

♠ K 9 5 2
♡ Q J 4
♢ A J 5
♣ 6 5 4

♠ A 6 4
♡ K 10 8 5
♢ K Q 7
♣ A 10 2

DEAL NO. 42

Contract: 3NT. Lead: ♠K.

♠ A 8 6
♡ A Q J 5
♢ K 7 2
♣ 6 5 2

♠ 9 4
♡ 10 9 7 4
♢ A Q 6
♣ A K 4 3

DEAL NO. 41

Contract: 3NT. Lead: ♣K.

The North-South hands, and the lead, are identical to *Deal 39*. So you should play the same way, by holding up ♣A for one round and then attacking the heart suit. This time East does have a third club when in with ♡A, but that means West only started with four clubs, so your contract is safe. The defence can take only three club tricks and ♡A.

♠	2
♡	0
◊	3
♣	1
TTA	6

DEAL NO. 42

Contract: 3NT. Lead: ♠K.

North: ♠ A 8 6 ♡ A Q J 5 ◊ K 7 2 ♣ 6 5 2

West: ♠ K Q J 7 3 ♡ 8 6 ◊ 10 9 5 ♣ Q 8 7

East: ♠ 10 5 2 ♡ K 3 2 ◊ J 8 4 3 ♣ J 10 9

South: ♠ 9 4 ♡ 10 9 7 4 ◊ A Q 6 ♣ A K 4 3

Never mind that you are not in 4♡ – how do you ensure 3NT? TTA = 7 but clearly extra tricks are available in hearts. In the meantime the defence are threatening to set up and take spade tricks. Do the arithmetic again . . . if West has five spades, East has three, so hold up till the third round and then take the heart finesse in complete safety. Assuming that West hasn't made a silly lead, the contract is 100% safe because he can never regain the lead unless the spades were 4-4 all the time.

♠	1
♡	1
◊	3
♣	2
TTA	7

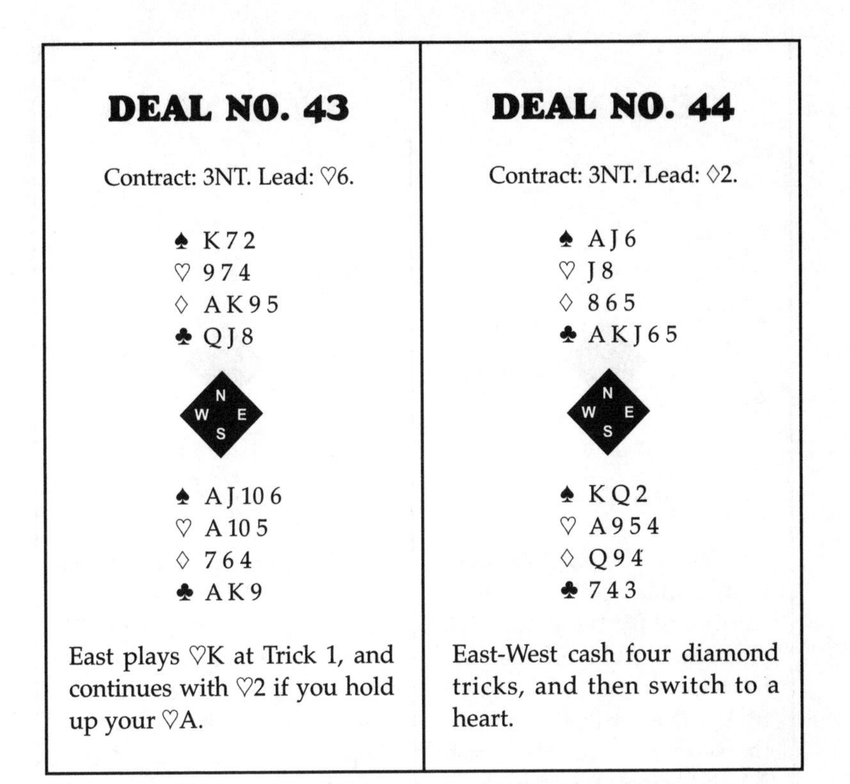

DEAL NO. 43

Contract: 3NT. Lead: ♡6.

♠ K 7 2
♡ 9 7 4
♢ A K 9 5
♣ Q J 8

♠ A J 10 6
♡ A 10 5
♢ 7 6 4
♣ A K 9

East plays ♡K at Trick 1, and continues with ♡2 if you hold up your ♡A.

DEAL NO. 44

Contract: 3NT. Lead: ♢2.

♠ A J 6
♡ J 8
♢ 8 6 5
♣ A K J 6 5

♠ K Q 2
♡ A 9 5 4
♢ Q 9 4
♣ 7 4 3

East-West cash four diamond tricks, and then switch to a heart.

DEAL NO. 43

Contract: 3NT. Lead: ♡6.

TTA leaves you one trick short and spades are the obvious candidate for the extra trick you need. Hold off the first heart lead, in case West has led from a five-card suit, and win the second round. Now cash ♠A and lead ♠J for a finesse. If East is able to win ♠Q he is welcome to it, for either he will be out of hearts, or West began originally with only four.

♠	2
♡	1
◇	2
♣	3
TTA	8

DEAL NO. 44

Contract: 3NT. Lead: ◇2.

North: ♠ A J 6 ♡ J 8 ◇ 8 6 5 ♣ A K J 6 5

West: ♠ 5 4 3 ♡ Q 7 3 ◇ A J 7 2 ♣ Q 9 2

East: ♠ 10 9 8 7 ♡ K 10 6 2 ◇ K 10 3 ♣ 10 8

South: ♠ K Q 2 ♡ A 9 5 4 ◇ Q 9 4 ♣ 7 4 3

You have to win with ♡A and then must plan to take all the remaining tricks. Although TTA is only 6, clubs will furnish the extra tricks you need if you are lucky. It is against the odds to hope somebody has ♣Q-x. Correct play is to finesse ♣J, hoping that West holds ♣Q-x or ♣Q-x-x. If he has, you can win ♣J, cash ♣A-K and finally ♣6-5 to land a lucky contract.

♠	3
♡	1
◇	0
♣	2
TTA	6

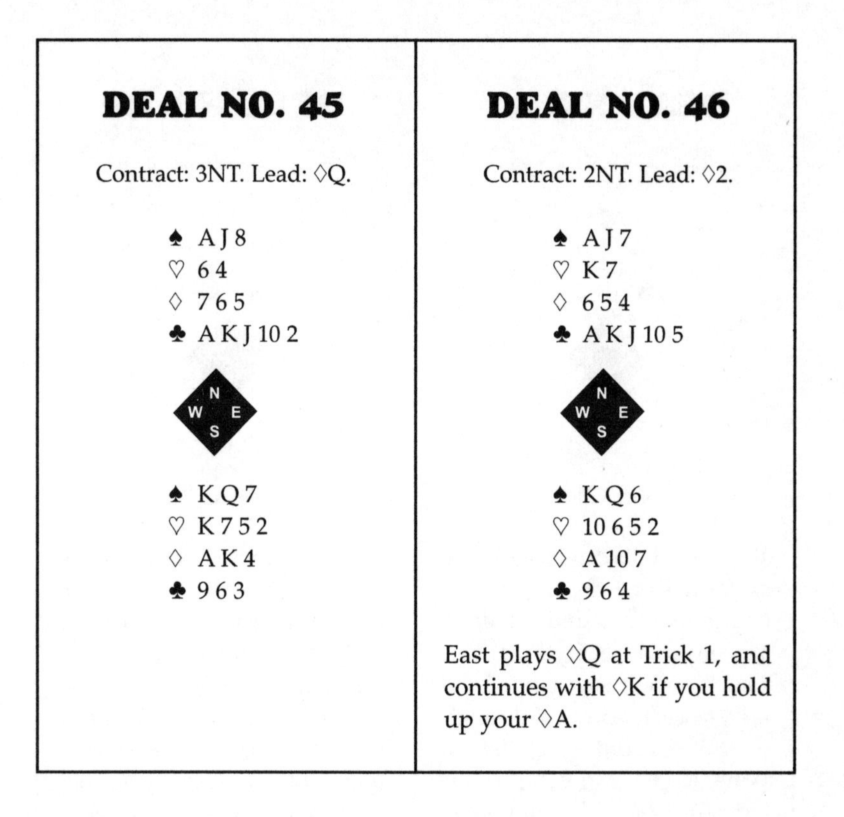

DEAL NO. 45

Contract: 3NT. Lead: ♢Q.

♠ A J 8
♡ 6 4
♢ 7 6 5
♣ A K J 10 2

♠ K Q 7
♡ K 7 5 2
♢ A K 4
♣ 9 6 3

DEAL NO. 46

Contract: 2NT. Lead: ♢2.

♠ A J 7
♡ K 7
♢ 6 5 4
♣ A K J 10 5

♠ K Q 6
♡ 10 6 5 2
♢ A 10 7
♣ 9 6 4

East plays ♢Q at Trick 1, and continues with ♢K if you hold up your ♢A.

DEAL NO. 45

Contract: 3NT. Lead: ♢Q.

TTA = 7. Clubs can provide the extra tricks all right, but your hearts look decidedly feeble. You must do everything you can to prevent East gaining the lead, since a heart lead through your ♡K could spell defeat. Win ♢A and cash ♣A-K. As it happens, ♣Q falls and your troubles are over. But if West had held ♣Q-5-4, you would give up the third round of clubs to him quite happily, as he cannot attack hearts. And if East had held ♣Q-x-x you were always going to be in trouble.

♠	3
♡	0
♢	2
♣	2
TTA	7

DEAL NO. 46

Contract: 2NT. Lead: ♢2.

TTA = 6. Clubs should provide the extra tricks *but* your hearts are vulnerable. This time it is West you must try to keep off lead, to prevent a possible killing heart switch. The key is to hold off the first two diamonds, thus ensuring that East, if he gets in with ♣Q, cannot play a diamond across to West's hand. Win the third round of diamonds, and then finesse ♣10 knowing that, even if East can win, he cannot attack hearts. You make two extra club tricks in safety to bring home the contract.

♠	3
♡	0
♢	1
♣	2
TTA	6

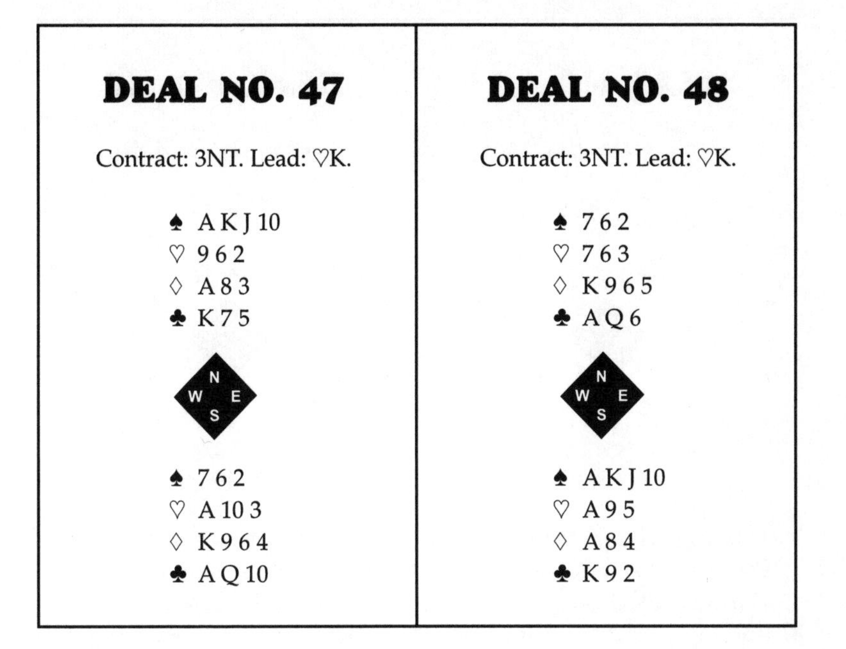
DEAL NO. 47
Contract: 3NT. Lead: ♡K.
♠ A K J 10
♡ 9 6 2
♢ A 8 3
♣ K 7 5
N
W E
S
♠ 7 6 2
♡ A 10 3
♢ K 9 6 4
♣ A Q 10
DEAL NO. 48
Contract: 3NT. Lead: ♡K.
♠ 7 6 2
♡ 7 6 3
♢ K 9 6 5
♣ A Q 6
N
W E
S
♠ A K J 10
♡ A 9 5
♢ A 8 4
♣ K 9 2

DEAL NO. 47

Contract: 3NT. Lead: ♡K.

This deal should be easy for you by now. TTA leaves you one trick short but, clearly, at least one extra trick is available in spades. Meanwhile, if West has led from a five-card suit, East will have only two hearts. Therefore hold up ♡A for one round, then cash ♠A in case somebody has a singleton ♠Q. Assuming that ♠Q doesn't fall, come back to hand and finesse ♠10 in safety. As it happens, East does have a third heart, but the defenders can take only three hearts and ♠Q while you notch up your contract.

♠	2
♡	1
♢	2
♣	3
TTA	8

DEAL NO. 48

Contract: 3NT. Lead: ♡K.

Again TTA = 8, again spades offer chances of extra tricks and again the defenders have attacked in your weak spot, hearts. This time, as you can see, West has led from a five-card suit and your contract could be in danger. Hold up ♡A for one round, and then cash ♠A-K, refusing the finesse – doing your best to prevent West getting back in to cash hearts. You don't care if East can win with ♠Q because, if he does have a third heart, the contract was safe in any case.

♠	2
♡	1
♢	2
♣	3
TTA	8

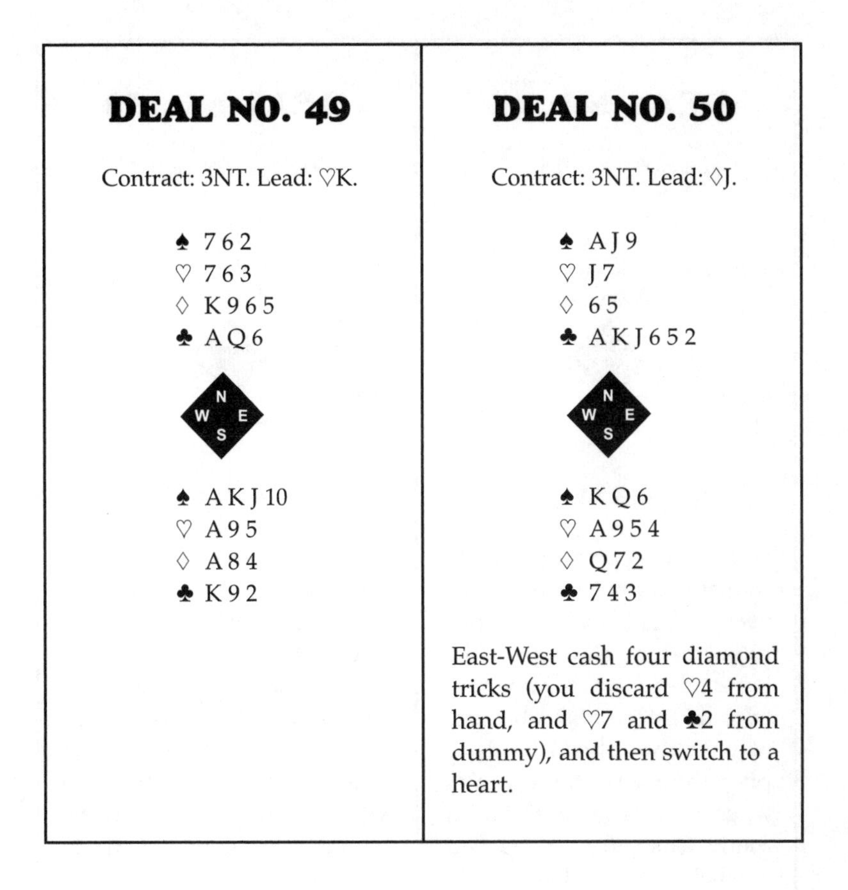

DEAL NO. 49

Contract: 3NT. Lead: ♡K.

♠ 7 6 2
♡ 7 6 3
◇ K 9 6 5
♣ A Q 6

♠ A K J 10
♡ A 9 5
◇ A 8 4
♣ K 9 2

DEAL NO. 50

Contract: 3NT. Lead: ◇J.

♠ A J 9
♡ J 7
◇ 6 5
♣ A K J 6 5 2

♠ K Q 6
♡ A 9 5 4
◇ Q 7 2
♣ 7 4 3

East-West cash four diamond tricks (you discard ♡4 from hand, and ♡7 and ♣2 from dummy), and then switch to a heart.

DEAL NO. 49

Contract: 3NT. Lead: ♡K.

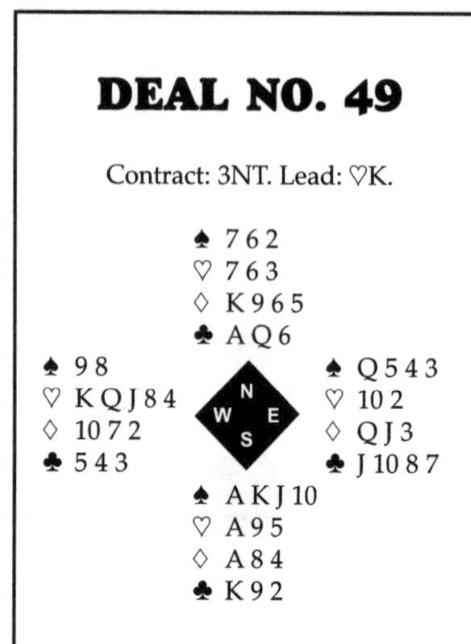

Here is a reprise of *Deal 48* so that you can clearly see the need to hold up ♡A for one round before playing off the top spades. Here, ♠Q does not fall but East has it and, because of your thoughtful hold-up play, cannot continue hearts when he gets in on the third round of spades. If you had not held up ♡A, East would have been able to play a heart across to West, who would have cashed enough tricks to defeat the contract.

♠	2
♡	1
◇	2
♣	3
TTA	8

DEAL NO. 50

Contract: 3NT. Lead: ◇J.

You have lost four tricks, so must take the remainder if you are going to make this contract. You met essentially the same problem on *Deal 44*. There you had eight clubs between your two hands and the correct play was to finesse ♣J. Here you have nine clubs and the correct percentage play is to cash ♣A-K because the odds just about favour the four outstanding clubs to be split 2-2. Assuming that ♣Q falls as expected, you will have enough club tricks to bring home the contract.

♠	3
♡	1
◇	0
♣	2
TTA	6

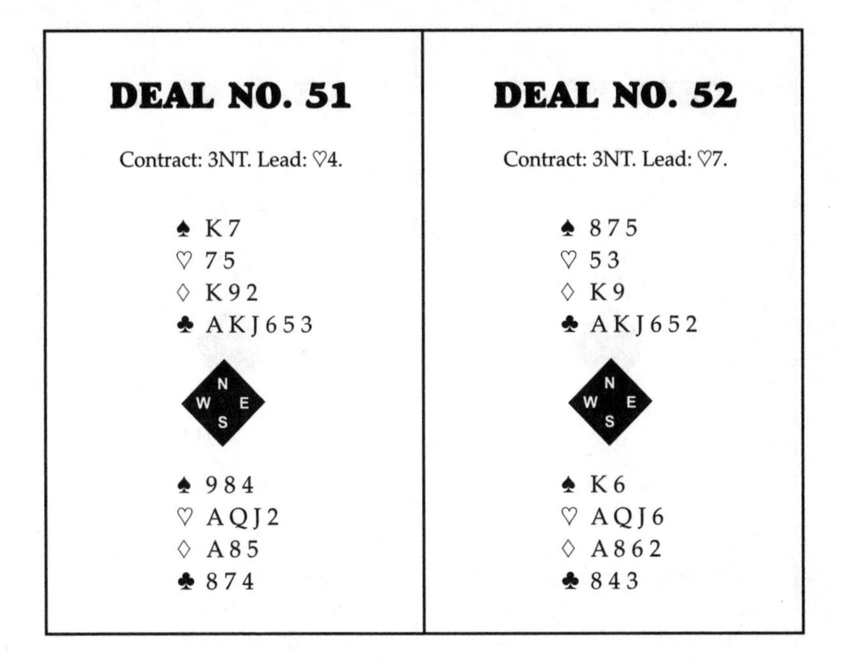
DEAL NO. 51
Contract: 3NT. Lead: ♡4.
♠ K 7
♡ 7 5
♢ K 9 2
♣ A K J 6 5 3
N
W E
S
♠ 9 8 4
♡ A Q J 2
♢ A 8 5
♣ 8 7 4
DEAL NO. 52
Contract: 3NT. Lead: ♡7.
♠ 8 7 5
♡ 5 3
♢ K 9
♣ A K J 6 5 2
N
W E
S
♠ K 6
♡ A Q J 6
♢ A 8 6 2
♣ 8 4 3

DEAL NO. 51

Contract: 3NT. Lead: ♡4.

TTA is 6 as a result of a favourable heart lead round to your ♡A-Q and clubs are the obvious place to look for the extra three tricks needed. If you needed all six clubs, your best play would be to cash ♣A-K, as in the previous deal. But you only need five club tricks and you would do better to try to protect your tenuous spade holding. Win ♡Q, cash ♣A, and then cross to ◊A and finesse ♣J. No matter if it loses to East's ♣Q, since East cannot attack spades and you have set up enough club tricks for your contract.

♠	0
♡	2
◊	2
♣	2
TTA	6

DEAL NO. 52

Contract: 3NT. Lead: ♡7.

North: ♠ 8 7 5 ♡ 5 3 ◊ K 9 ♣ A K J 6 5 2

West: ♠ A J 9 ♡ K 10 8 7 4 ◊ J 4 ♣ Q 9 7

East: ♠ Q 10 4 3 2 ♡ 9 2 ◊ Q 10 7 5 3 ♣ 10

South: ♠ K 6 ♡ A Q J 6 ◊ A 8 6 2 ♣ 8 4 3

This is the other side of the coin from *Deal 51*. This time it is South who has the tenuous spade holding and you must play to try to keep East off lead. So win ♡Q and then play off ♣A-K, spurning the finesse. No matter if West is able to win ♣Q which could have been finessed. West is unable to attack spades and again you have set up enough club tricks for your contract.

♠	0
♡	2
◊	2
♣	2
TTA	6

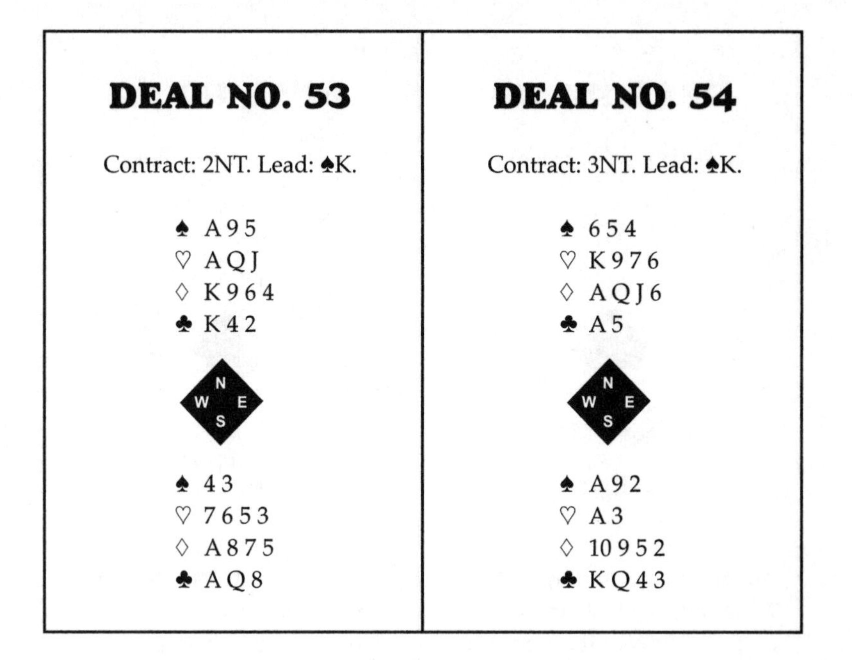

DEAL NO. 53

Contract: 2NT. Lead: ♠K.

North:
♠ A 9 5
♡ A Q J
♢ K 9 6 4
♣ K 4 2

South:
♠ 4 3
♡ 7 6 5 3
♢ A 8 7 5
♣ A Q 8

DEAL NO. 54

Contract: 3NT. Lead: ♠K.

North:
♠ 6 5 4
♡ K 9 7 6
♢ A Q J 6
♣ A 5

South:
♠ A 9 2
♡ A 3
♢ 10 9 5 2
♣ K Q 4 3

DEAL NO. 53

Contract: 2NT. Lead: ♠K.

Once again TTA leaves you one trick short and the defence have attacked your weakest spot. By now it should be routine to hold up ♠A till the third round, to exhaust East of spades if they happen to be 5-3. In theory you could now play diamonds to garner your extra trick, but that risks West gaining the lead. Much better to take a simple heart finesse. Even if ♡J loses to ♡K, ♡Q is still there to bring your TTA up to the required 8.

♠	1
♡	1
◊	2
♣	3
TTA	7

DEAL NO. 54

Contract: 3NT. Lead: ♠K.

West	North / South	East
	♠ 6 5 4 ♡ K 9 7 6 ◊ A Q J 6 ♣ A 5	
♠ K Q J 10 7 ♡ J 10 8 ◊ 8 7 4 ♣ 8 6	N / W E / S	♠ 8 3 ♡ Q 5 4 2 ◊ K 3 ♣ J 10 9 7 2
	♠ A 9 2 ♡ A 3 ◊ 10 9 5 2 ♣ K Q 4 3	

This too should be routine by now. Although TTA is only 7, diamonds can clearly provide two extra tricks even if the finesse loses. It is just a matter of making sure East can do no mischief in spades if he does get in with ◊K. Arithmetic again! If West has five spades, East has two. Therefore hold up ♠A until the second round, then take the diamond finesse. Holding up aces in this way is a fundamental and important technique and we make no excuses for including several deals to demonstrate it.

♠	1
♡	2
◊	1
♣	3
TTA	7

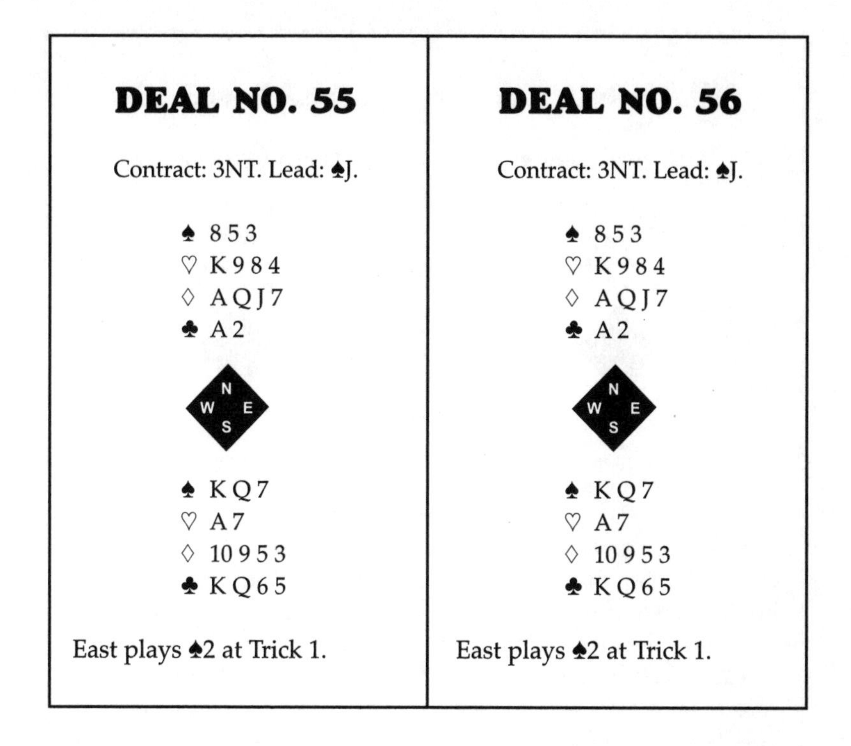

DEAL NO. 55

Contract: 3NT. Lead: ♠J.

♠ 8 5 3
♡ K 9 8 4
◊ A Q J 7
♣ A 2

N / W E / S

♠ K Q 7
♡ A 7
◊ 10 9 5 3
♣ K Q 6 5

East plays ♠2 at Trick 1.

DEAL NO. 56

Contract: 3NT. Lead: ♠J.

♠ 8 5 3
♡ K 9 8 4
◊ A Q J 7
♣ A 2

N / W E / S

♠ K Q 7
♡ A 7
◊ 10 9 5 3
♣ K Q 6 5

East plays ♠2 at Trick 1.

DEAL NO. 55

Contract: 3NT. Lead: ♠J.

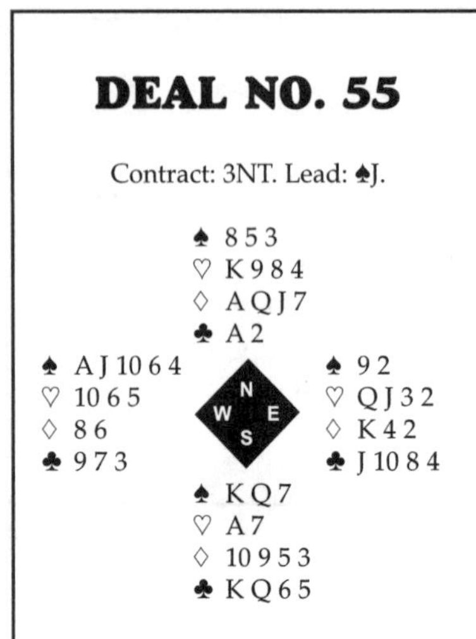

Almost the same as *Deal 54,* except that South holds ♠K-Q instead of ♠A. If you win Trick 1 and take the losing diamond finesse, East will return his second and last spade to beat you. So . . . don't win Trick 1! What can the defenders do? If they continue spades, East will have none left when in with ◇K and, if they do anything else, your ♠K-Q remains as a stopper when East gets in. In effect your ♠K-Q perform the same task as ♠A in *Deal 54,* but it is much harder to see. If you got this one right, maybe you shouldn't be reading this book!

♠	0
♡	2
◇	1
♣	3
TTA	6

DEAL NO. 56

Contract: 3NT. Lead: ♠J.

North: ♠ 8 5 3 ♡ K 9 8 4 ◇ A Q J 7 ♣ A 2

West: ♠ A J 10 6 ♡ 10 6 5 ◇ 8 6 ♣ 9 7 4 3

East: ♠ 9 4 2 ♡ Q J 3 2 ◇ K 4 2 ♣ J 10 8

South: ♠ K Q 7 ♡ A 7 ◇ 10 9 5 3 ♣ K Q 6 5

You are right – this is the same as *Deal 55* and again you have to take the diamond finesse to increase your TTA of 6 to 9. Again you must refuse to win Trick 1 in case West has five spades. Say West persists with ♠6 to East's ♠9 and your ♠K. When you do take the losing diamond finesse, East has a spade left, but that means West started with only four. *Deal 55* shows why the spade hold-up is essential if West has five spades, and this deal shows that it doesn't cost if the spades were, after all, 4-3.

♠	0
♡	2
◇	1
♣	3
TTA	6

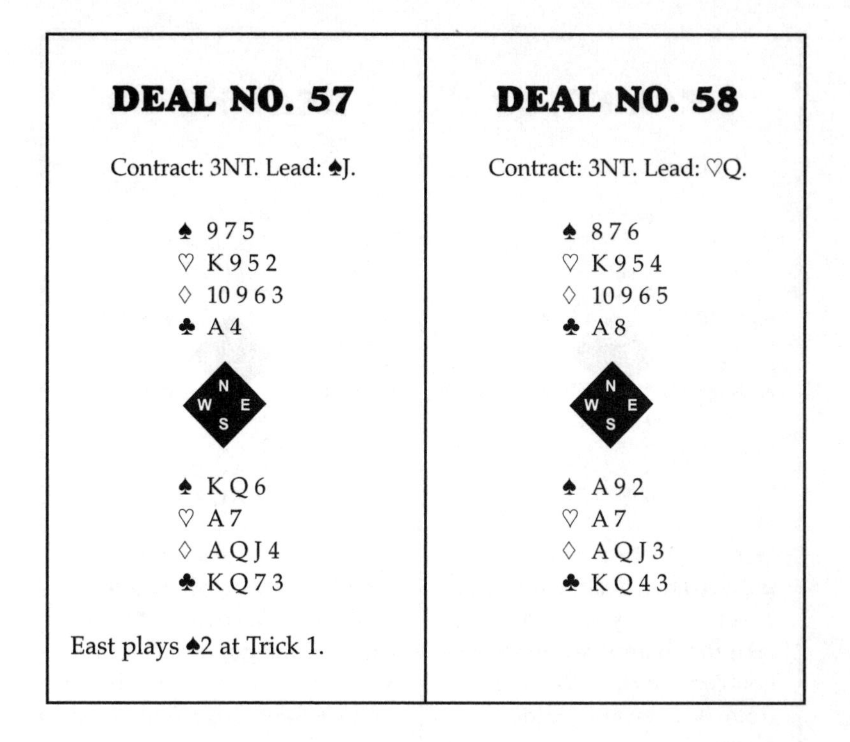

DEAL NO. 57
Contract: 3NT. Lead: ♠J.
♠ 9 7 5
♡ K 9 5 2
◊ 10 9 6 3
♣ A 4
N
W E
S
♠ K Q 6
♡ A 7
◊ A Q J 4
♣ K Q 7 3
East plays ♠2 at Trick 1.
DEAL NO. 58
Contract: 3NT. Lead: ♡Q.
♠ 8 7 6
♡ K 9 5 4
◊ 10 9 6 5
♣ A 8
N
W E
S
♠ A 9 2
♡ A 7
◊ A Q J 3
♣ K Q 4 3

DEAL NO. 57

Contract: 3NT. Lead: ♠J.

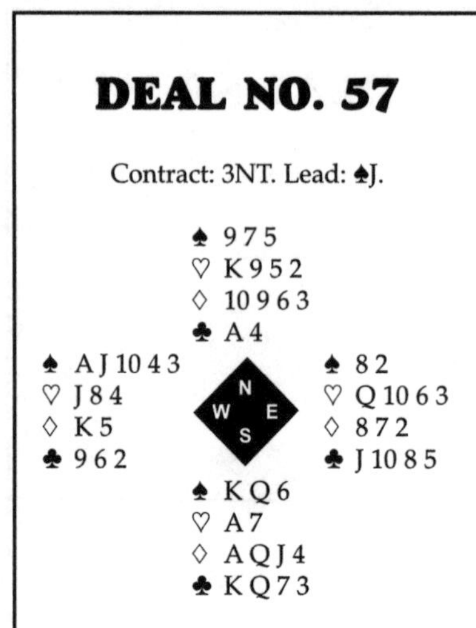

Here is another take on the previous two deals. Once again TTA is only 6, you will have to take the diamond finesse and you can see that West has led from a five-card spade suit. However, here the diamond finesse will be taken into the West hand. Do you see the difference that makes? Just win with ♠K, cross to dummy and finesse in diamonds. Your ♠Q-6 still stops the spades if West is able to win ◇K.

♠	0
♡	2
◇	1
♣	3
TTA	6

DEAL NO. 58

Contract: 3NT. Lead: ♡Q.

On a heart lead this deal should present no problems. Just win ♡A, cross to ♣A and take the diamond finesse. If it wins, you will make ten tricks (TTA + three extra diamonds), while if it loses, the contract is still perfectly safe because you still have all the suits stopped.

♠	1
♡	2
◇	1
♣	3
TTA	7

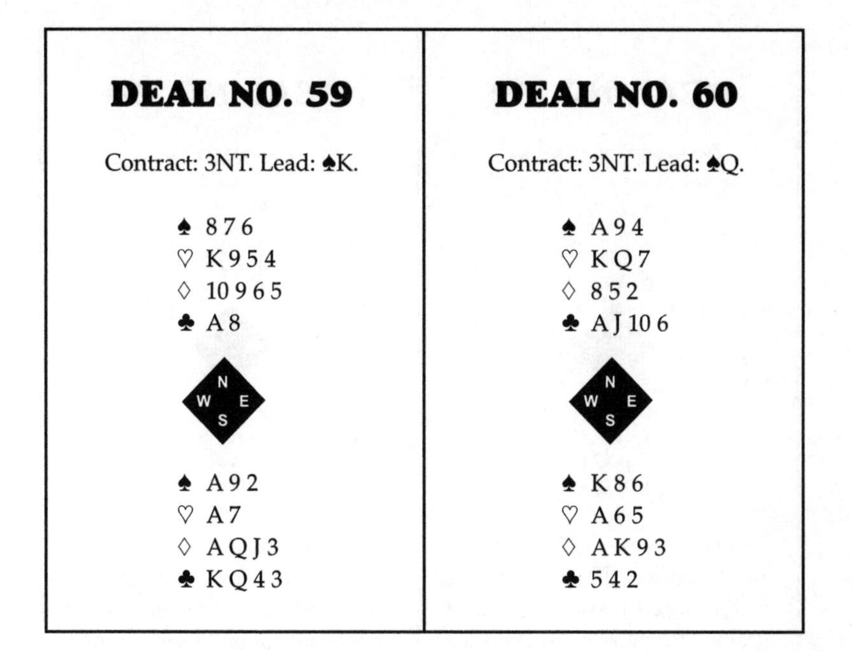
DEAL NO. 59
Contract: 3NT. Lead: ♠K.
♠ 8 7 6
♡ K 9 5 4
♢ 10 9 6 5
♣ A 8
N
W
E
S
♠ A 9 2
♡ A 7
♢ A Q J 3
♣ K Q 4 3
DEAL NO. 60
Contract: 3NT. Lead: ♠Q.
♠ A 9 4
♡ K Q 7
♢ 8 5 2
♣ A J 10 6
N
W
E
S
♠ K 8 6
♡ A 6 5
♢ A K 9 3
♣ 5 4 2

DEAL NO. 59

Contract: 3NT. Lead: ♠K.

This is the same as *Deal 58* but the defenders have started a much more threatening spade attack. Now you must hold up ♠A for one round – in case West has led from a five-card suit – and then consider how to keep West from regaining the lead. Do you see it? Yes, refuse the diamond finesse and just cash ◊A. You don't care if East gains the lead and, every now and then, as above, West will drop an annoyed singleton ◊K.

♠ 1
♡ 2
◊ 1
♣ 3
TTA 7

DEAL NO. 60

Contract: 3NT. Lead: ♠Q.

North: ♠ A 9 4 ♡ K Q 7 ◊ 8 5 2 ♣ A J 10 6

West: ♠ Q J 10 7 3 ♡ 9 ◊ 10 7 6 4 ♣ Q 9 3

East: ♠ 5 2 ♡ J 10 8 4 3 2 ◊ Q J ♣ K 8 7

South: ♠ K 8 6 ♡ A 6 5 ◊ A K 9 3 ♣ 5 4 2

TTA = 8. Where do you go for your extra trick? In theory diamonds could break 3-3 but that is only about a 36% chance. Clubs offer much better odds. Win the spade, and finesse ♣J. If it wins, your troubles are over, but no doubt East will win with ♣Q or ♣K. Now win the likely spade continuation, and finesse ♣10. It is to be hoped that this will win, as the chances of East holding both ♣K and ♣Q are only 25%. In fact, if clubs turn out to be 3-3, you will make an overtrick!

♠ 2
♡ 3
◊ 2
♣ 1
TTA 8

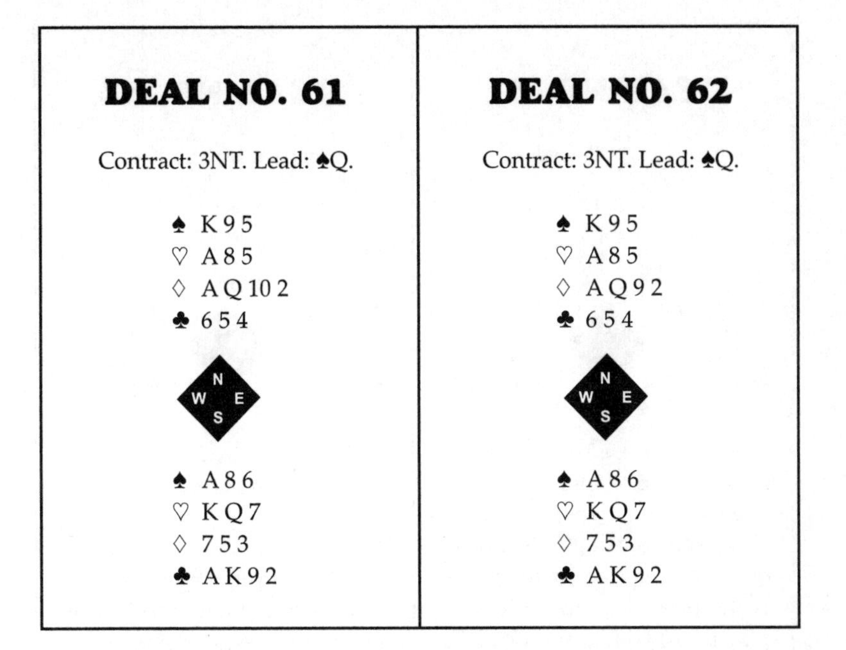

DEAL NO. 61

Contract: 3NT. Lead: ♠Q.

♠ K 9 5
♡ A 8 5
♢ A Q 10 2
♣ 6 5 4

♠ A 8 6
♡ K Q 7
♢ 7 5 3
♣ A K 9 2

DEAL NO. 62

Contract: 3NT. Lead: ♠Q.

♠ K 9 5
♡ A 8 5
♢ A Q 9 2
♣ 6 5 4

♠ A 8 6
♡ K Q 7
♢ 7 5 3
♣ A K 9 2

DEAL NO. 61

Contract: 3NT. Lead: ♠Q.

You need to bring TTA up by one trick and clearly diamonds is the best place to look. Best play is to lead to dummy's ◊10. If it loses to ◊J you still have the chance of finessing ◊Q. As the cards lie, finessing ◊Q immediately does give you the extra trick you need but now West, with ◊K-J equals against dummy's Ace, must inevitably take a diamond trick. If you finesse ◊10 initially, and follow up with a finesse of ◊Q after, West's holding is useless and you end up with eleven tricks.

♠	2
♡	3
◊	1
♣	2
TTA	8

DEAL NO. 62

Contract: 3NT. Lead: ♠Q.

North: ♠ K 9 5 ♡ A 8 5 ◊ A Q 9 2 ♣ 6 5 4

West: ♠ Q J 10 7 2 ♡ 9 6 ◊ J 10 6 4 ♣ 8 7

East: ♠ 4 3 ♡ J 10 4 3 2 ◊ K 8 ♣ Q J 10 3

South: ♠ A 8 6 ♡ K Q 7 ◊ 7 5 3 ♣ A K 9 2

Deal 61 again, but dummy's ◊10 has shrunk into ◊9. This time correct play is to lead to ◊9 in case West holds ◊J-10. This works as the cards lie, because East has to play ◊K on ◊9, promoting dummy's ◊Q. If West had 'split his honours' by playing ◊10 or ◊J, you would have finessed ◊Q. Yes, East would have won ◊K, but then dummy's ◊A-9 would still be poised over West's remaining honour and a second finesse would have seen you home. If East had been able to win with, say, ◊J, you would then try finessing ◊Q. If that also lost, your last resort would be a 3-3 diamond break.

♠	2
♡	3
◊	1
♣	2
TTA	8

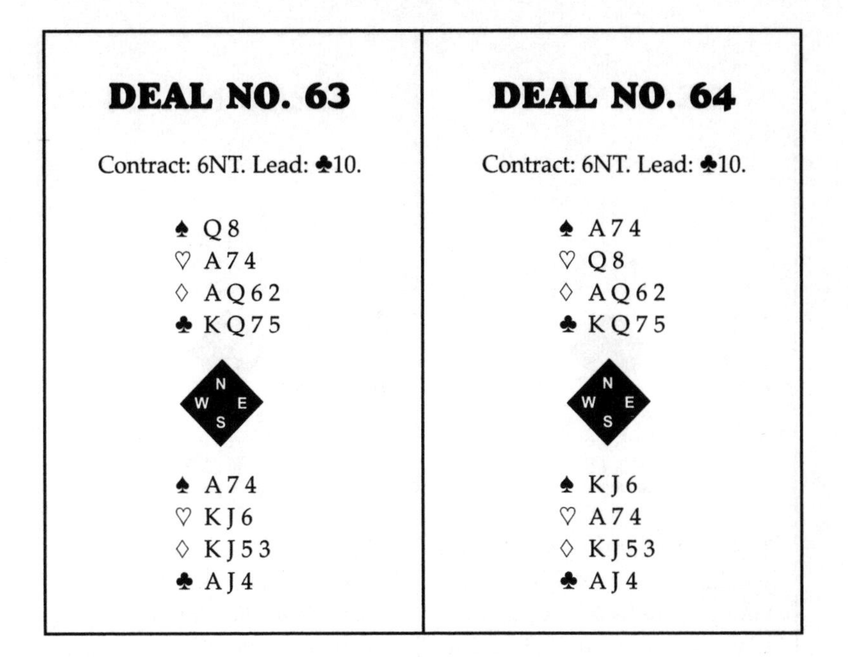
DEAL NO. 63
Contract: 6NT. Lead: ♣10.
♠ Q 8
♡ A 7 4
◊ A Q 6 2
♣ K Q 7 5
N
W E
S
♠ A 7 4
♡ K J 6
◊ K J 5 3
♣ A J 4
DEAL NO. 64
Contract: 6NT. Lead: ♣10.
♠ A 7 4
♡ Q 8
◊ A Q 6 2
♣ K Q 7 5
N
W E
S
♠ K J 6
♡ A 7 4
◊ K J 5 3
♣ A J 4

DEAL NO. 63

Contract: 6NT. Lead: ♣10.

TTA = 11, one trick short. You will have to make ♠Q or ♡J for your twelfth trick – but which? If you try finessing ♡J and it loses, you will have no further chance because either opponent can take ♠K when you lead low towards dummy's ♠Q. On the other hand, if you lead to dummy's ♠Q first and it loses to East's ♠K, you can always try ♡J as a second chance. Correct play is therefore to try leading up to ♠Q at Trick 2, hoping that West holds ♠K.

♠	1
♡	2
♢	4
♣	4
TTA	11

DEAL NO. 64

Contract: 6NT. Lead: ♣10.

West	North	East
	♠ A 7 4 ♡ Q 8 ♢ A Q 6 2 ♣ K Q 7 5	
♠ 10 9 5 ♡ J 10 6 ♢ 8 7 ♣ 10 9 8 6 3	N W E S	♠ Q 8 3 2 ♡ K 9 5 3 2 ♢ 10 9 4 ♣ 2
	♠ K J 6 ♡ A 7 4 ♢ K J 5 3 ♣ A J 4	

This should be easy if the lesson of *Deal 63* has sunk home! Win the club and try a heart towards ♡Q in dummy immediately. This loses but, in the fullness of time, you can try cashing ♠A and finessing ♠J. As it happens this works, and you make the contract.

♠	2
♡	1
♢	4
♣	4
TTA	11

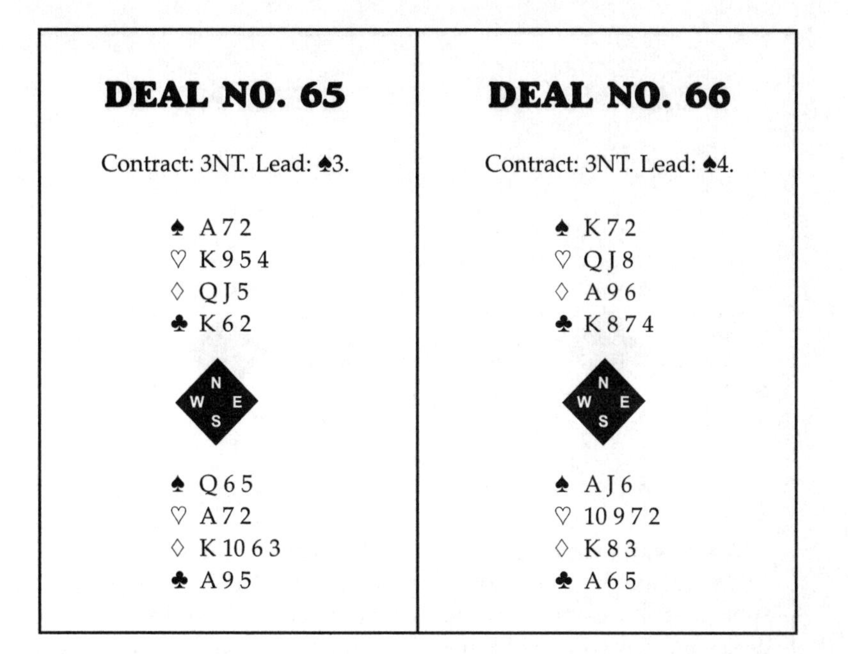

DEAL NO. 65

Contract: 3NT. Lead: ♠3.

North:
♠ A 7 2
♡ K 9 5 4
◊ Q J 5
♣ K 6 2

South:
♠ Q 6 5
♡ A 7 2
◊ K 10 6 3
♣ A 9 5

DEAL NO. 66

Contract: 3NT. Lead: ♠4.

North:
♠ K 7 2
♡ Q J 8
◊ A 9 6
♣ K 8 7 4

South:
♠ A J 6
♡ 10 9 7 2
◊ K 8 3
♣ A 6 5

DEAL NO. 65

Contract: 3NT. Lead: ♠3.

TTA = 5, way short of the nine tricks required. You should spot that knocking out the defenders' ◇A will yield three extra tricks in that suit. Also, if you play low in dummy at Trick 1, you will be guaranteed an extra spade trick. Either West has led from ♠K, in which case you make ♠Q at Trick 1, or East plays ♠K, in which case you make ♠Q later. A-x-x opposite Q-x-x will always yield two tricks if a defender has to lead round to the Q-x-x. It is only a 50% chance if you have to lead the suit yourself.

♠	1
♡	2
◇	0
♣	2
TTA	5

DEAL NO. 66

Contract: 3NT. Lead: ♠4.

TTA leaves you three tricks short but you should see that the opening lead has given you a trick straight away. Just play low in dummy. Either East will play low, in which case you win with ♠J, or he plays ♠Q, in which case you win with ♠A and make ♠J later. Having won Trick 1, lead a low heart to dummy to knock out the defenders' ♡K. Win the return, and then play another heart to knock out ♡A. Your ♡10-9 will provide the two extra tricks required.

♠	2
♡	0
◇	2
♣	2
TTA	6

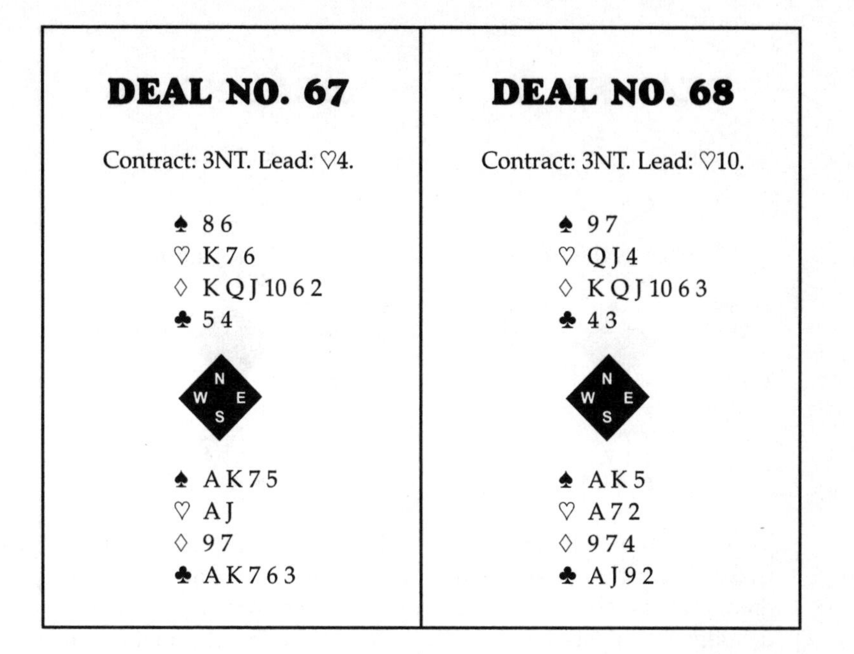
DEAL NO. 67
Contract: 3NT. Lead: ♡4.
♠ 8 6
♡ K 7 6
◊ K Q J 10 6 2
♣ 5 4
N
W E
S
♠ A K 7 5
♡ A J
◊ 9 7
♣ A K 7 6 3
DEAL NO. 68
Contract: 3NT. Lead: ♡10.
♠ 9 7
♡ Q J 4
◊ K Q J 10 6 3
♣ 4 3
N
W E
S
♠ A K 5
♡ A 7 2
◊ 9 7 4
♣ A J 9 2

TTA is only 6 but there are five extra tricks available in diamonds as soon as ♢A is dislodged, and you can win ♡J at Trick 1 as well. Twelve tricks! Unfortunately, if you win with ♡J, East will win the second diamond trick, not the first, and how then will you cross to dummy to enjoy those lovely diamonds? Your now-singleton ♡A blocks the suit and you cannot even make nine tricks! The remedy is simply to win ♡A at Trick 1 and go after the diamonds. Dummy has ♡K as an entry and you make the contract comfortably.

♠	2
♡	2
♢	0
♣	2
TTA	6

This is one of the most difficult deals in this book. Did you play ♡Q at Trick 1, certain that you must thereby make two heart tricks? So you will, but East will not play ♡K. West will hold up ♢A until the third round. Now your ♡J is not an entry to dummy and all those winning diamonds, since East has clung on to his ♡K. The solution? Play low in dummy at Trick 1 and win with ♡A. Now dummy's ♡Q-J will guarantee a sure entry to the diamonds regardless of when East decides to take his ♡K.

♠	2
♡	1
♢	0
♣	1
TTA	4

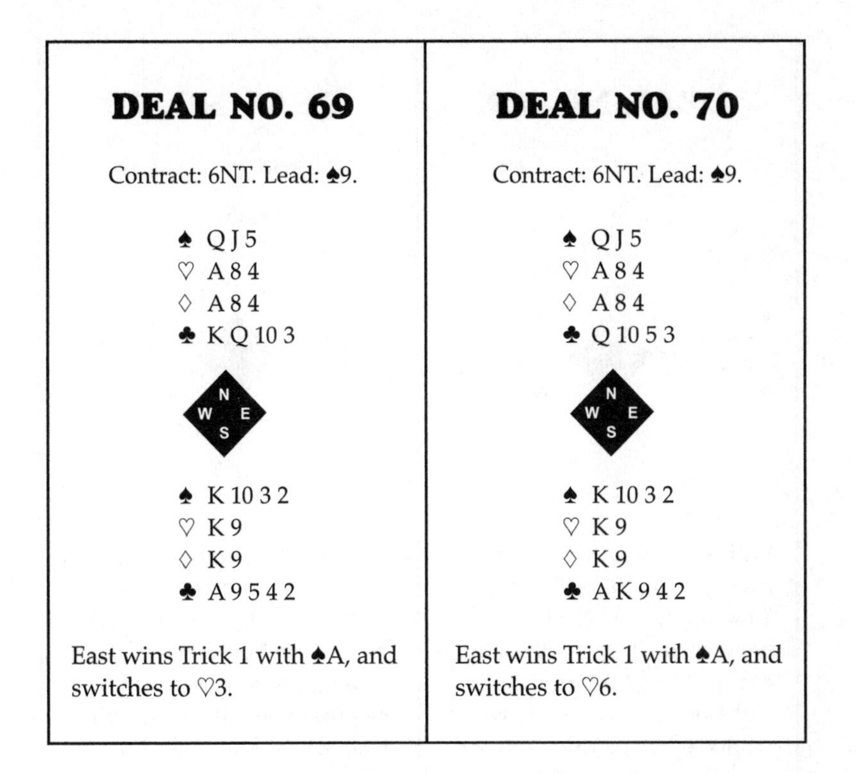

DEAL NO. 69

Contract: 6NT. Lead: ♠9.

♠ Q J 5
♡ A 8 4
♢ A 8 4
♣ K Q 10 3

♠ K 10 3 2
♡ K 9
♢ K 9
♣ A 9 5 4 2

East wins Trick 1 with ♠A, and switches to ♡3.

DEAL NO. 70

Contract: 6NT. Lead: ♠9.

♠ Q J 5
♡ A 8 4
♢ A 8 4
♣ Q 10 5 3

♠ K 10 3 2
♡ K 9
♢ K 9
♣ A K 9 4 2

East wins Trick 1 with ♠A, and switches to ♡6.

DEAL NO. 69

Contract: 6NT. Lead: ♠9.

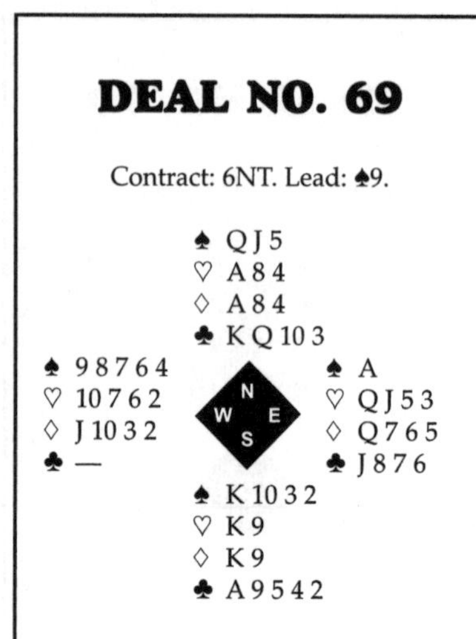

With ♠A out of the way, three extra spade tricks bring your TTA up to 10. Now all you have to do is play the clubs correctly. If the outstanding clubs are 3-1, or 2-2, it won't matter what you do. You will always make five club tricks. To guard against them being 4-0, cash ♣K first. Then, if East shows out, you can finesse ♣10, while if West shows out you can finesse ♣9. If you make the mistake of cashing your ♣A first, you can only pick up four clubs in the West hand.

♠	0
♡	2
◊	2
♣	3
TTA	7

DEAL NO. 70

Contract: 6NT. Lead: ♠9.

North: ♠ Q J 5 ♡ A 8 4 ◊ A 8 4 ♣ Q 10 5 3

West: ♠ 9 8 7 6 4 ♡ 10 7 ◊ J 10 ♣ J 8 7 6

East: ♠ A ♡ Q J 6 5 3 2 ◊ Q 7 6 5 3 2 ♣ —

South: ♠ K 10 3 2 ♡ K 9 ◊ K 9 ♣ A K 9 4 2

As in *Deal 69*, your TTA climbs to 10 as soon as ♠A has gone and it only remains to decide how to play the clubs. Think it through. If you play dummy's ♣Q first you will be all right if East has all four clubs but you will be unable to pick up four clubs with West. If you play ♣A first, you will retain ♣Q-10 in dummy and ♣K-9 in hand, and can finesse either way if it proves necessary. So it is correct to play ♣A first to see how the land lies.

♠	0
♡	2
◊	2
♣	3
TTA	7

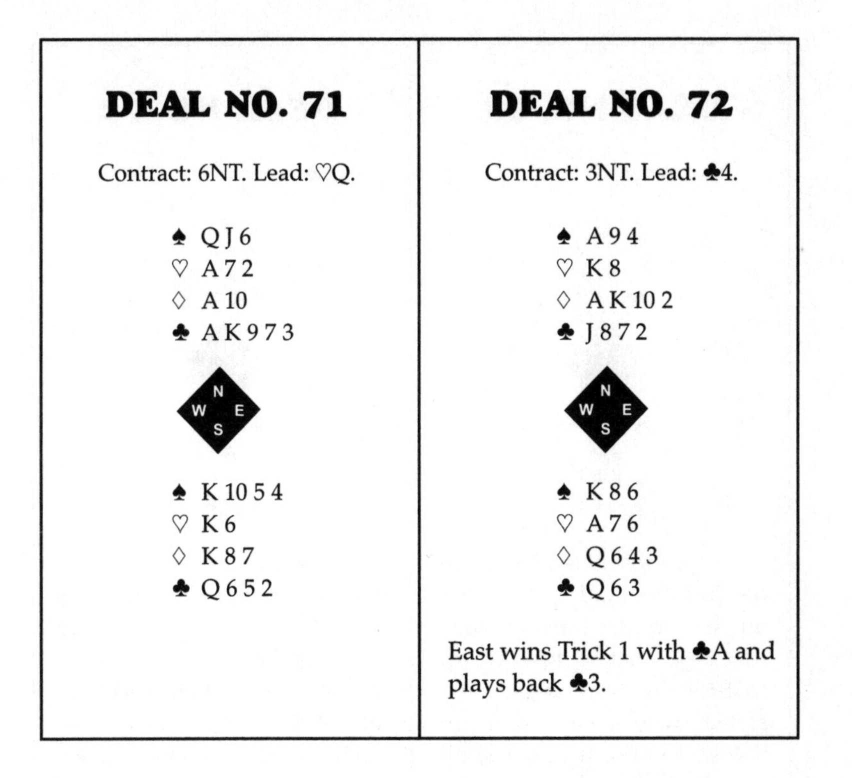
DEAL NO. 71
Contract: 6NT. Lead: ♡Q.
♠ Q J 6
♡ A 7 2
◊ A 10
♣ A K 9 7 3
N
W E
S
♠ K 10 5 4
♡ K 6
◊ K 8 7
♣ Q 6 5 2
DEAL NO. 72
Contract: 3NT. Lead: ♣4.
♠ A 9 4
♡ K 8
◊ A K 10 2
♣ J 8 7 2
N
W E
S
♠ K 8 6
♡ A 7 6
◊ Q 6 4 3
♣ Q 6 3
East wins Trick 1 with ♣A and plays back ♣3.

DEAL NO. 71

Contract: 6NT. Lead: ♡Q.

This time the defenders have not been so kind as to knock out ♠A, so that must be your first task. That brings TTA up to 10. Now, how to play the clubs? There is only a problem if they are 4-0. If East has all four, there is nothing you can do. Your ♣Q cannot single-handedly capture his ♣J-10. But if West has all four, dummy's ♣A-K-9 enable you to pick up the ♣J-10. So correct play is to cash ♣Q first, to cater for the 4-0 break which you can cope with.

♠	0
♡	2
◇	2
♣	3
TTA	7

DEAL NO. 72

Contract: 3NT. Lead: ♣4.

In clubs you have one of those holdings where you are sure to make a trick if the defence open up the suit. Play low in dummy and either East will play ♣A or ♣K, in which case your ♣J-Q become equals against the other high honour, or East plays low and you win ♣Q immediately. That brings TTA to 8. Diamonds should provide your ninth trick. If they are 4-1, you can only cope if West has the length. So cash ◇A and cross to ◇Q and, if East does show out, ◇K-10 remain in dummy for the marked finesse against West.

♠	2
♡	2
◇	3
♣	0
TTA	7

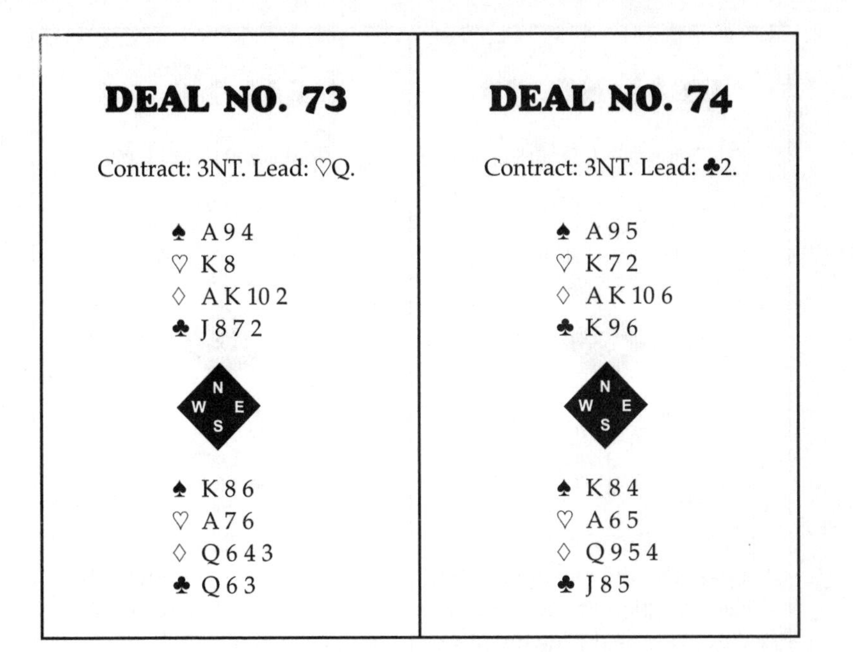
DEAL NO. 73
Contract: 3NT. Lead: ♡Q.
♠ A 9 4
♡ K 8
◇ A K 10 2
♣ J 8 7 2
N
W E
S
♠ K 8 6
♡ A 7 6
◇ Q 6 4 3
♣ Q 6 3
DEAL NO. 74
Contract: 3NT. Lead: ♣2.
♠ A 9 5
♡ K 7 2
◇ A K 10 6
♣ K 9 6
N
W E
S
♠ K 8 4
♡ A 6 5
◇ Q 9 5 4
♣ J 8 5

DEAL NO. 73

Contract: 3NT. Lead: ♡Q.

What a difference a lead makes! On the previous deal West was good enough to lead a club. This deal is included to show you just how useful that lead was. TTA = 7. If you play the diamonds right – ♢A and then ♢Q – your total is up to 8. But now you have to play the clubs yourself for that extra trick . . . and there is no sensible way to do it. ♣J is destined to be captured by ♣A, ♣Q by ♣K, and by the time you have played three rounds to set up ♣8 in dummy, the defence will surely have already beaten you.

♠	2
♡	2
♢	3
♣	0
TTA	7

DEAL NO. 74

Contract: 3NT. Lead: ♣2.

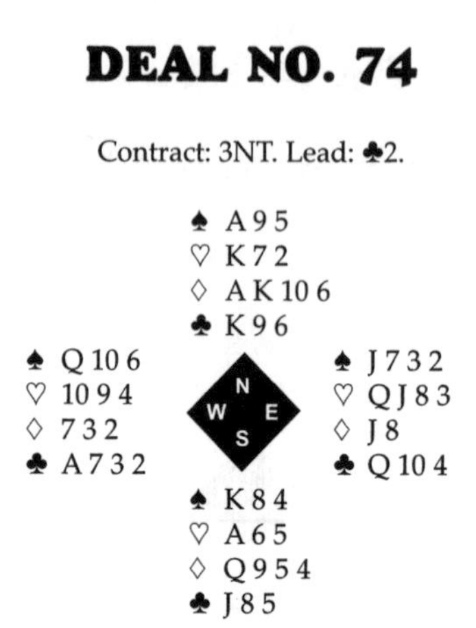

TTA = 7, but diamonds should provide one extra trick, thus bringing the total to 8. What about the ninth? Well, in clubs you have ♣K-x-x opposite ♣J-x-x and you should realise by now that this combination will provide a certain trick if the defence opens up the suit. Play low from dummy. Either East will win ♣Q, in which case your ♣K and ♣J are equals against the ace, or he plays the ace, in which case your ♣K is a winner, or he plays low, in which case you take your ♣J immediately.

♠	2
♡	2
♢	3
♣	0
TTA	7

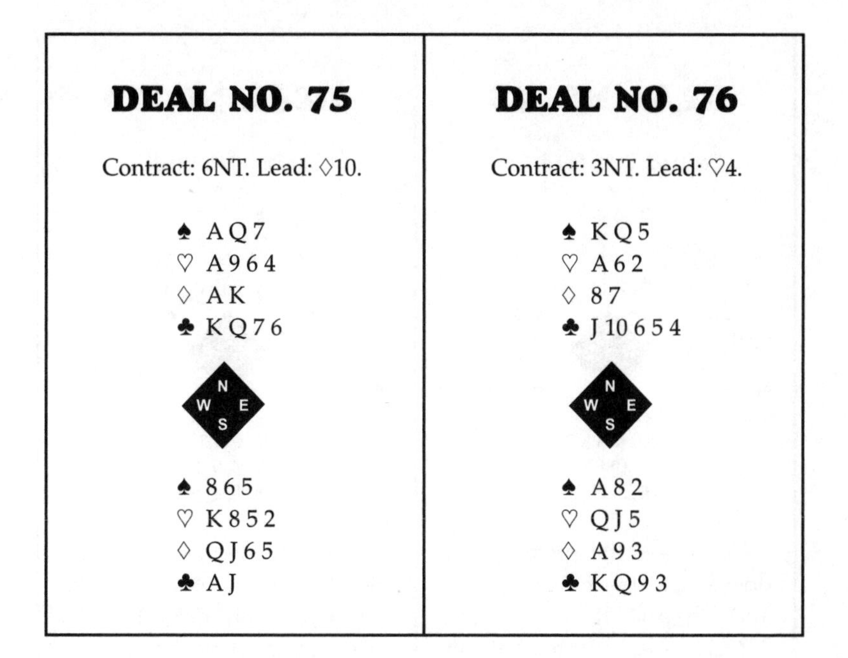
DEAL NO. 75
Contract: 6NT. Lead: ◊10.
♠ A Q 7
♡ A 9 6 4
◊ A K
♣ K Q 7 6
N
W E
S
♠ 8 6 5
♡ K 8 5 2
◊ Q J 6 5
♣ A J
DEAL NO. 76
Contract: 3NT. Lead: ♡4.
♠ K Q 5
♡ A 6 2
◊ 8 7
♣ J 10 6 5 4
N
W E
S
♠ A 8 2
♡ Q J 5
◊ A 9 3
♣ K Q 9 3

DEAL NO. 75

Contract: 6NT. Lead: ◊10.

TTA = 11 and the opening lead does you no harm. Play off ♡A and ♡K first. If hearts break 3-2, give up a heart to establish your fourth heart and twelfth trick. If the hearts don't break, you can fall back on the spade finesse. Note that you cannot try the finesse first because, if it loses, there is obviously no sense in giving up a heart trick as well!

♠	1
♡	2
◊	4
♣	4
TTA	11

DEAL NO. 76

Contract: 3NT. Lead: ♡4.

North: ♠ K Q 5 ♡ A 6 2 ◊ 8 7 ♣ J 10 6 5 4

West: ♠ 10 9 4 3 ♡ 10 8 7 4 3 ◊ 5 2 ♣ 7 2

East: ♠ J 7 6 ♡ K 9 ◊ K Q J 10 6 4 ♣ A 8

South: ♠ A 8 2 ♡ Q J 5 ◊ A 9 3 ♣ K Q 9 3

TTA is a lowly 5, but you can clearly drive out ♣A and make four extra club tricks. You can also guarantee two heart tricks by playing low from dummy at Trick 1, but is this wise? A glance at the East-West hands will tell you the answer. East will win ♡K and switch to ◊K, setting up diamonds while retaining ♣A as an entry. The moral is not to take a finesse unless you really have to, or unless you know it is safe even if it loses.

♠	3
♡	1
◊	1
♣	0
TTA	5

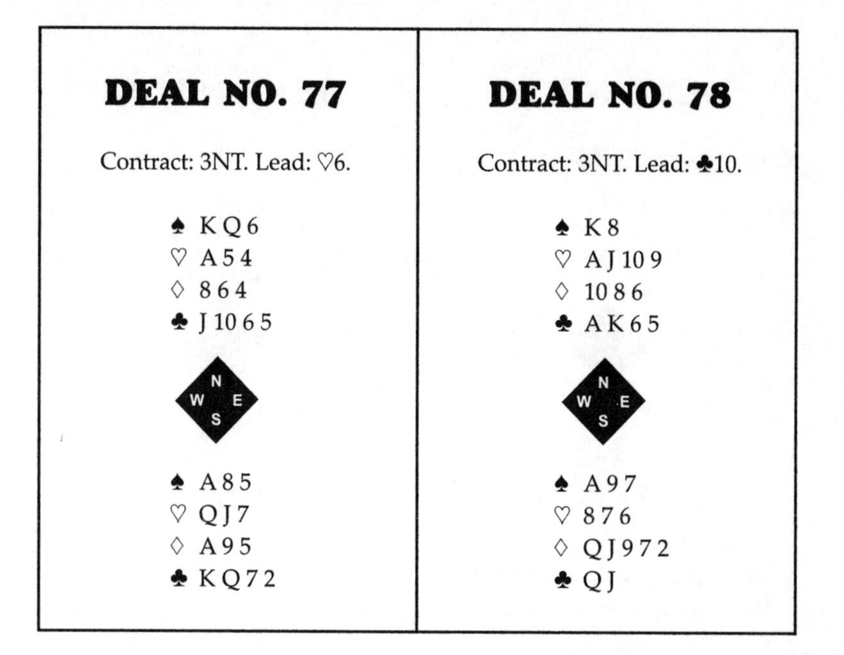
DEAL NO. 77
Contract: 3NT. Lead: ♡6.
♠ K Q 6
♡ A 5 4
◇ 8 6 4
♣ J 10 6 5
N
W E
S
♠ A 8 5
♡ Q J 7
◇ A 9 5
♣ K Q 7 2
DEAL NO. 78
Contract: 3NT. Lead: ♣10.
♠ K 8
♡ A J 10 9
◇ 10 8 6
♣ A K 6 5
N
W E
S
♠ A 9 7
♡ 8 7 6
◇ Q J 9 7 2
♣ Q J

DEAL NO. 77

Contract: 3NT. Lead: ♡6.

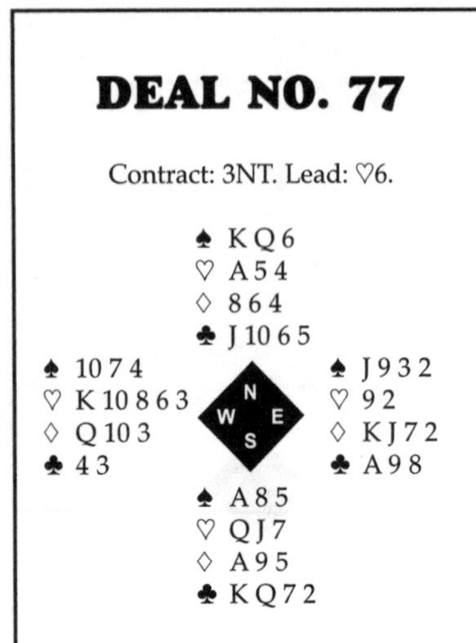

Again TTA = 5 and again you must plan to knock out ♣A, but this time clubs will furnish only three extra tricks. So this time you must play low from dummy on the opening lead to guarantee your two heart tricks. You hope either that East does not hold ♡K or that, if he does, no lethal diamond switch will be forthcoming. As it happens, East does not hold ♡K, so you can win Trick 1 in hand and set about the clubs in peace.

♠	3
♡	1
♢	1
♣	0
TTA	5

DEAL NO. 78

Contract: 3NT. Lead: ♣10.

North: ♠ K 8 ♡ A J 10 9 ♢ 10 8 6 ♣ A K 6 5

West: ♠ 10 4 3 ♡ Q 5 ♢ K 5 4 ♣ 10 9 8 7 4

East: ♠ Q J 6 5 2 ♡ K 4 3 2 ♢ A 3 ♣ 3 2

South: ♠ A 9 7 ♡ 8 7 6 ♢ Q J 9 7 2 ♣ Q J

You need two tricks to bring TTA up to 9 and you should have time to make use of your diamonds. Win with ♣Q and play ♢2 to dummy's ♢10 to knock out ♢K. Win whatever the defenders return, and play another diamond to knock out ♢A. You then have three more diamond tricks and, even if the defence has attacked hearts, you will make the contract easily.

♠	2
♡	1
♢	0
♣	4
TTA	7

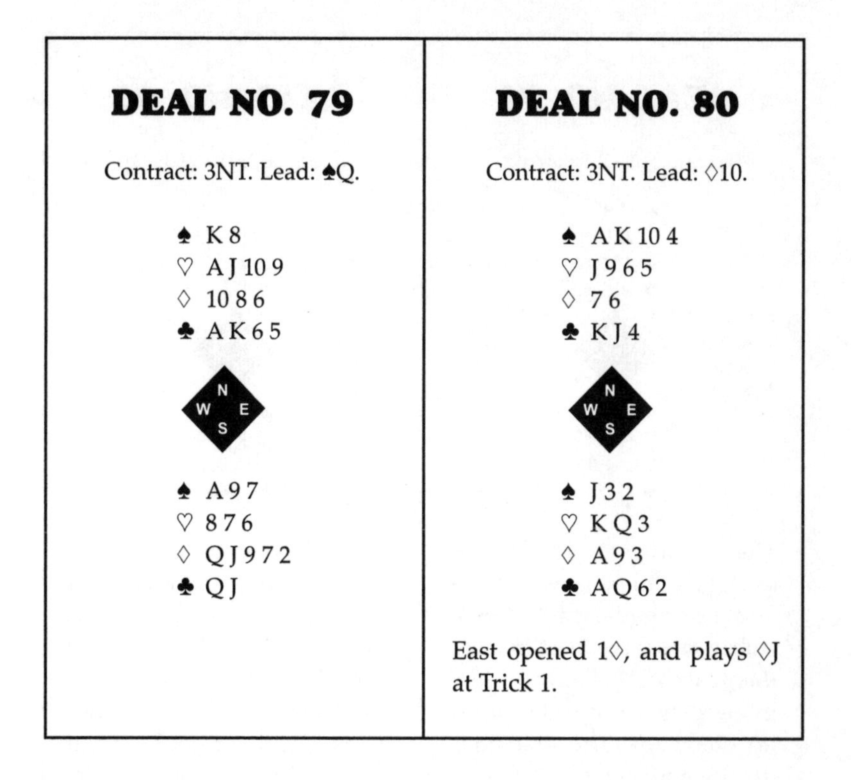

DEAL NO. 79

Contract: 3NT. Lead: ♠Q.

North:
♠ K 8
♡ A J 10 9
♢ 10 8 6
♣ A K 6 5

South:
♠ A 9 7
♡ 8 7 6
♢ Q J 9 7 2
♣ Q J

DEAL NO. 80

Contract: 3NT. Lead: ♢10.

North:
♠ A K 10 4
♡ J 9 6 5
♢ 7 6
♣ K J 4

South:
♠ J 3 2
♡ K Q 3
♢ A 9 3
♣ A Q 6 2

East opened 1♢, and plays ♢J at Trick 1.

DEAL NO. 79

Contract: 3NT. Lead: ♠Q.

This is the same as *Deal 78*, except that the defenders have attacked spades rather than clubs. Do you see the difference this makes? You have to lose the lead twice in order to set up diamonds. The first time, the defence will knock out your ♠A. The second time, they will cash spade winners and defeat you. Your best chance is to forget the diamonds and try the double finesse in hearts. Play a heart to ♡J, which will probably lose. Then, when you regain the lead, play a heart to ♡10. You will make the contract so long as East does not hold both ♡K and ♡Q.

♠	2
♡	1
◇	0
♣	4
TTA	7

DEAL NO. 80

Contract: 3NT. Lead: ◇10.

This deal looks awfully similar to several others. Surely it is just a case of doing the sums and holding up ◇A till the third round before knocking out ♡A? You have to assume that West holds ♡A, don't you? And, if he does, don't you end up with an overtrick? Well, think about it. See if you can spot the catch and how to get round it. All will be revealed at the start of the final section of this book.

♠	2
♡	0
◇	1
♣	4
TTA	7

SECTION 2
TRUMP CONTRACTS

TRUMP CONTRACTS

In this section we change the emphasis from no-trump to suit contracts – and by doing so add a totally new dimension to the game! In no-trumps sound technique is to count 'top tricks available' because nobody can stop you cashing winners – the opposition either follow suit or discard. Not so in a trump contract! If you try to cash the ace, king, queen in a suit, what will happen more often than not is that one of the defenders will trump one of your winners. 'Why not draw the opponents' trumps then?' you might say. Quite often this will be the right approach – but not always! The fact is that playing in a trump contract provides a declarer with options that just do not exist when playing in no-trumps.

Instead of counting 'Top Tricks Available' you will find that it makes more sense to count instead what we call 'Total Losing Tricks' (TLT) – the number of *potential* losers in each suit, *from declarer's point of view.* If the total number of potential losers is greater than you can afford, then you have to try to do something about it. Here is an example:

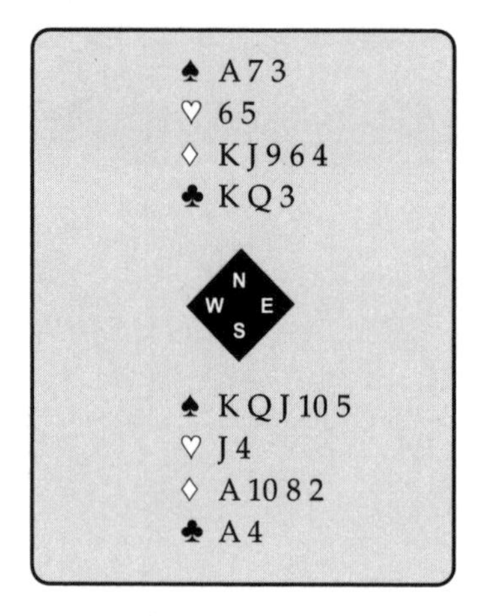

West leads ♡A against your contract of 4♠. You count up your potential losers: none in spades, two in hearts, one in diamonds (the queen) and none in clubs. That comes to three at most and you can see that you may well not lose a diamond. The defence cashes two top hearts and switches to a club but you simply win, draw the opponents' trumps in as many rounds as it takes, and make either ten or eleven tricks depending on whether you lose a trick to ♢Q.

In the above example you elected to play in a trump suit because you needed trumps to stop the run of the defenders' hearts – without trumps they could take at least the first five heart tricks. The trumps themselves did not provide any extra tricks. However, that is not always the case:

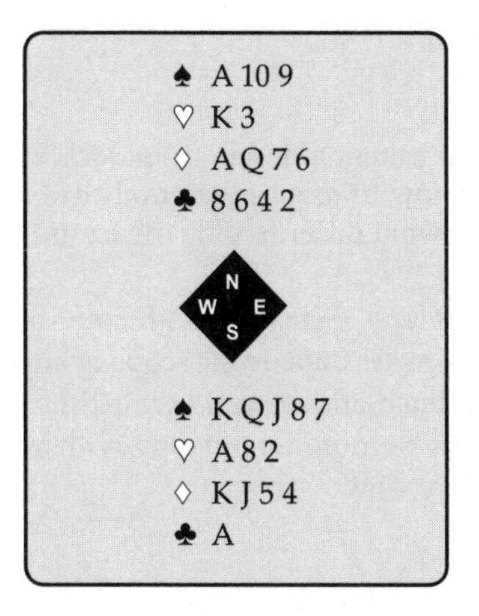

You have done well to bid to 7♠ and the lead is ♡Q. You count up the total losing tricks from declarer's perspective – none in spades, one in hearts, none in diamonds and none in clubs. One is too many in a grand slam, so you have to do something about it. Can you see how wrong it would be to win the opening lead, draw the enemy trumps and hope for the best? That's right, you would end up with the heart loser that you were worried about from the start. Instead, win ♡K, draw just two rounds of trumps, and cash ♡A. Then trump your small heart in dummy. You have to remember to draw any remaining trumps now, of course, and you can do that by entering your hand with ♣A.

Could anything go wrong? Well, somebody might trump the second heart, but only if the suit splits an unlikely 7–1. Besides, no other play would land your contract. Here you can see the power of playing in a trump suit to gain extra tricks from those trumps. If you had played the above hand in no-trumps you would have been unable to make more than twelve tricks.

The deals in this section will take you through counting potential losers in suits and trying to reduce them if there are too many. Sometimes the number of losers you count in the trump suit may appear unrealistic. A-x-x-x opposite K-x-x-x, for example, could be counted as two potential losers because the suit might break 5-0 or 4-1. However, with the usual 3-2 break you can mentally reduce the losers to one. All the techniques that you need when playing no-trump contacts – knocking out stoppers, finessing, counting the suits – are still very much applicable. So try the following three-step process which you should apply on all trump contracts the moment dummy has been tabled:

- count your potential losers from declarer's perspective
- work out how to reduce the number of losers if need be
- decide on what order to play the cards

As before, the deals will increase in difficulty as you work through them but none of them are outside the scope of anyone who follows the basic principles outlined above. And by the time you reach the end of this section you will be more than happy with your ability to handle trump contracts. Play well!

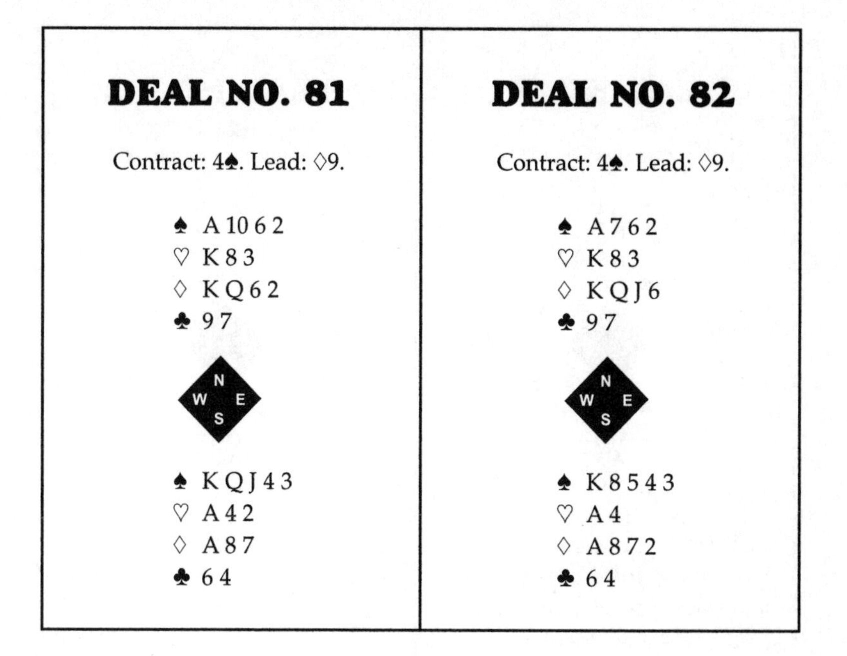
DEAL NO. 81
Contract: 4♠. Lead: ♢9.
♠ A 10 6 2
♡ K 8 3
♢ K Q 6 2
♣ 9 7
N
W E
S
♠ K Q J 4 3
♡ A 4 2
♢ A 8 7
♣ 6 4
DEAL NO. 82
Contract: 4♠. Lead: ♢9.
♠ A 7 6 2
♡ K 8 3
♢ K Q J 6
♣ 9 7
N
W E
S
♠ K 8 5 4 3
♡ A 4
♢ A 8 7 2
♣ 6 4

DEAL NO. 81

Contract: 4♠. Lead: ♢9.

TLT tells you that you only have three losers, so win ♢A and then play as many rounds of trumps as it takes to draw all the opponents' trumps. (It does not matter in which order you cash them.) Having drawn trumps, you can cash ♢K-Q followed by ♡A-K. Note that if you tried to cash the red suits first, before drawing trumps, either opponent might have been able to win one of those tricks by trumping.

♠	0
♡	1
♢	0
♣	2
TLT	3

DEAL NO. 82

Contract: 4♠. Lead: ♢9.

North: ♠ A 7 6 2 ♡ K 8 3 ♢ K Q J 6 ♣ 9 7

West: ♠ J 10 9 ♡ Q 10 7 6 ♢ 9 3 ♣ K J 10 3

East: ♠ Q ♡ J 9 5 2 ♢ 10 5 4 ♣ A Q 8 5 2

South: ♠ K 8 5 4 3 ♡ A 4 ♢ A 8 7 2 ♣ 6 4

TLT suggests that you might have two losing trumps but you must hope that this is wrong. Win the diamond lead in either hand and play a top trump and, if both opponents follow, play the other top trump and notice whether or not there is still a trump outstanding. There is no harm in playing a third round if there is, but no necessity either. Just try to cash the three remaining top diamonds and the ♡A-K. The opponent holding the top trump will use it at some time, but that and the ♣A-K are all you will lose.

♠	2
♡	0
♢	0
♣	2
TLT	4

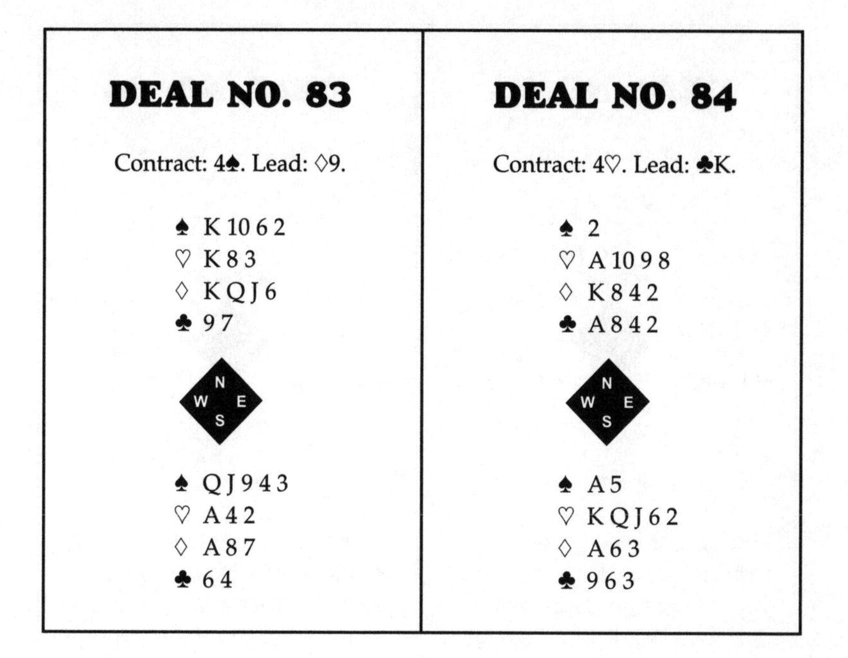

DEAL NO. 83

Contract: 4♠. Lead: ♢9.

♠ K 10 6 2
♡ K 8 3
♢ K Q J 6
♣ 9 7

♠ Q J 9 4 3
♡ A 4 2
♢ A 8 7
♣ 6 4

DEAL NO. 84

Contract: 4♡. Lead: ♣K.

♠ 2
♡ A 10 9 8
♢ K 8 4 2
♣ A 8 4 2

♠ A 5
♡ K Q J 6 2
♢ A 6 3
♣ 9 6 3

DEAL NO. 83

Contract: 4♠. Lead: ♢9.

You are missing the ace of trumps but that doesn't mean you can ignore them! Win the diamond lead with ♢A and keep playing trump honours until the ace is played, being careful to remember how many trumps the defence still holds. The opponents may cash ♣A-K at this stage but, after that, you will be able to regain the lead. Draw any outstanding trumps, then play your three winning diamonds and your two top hearts. The losing heart in the TLT table will be discarded on a top diamond from dummy.

♠	1
♡	1
♢	0
♣	2
TLT	4

DEAL NO. 84

Contract: 4♡. Lead: ♣K.

North
♠ 2
♡ A 10 9 8
♢ K 8 4 2
♣ A 8 4 2

West
♠ Q 10 8 7
♡ 7 5
♢ Q 10 5
♣ K Q J 5

East
♠ K J 9 6 4 3
♡ 4 3
♢ J 9 7
♣ 10 7

South
♠ A 5
♡ K Q J 6 2
♢ A 6 3
♣ 9 6 3

Win ♣A and immediately play ♠A followed by trumping ♠5 with ♡8. Then play ♡A and as many other rounds of trumps as it takes to make sure that neither opponent has any left. Only then can you cash your two top diamonds. Have you noticed how you gained a trick by trumping that little spade in dummy? The losing spade in the TLT table just vanished!

♠	1
♡	0
♢	1
♣	2
TLT	4

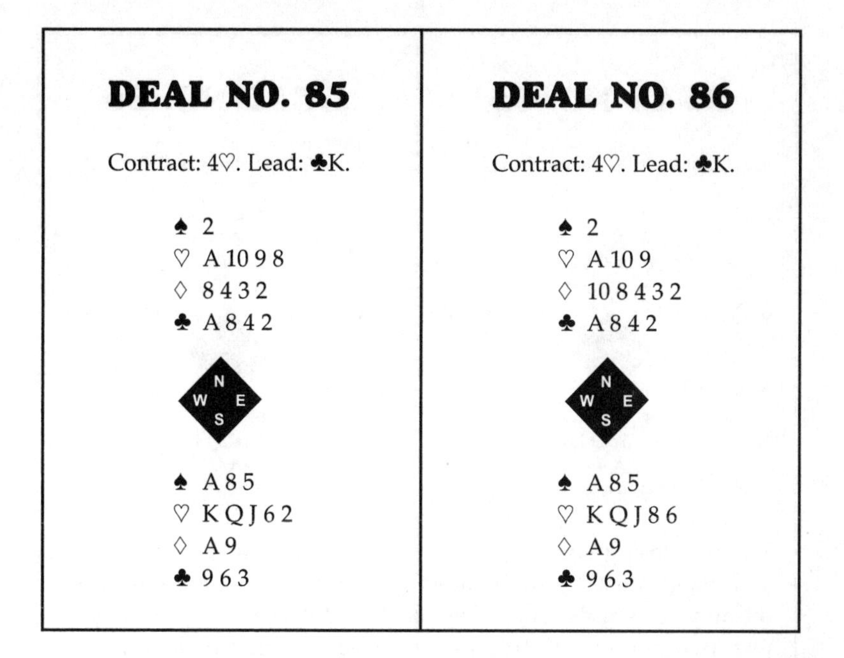
DEAL NO. 85
Contract: 4♡. Lead: ♣K.
♠ 2
♡ A 10 9 8
◊ 8 4 3 2
♣ A 8 4 2
N
W E
S
♠ A 8 5
♡ K Q J 6 2
◊ A 9
♣ 9 6 3
DEAL NO. 86
Contract: 4♡. Lead: ♣K.
♠ 2
♡ A 10 9
◊ 10 8 4 3 2
♣ A 8 4 2
N
W E
S
♠ A 8 5
♡ K Q J 8 6
◊ A 9
♣ 9 6 3

DEAL NO. 85

Contract: 4♡. Lead: ♣K.

The two losing spades in the TLT table must be ruffed in dummy, so win ♣A and, after just two rounds of trumps, play ♠A and ruff a spade in dummy. Return to hand with ◊A, and then ruff the last spade. In all you will make five hearts, the ♠A, two ruffs, and the minor suit aces. It was important to work out where your tricks were coming from and to understand that there are times when you cannot afford to draw all the out-standing trumps.

♠	2
♡	0
◊	1
♣	2
TLT	5

DEAL NO. 86

Contract: 4♡. Lead: ♣K.

North: ♠ 2 ♡ A 10 9 ◊ 10 8 4 3 2 ♣ A 8 4 2

West: ♠ Q 10 7 3 ♡ 7 2 ◊ Q 6 5 ♣ K Q J 5

East: ♠ K J 9 6 4 ♡ 5 4 3 ◊ K J 7 ♣ 10 7

South: ♠ A 8 5 ♡ K Q J 8 6 ◊ A 9 ♣ 9 6 3

This time you can only afford to draw one round of trumps. Why? Because, as before, you need to trump both your two losing spades in dummy and to do that you need dummy to have two trumps! So, after drawing just *one* round of trumps, follow the line detailed in the previous hand to deal with the two losing spades in the TLT count.

♠	2
♡	0
◊	1
♣	2
TLT	5

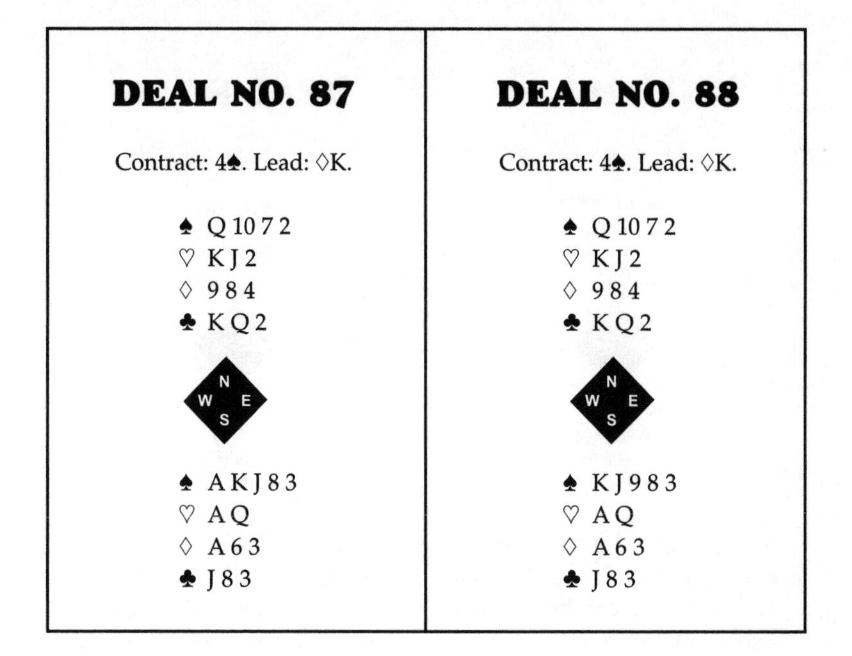
DEAL NO. 87
Contract: 4♠. Lead: ♢K.
♠ Q 10 7 2
♡ K J 2
♢ 9 8 4
♣ K Q 2
N
W E
S
♠ A K J 8 3
♡ A Q
♢ A 6 3
♣ J 8 3
DEAL NO. 88
Contract: 4♠. Lead: ♢K.
♠ Q 10 7 2
♡ K J 2
♢ 9 8 4
♣ K Q 2
N
W E
S
♠ K J 9 8 3
♡ A Q
♢ A 6 3
♣ J 8 3

DEAL NO. 87

Contract: 4♠. Lead: ◊K.

Win ◊A and draw trumps in as many rounds as it takes. The most you can lose now is two diamonds and a club, but it is always nice to make overtricks. After drawing trumps play ♡A followed by the queen *which you should overtake with the king in dummy!* Cash ♡J and throw away a diamond from hand. Now you can lead top clubs until the ace appears and, although the defence will win a diamond, that will be their last trick. TLT said you had two losing diamonds but you managed to throw one of them away.

♠	0
♡	0
◊	2
♣	1
TLT	3

DEAL NO. 88

Contract: 4♠. Lead: ◊K.

If you try to draw trumps the opponents will take the two black aces and two diamond tricks for one down. Win ◊A and, before touching trumps, play ♡A followed by the queen *which you overtake with the king in dummy.* Cash ♡J throwing a diamond from hand and, if everyone follows, you can turn your attention to the trump suit. When the defenders win the ace, they can now only cash one diamond, not the two predicted by the TLT count. Do you see the importance of forward planning?

♠	1
♡	0
◊	2
♣	1
TLT	4

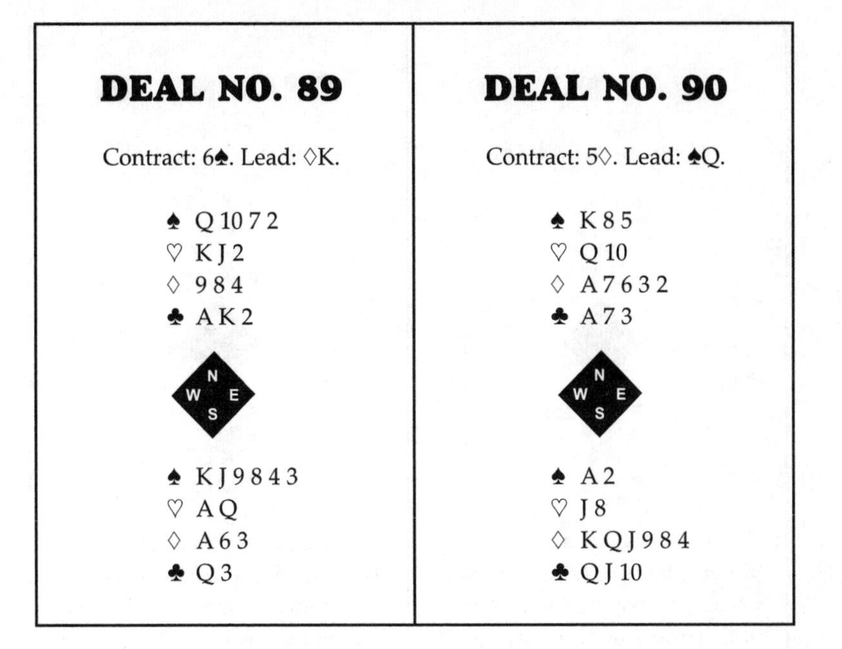
DEAL NO. 89
Contract: 6♠. Lead: ♢K.
♠ Q 10 7 2
♡ K J 2
♢ 9 8 4
♣ A K 2
N
W E
S
♠ K J 9 8 4 3
♡ A Q
♢ A 6 3
♣ Q 3
DEAL NO. 90
Contract: 5♢. Lead: ♠Q.
♠ K 8 5
♡ Q 10
♢ A 7 6 3 2
♣ A 7 3
N
W E
S
♠ A 2
♡ J 8
♢ K Q J 9 8 4
♣ Q J 10

DEAL NO. 89

Contract: 6♠. Lead: ♢K.

You have bid to a good slam but you have to take care. Win ♢A and realise that you cannot pull trumps as the opponents will win two diamonds plus the ace of trumps. Get rid of one diamond by playing the hearts as in *Deal 88*, then play ♣Q and ♣A-K, on which you discard your other diamond loser. Only then attack trumps. Your only loser will be the ace of trumps because you have escaped the two diamond losers predicted by the TLT.

♠	1
♡	0
♢	2
♣	0
TLT	3

DEAL NO. 90

Contract: 5♢. Lead: ♠Q.

North: ♠ K 8 5 ♡ Q 10 ♢ A 7 6 3 2 ♣ A 7 3

West: ♠ Q J 10 9 ♡ K 7 5 3 ♢ 10 ♣ K 9 6 5

East: ♠ 7 6 4 3 ♡ A 9 6 4 2 ♢ 5 ♣ 8 4 2

South: ♠ A 2 ♡ J 8 ♢ K Q J 9 8 4 ♣ Q J 10

Although you have escaped a heart lead, there is no way you are going to avoid ultimately losing two heart tricks – which means that you cannot afford to lose a club. Win the spade in either hand, and then draw all the defenders' trumps ending in hand to lead ♣Q. If West plays the king your troubles are over but, if he doesn't, you must resist the impulse to play the ace from dummy, playing low instead. If the queen wins, repeat the manoeuvre and lead the jack. If East has the king of clubs, *tant pis* – you did your best.

♠	0
♡	2
♢	0
♣	1
TLT	3

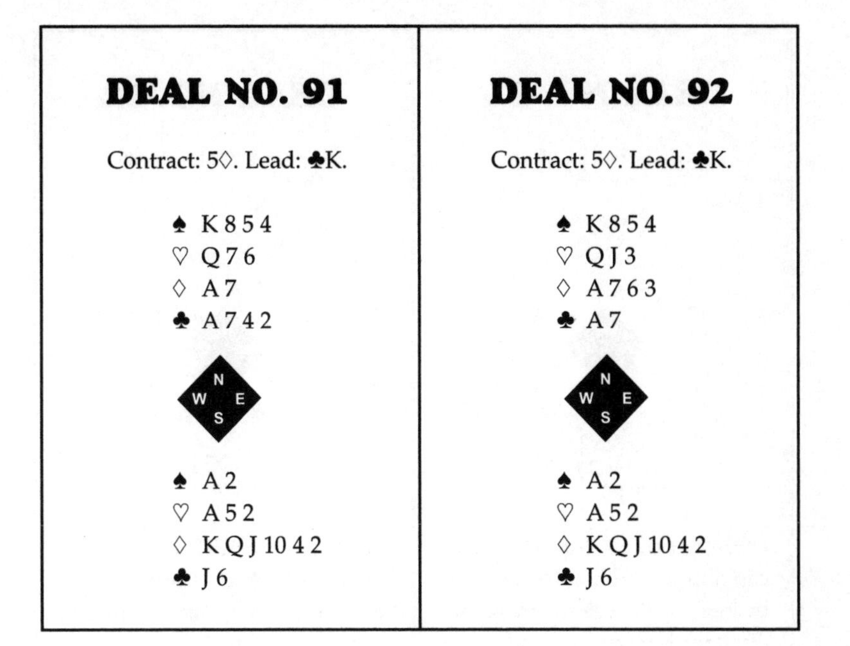
DEAL NO. 91
Contract: 5♢. Lead: ♣K.
♠ K 8 5 4
♡ Q 7 6
♢ A 7
♣ A 7 4 2
N
W E
S
♠ A 2
♡ A 5 2
♢ K Q J 10 4 2
♣ J 6
DEAL NO. 92
Contract: 5♢. Lead: ♣K.
♠ K 8 5 4
♡ Q J 3
♢ A 7 6 3
♣ A 7
N
W E
S
♠ A 2
♡ A 5 2
♢ K Q J 10 4 2
♣ J 6

DEAL NO. 91

Contract: 5♢. Lead: ♣K.

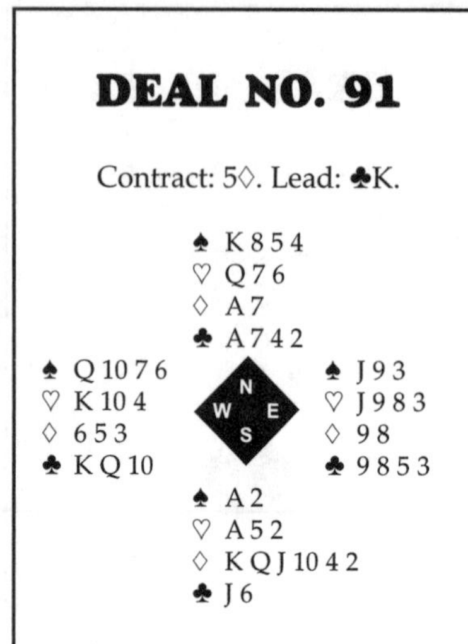

With a certain club loser you can only afford to lose one trick in hearts. Win ♣A, draw the outstanding trumps ending in hand, and play ♡A followed by a low heart. If West plays low, play ♡Q and hope that West has ♡K. Avoid the mistake, as already described in the *No-Trumps Section*, of 'finessing' ♡Q, which can never gain. You need West to have ♡K – a 50% chance.

♠	0
♡	2
♢	0
♣	1
TLT	3

DEAL NO. 92

Contract: 5♢. Lead: ♣K.

North: ♠ K 8 5 4 ♡ Q J 3 ♢ A 7 6 3 ♣ A 7

West: ♠ Q 10 7 6 ♡ K 10 4 ♢ 5 ♣ K Q 10 4 2

East: ♠ J 9 3 ♡ 9 8 7 6 ♢ 9 8 ♣ 9 8 5 3

South: ♠ A 2 ♡ A 5 2 ♢ K Q J 10 4 2 ♣ J 6

Here your contract is secure. Win with ♣A, draw trumps and make two hearts either by playing ace and then a small one towards dummy, or by leading the queen from table, letting it run if East plays low. Either way you are certain of making two heart tricks, and will just lose one heart and one club – as predicted by the TLT.

♠	0
♡	1
♢	0
♣	1
TLT	2

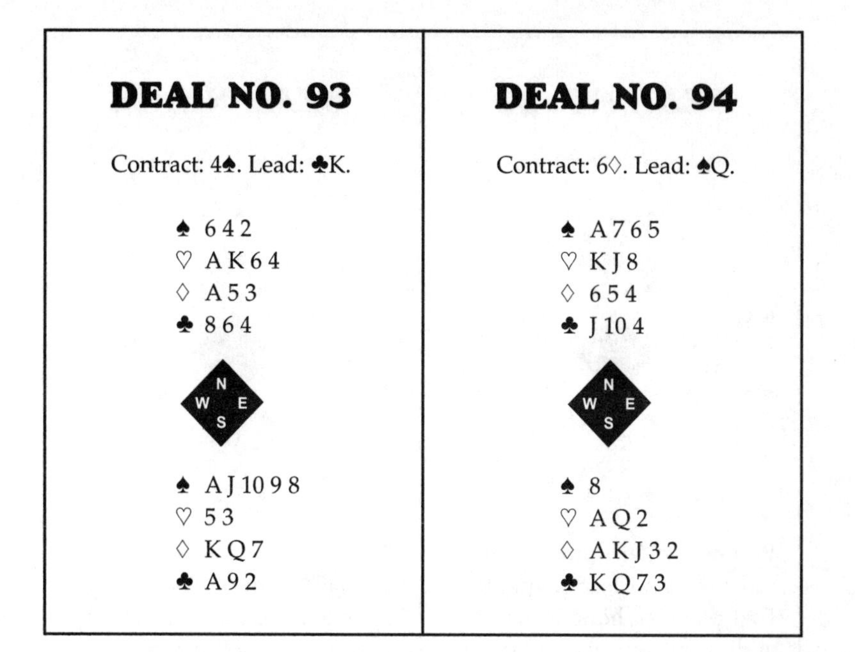
DEAL NO. 93
Contract: 4♠. Lead: ♣K.
♠ 6 4 2
♡ A K 6 4
◊ A 5 3
♣ 8 6 4
N
W E
S
♠ A J 10 9 8
♡ 5 3
◊ K Q 7
♣ A 9 2
DEAL NO. 94
Contract: 6◊. Lead: ♠Q.
♠ A 7 6 5
♡ K J 8
◊ 6 5 4
♣ J 10 4
N
W E
S
♠ 8
♡ A Q 2
◊ A K J 3 2
♣ K Q 7 3

DEAL NO. 93

Contract: 4♠. Lead: ♣K.

Win ♣A, enter dummy with a red card, and lead a spade. If East plays an honour, win ♠A and drive out the other top trump. If East plays low, play ♠J. West might win and take two club tricks but, when you regain the lead, play another trump from dummy. If East plays the remaining honour, win and draw trumps; if not, play ♠10 from hand. If West follows low, draw the last trump; if West shows out, return to dummy to repeat the procedure. You need East to hold ♠K or ♠Q.

♠	2
♡	0
◇	0
♣	2
TLT	4

DEAL NO. 94

Contract: 6◇. Lead: ♠Q.

North: ♠ A 7 6 5 ♡ K J 8 ◇ 6 5 4 ♣ J 10 4

West: ♠ Q J 10 4 ♡ 10 7 6 ◇ 10 7 ♣ 8 6 5 2

East: ♠ K 9 3 2 ♡ 9 5 4 3 ◇ Q 9 8 ♣ A 9

South: ♠ 8 ♡ A Q 2 ◇ A K J 3 2 ♣ K Q 7 3

TLT shows three possible losing trump tricks but you have to hope there are none! It is against the odds to play the ◇A-K hoping the queen will fall, whereas there is a 50% chance that ◇Q is on your right. Lead a low diamond from dummy and, if East plays low, insert the ◇J. If it wins, play the ace and king next and hopefully the opposing trumps will be drawn. Now you can afford to knock out ♣A. Note that finding a defender with singleton ◇Q does not help, as his partner will hold ◇10-9-8-7 and a certain trump trick.

♠	0
♡	0
◇	3!
♣	1
TLT	4

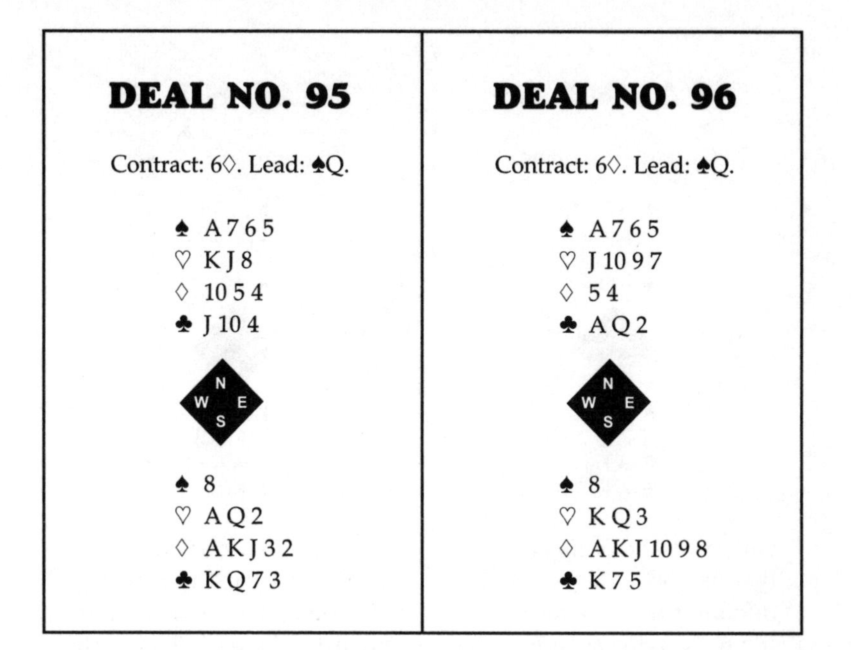
DEAL NO. 95
Contract: 6♢. Lead: ♠Q.
♠ A 7 6 5
♡ K J 8
♢ 10 5 4
♣ J 10 4
N
W E
S
♠ 8
♡ A Q 2
♢ A K J 3 2
♣ K Q 7 3
DEAL NO. 96
Contract: 6♢. Lead: ♠Q.
♠ A 7 6 5
♡ J 10 9 7
♢ 5 4
♣ A Q 2
N
W E
S
♠ 8
♡ K Q 3
♢ A K J 10 9 8
♣ K 7 5

DEAL NO. 95

Contract: 6♢. Lead: ♠Q.

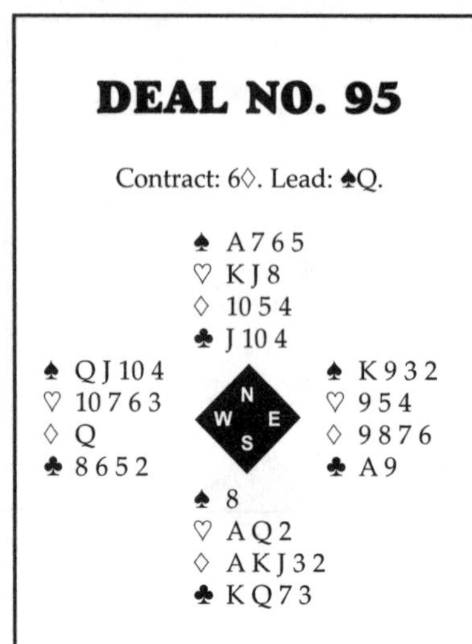

Superficially this appears to be the same as *Deal 94*, but now dummy has ♢10 and you can improve on the chances of not losing a trump. How? Simply by playing ♢A at trick two; if nothing exciting happens, cross to dummy with a heart to take the trump finesse by playing low to the jack. The extra chance is that West might have ♢Q singleton. Now that dummy has ♢10, a defender holding ♢9-8-7-6 does not have a certain trump trick.

♠	0
♡	0
♢	2
♣	1
TLT	3

DEAL NO. 96

Contract: 6♢. Lead: ♠Q.

North: ♠ A 7 6 5 ♡ J 10 9 7 ♢ 5 4 ♣ A Q 2
West: ♠ Q J 10 4 2 ♡ 8 4 2 ♢ 6 ♣ 9 6 4 3
East: ♠ K 9 3 ♡ A 6 5 ♢ Q 7 3 2 ♣ J 10 8
South: ♠ 8 ♡ K Q 3 ♢ A K J 10 9 8 ♣ K 7 5

Again, with a certain loser in hearts, you must play trumps to avoid the possible loser predicted by TLT. Taking the finesse is more likely to succeed than playing ♢A-K but you might be tempted to play a top diamond first, in case West has ♢Q singleton. Don't! West might have a singleton, but it is four times more likely that it is a small card than the queen. So take a finesse immediately by playing low to ♢J and, if successful, re-enter dummy with a club to repeat the process.

♠	0
♡	1
♢	1
♣	0
TLT	2

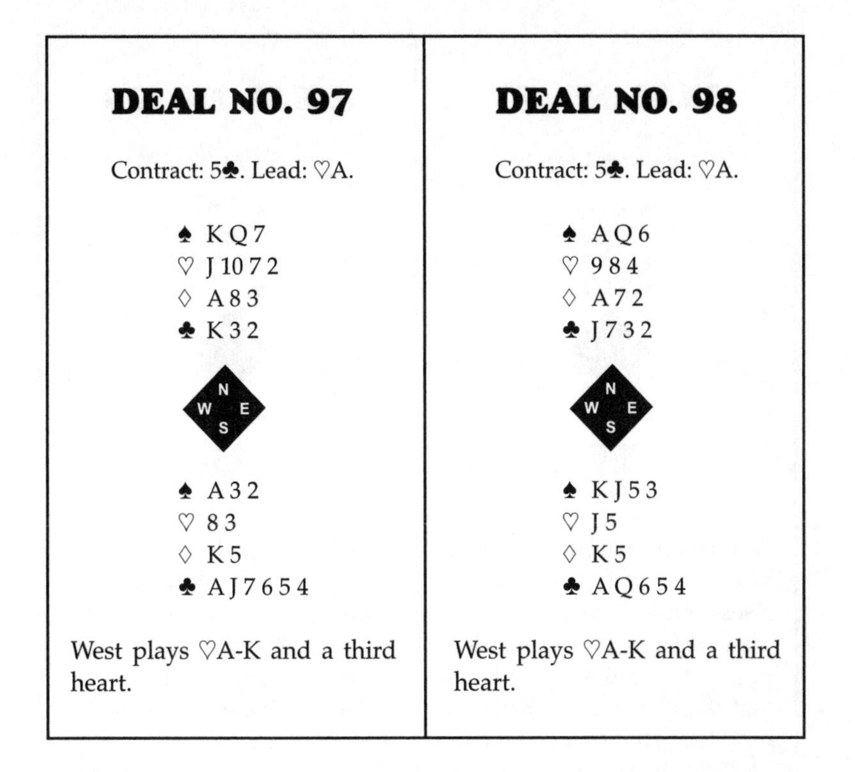

DEAL NO. 97

Contract: 5♣. Lead: ♡A.

♠ K Q 7
♡ J 10 7 2
♢ A 8 3
♣ K 3 2

♠ A 3 2
♡ 8 3
♢ K 5
♣ A J 7 6 5 4

West plays ♡A-K and a third heart.

DEAL NO. 98

Contract: 5♣. Lead: ♡A.

♠ A Q 6
♡ 9 8 4
♢ A 7 2
♣ J 7 3 2

♠ K J 5 3
♡ J 5
♢ K 5
♣ A Q 6 5 4

West plays ♡A-K and a third heart.

DEAL NO. 97

Contract: 5♣. Lead: ♡A.

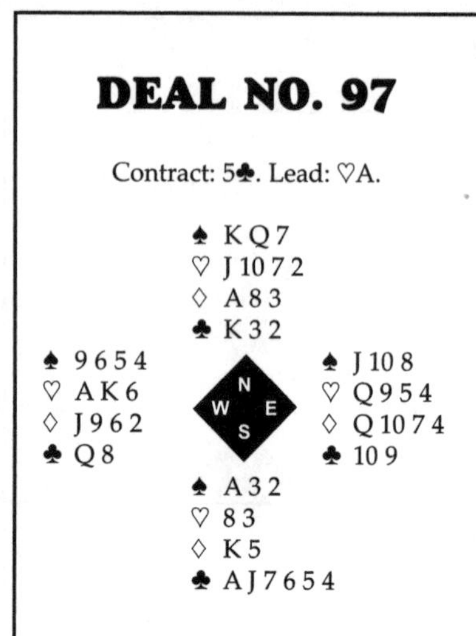

You ruff the third round of hearts, and note you have no losers outside the trump suit. There are two courses of action possible: lead ♣A-K and hope that the queen falls, or play a low club to the king and then a low club from table, finessing against the queen if East plays low. The chances of success are similar but, with *nine* cards between the two hands, the first line is slightly preferable. Note that the TLT prediction of two club losers is highly pessimistic, requiring West to have all four outstanding clubs.

♠	0
♡	2
◇	0
♣	2
TLT	4

DEAL NO. 98

Contract: 5♣. Lead: ♡A.

North: ♠ A Q 6 ♡ 9 8 4 ◇ A 7 2 ♣ J 7 3 2

West: ♠ 10 8 7 4 ♡ A K 6 2 ◇ J 9 6 ♣ 10 8

East: ♠ 9 2 ♡ Q 10 7 3 ◇ Q 10 8 4 3 ♣ K 9

South: ♠ K J 5 3 ♡ J 5 ◇ K 5 ♣ A Q 6 5 4

After ruffing the third heart you need to avoid the possible trump losers predicted by TLT. Playing ♣A will only work when the king is singleton so it must be better to finesse. Do *not* enter dummy to lead ♣J! If East *does* hold the singleton king, you have promoted a trump trick for West's ♣10-9-8. Play a *low* club from dummy with the intention of finessing. This works whenever East has the singleton *or* doubleton king.

♠	0
♡	2
◇	0
♣	2
TLT	4

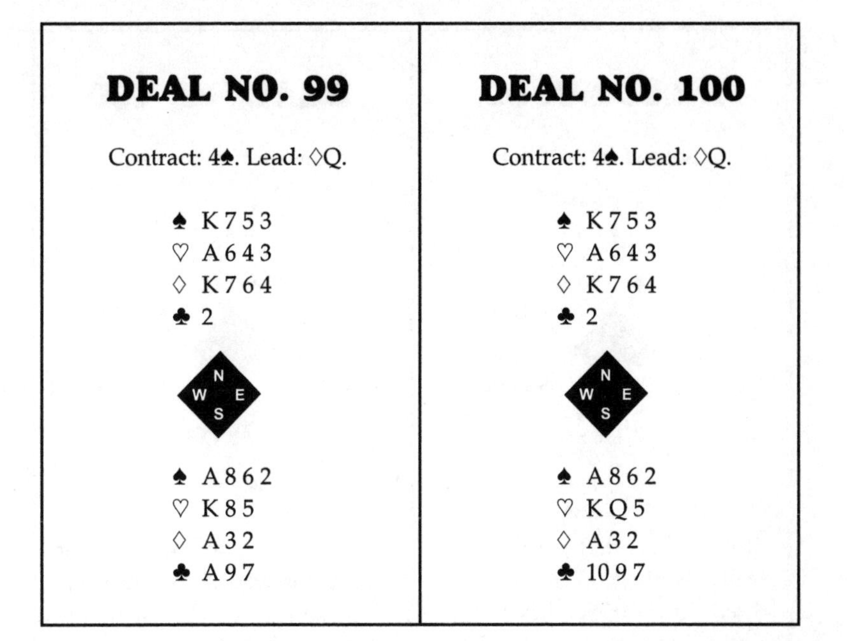
DEAL NO. 99
Contract: 4♠. Lead: ◊Q.
♠ K 7 5 3
♡ A 6 4 3
◊ K 7 6 4
♣ 2
N
W E
S
♠ A 8 6 2
♡ K 8 5
◊ A 3 2
♣ A 9 7
DEAL NO. 100
Contract: 4♠. Lead: ◊Q.
♠ K 7 5 3
♡ A 6 4 3
◊ K 7 6 4
♣ 2
N
W E
S
♠ A 8 6 2
♡ K Q 5
◊ A 3 2
♣ 10 9 7

DEAL NO. 99

Contract: 4♠. Lead: ◊Q.

TLT predicts that if things go really badly you might lose three trump tricks, but that is really highly unlikely. It is more reasonable to assume that there is just one if the defence's trumps break 3-2. Win ◊A and cash ♠A-K. If there is a trump outstanding leave it alone. Play ♣A, ruff a club on table, return to hand with ♡K and ruff your remaining club. Then play red-suit winners. The defender with the last trump may ruff but the trump losers will be held to one and the club losers will vanish.

♠	3!
♡	1
◊	1
♣	2
TLT	7

DEAL NO. 100

Contract: 4♠. Lead: ◊Q.

This deal is similar to *99* but we have traded the ♣A for ♡Q. Suppose you win the diamond in hand and play the two top trumps. When you lose the lead in clubs, the defender with the last trump may play it, which means you can only ruff one club. So win the diamond in hand, draw just one round of spades with ♠K and lead a club. Win the return, play ♠A and ruff a club in dummy. A heart to hand lets you ruff your last club and then play out winners until someone wins the outstanding trump.

♠	3
♡	0
◊	1
♣	3
TLT	7

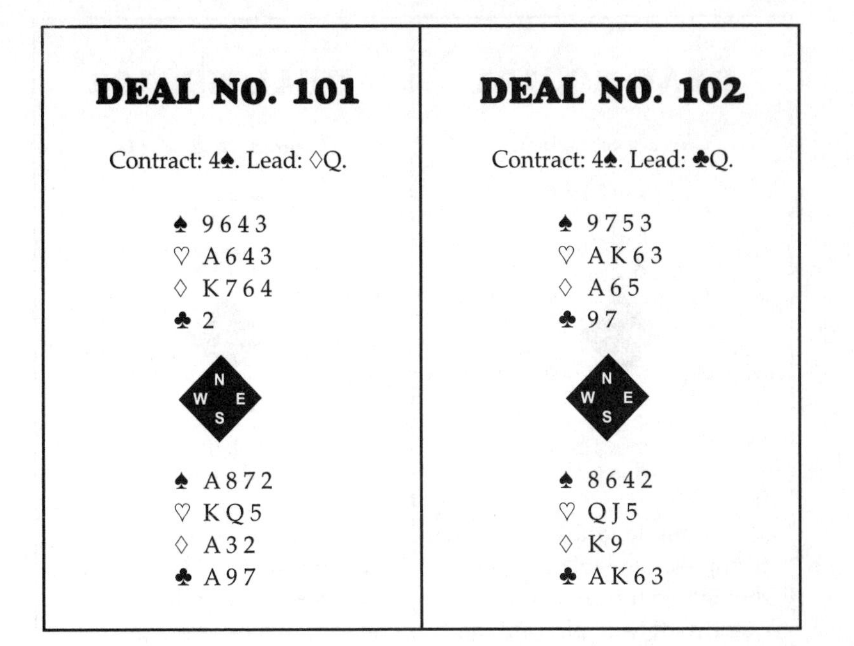

DEAL NO. 101

Contract: 4♠. Lead: ♢Q.

North:
♠ 9 6 4 3
♡ A 6 4 3
♢ K 7 6 4
♣ 2

South:
♠ A 8 7 2
♡ K Q 5
♢ A 3 2
♣ A 9 7

DEAL NO. 102

Contract: 4♠. Lead: ♣Q.

North:
♠ 9 7 5 3
♡ A K 6 3
♢ A 6 5
♣ 9 7

South:
♠ 8 6 4 2
♡ Q J 5
♢ K 9
♣ A K 6 3

You want to draw as many trumps as possible but retain the right to trump two clubs in dummy. If you play ♠A and another, the defence might play a third round leaving only one trump in dummy. Win ♢A, and *play a small spade from both hands.* Win the return and cash ♠A. It is to be hoped that there is only one trump outstanding now, so play ♣A, ruff a club, return to hand with a heart and ruff the last club. Then play winners and you will find that all the defence can make are two trumps and, maybe, a diamond.

♠	4!
♡	0
♢	1
♣	2
TLT	7

Don't panic when you are missing loads of top trumps! Here 4♠ is the right contract, and will almost certainly make as long as the adverse trumps break 3-2. Win ♣A and play a trump. Win the return and play another trump; if everybody follows, in the fullness of time you will make four hearts, two diamonds, two clubs and your two last trumps separately – ten tricks! The TLT is reduced to 3 because you lose just three spades. One club loser is ruffed and the other discarded on a top heart.

♠	5!
♡	0
♢	0
♣	2
TLT	7

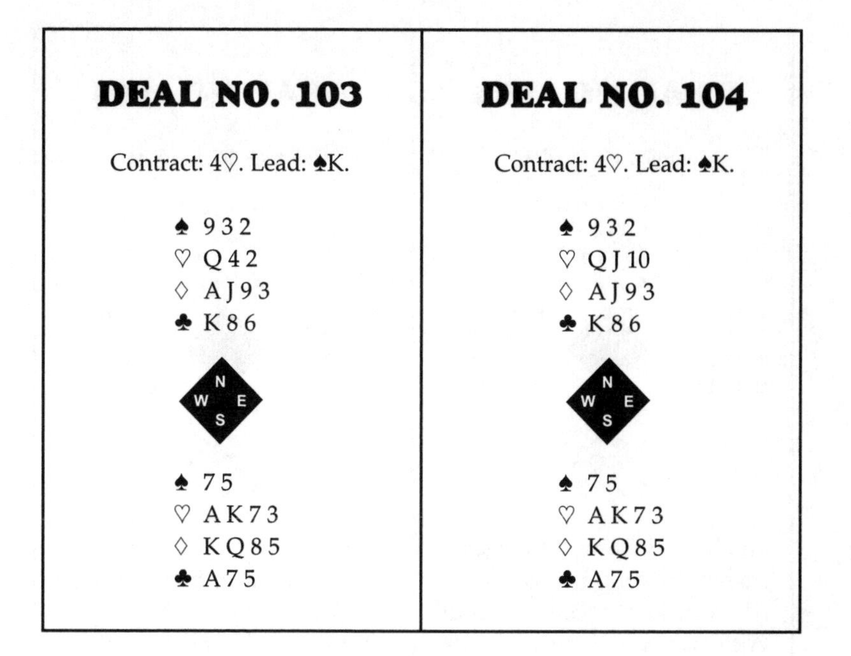
DEAL NO. 103
Contract: 4♡. Lead: ♠K.
♠ 9 3 2
♡ Q 4 2
◊ A J 9 3
♣ K 8 6
N
W
E
S
♠ 7 5
♡ A K 7 3
◊ K Q 8 5
♣ A 7 5
DEAL NO. 104
Contract: 4♡. Lead: ♠K.
♠ 9 3 2
♡ Q J 10
◊ A J 9 3
♣ K 8 6
N
W
E
S
♠ 7 5
♡ A K 7 3
◊ K Q 8 5
♣ A 7 5

DEAL NO. 103

Contract: 4♡. Lead: ♠K.

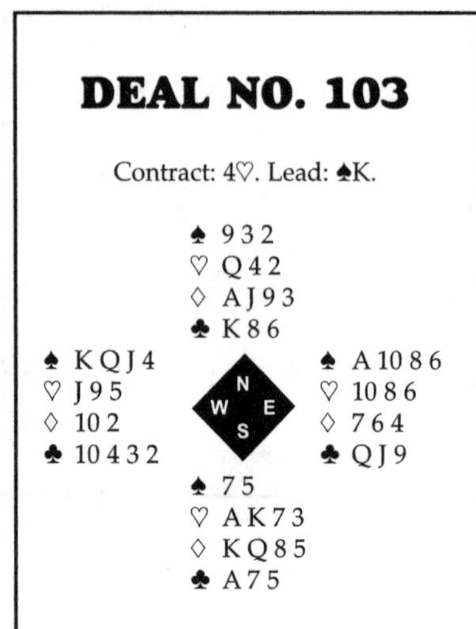

You have done well to reach a fragile 4♡ contract with only seven trumps between you! With two certain spade losers and a sure club loser you have to hope the outstanding trumps break 3-3. Ruff the third spade and play the three top hearts in any order. If the opponents follow to three rounds, you will make game with four heart tricks, four diamond tricks and two club tricks. You had to assume that the TLT count of 3 for the trump suit was way out.

♠	2
♡	3
◊	0
♣	1
TLT	6

DEAL NO. 104

Contract: 4♡. Lead: ♠K.

Now dummy has much better trumps. Usually they will split no worse than 4-2, so you should be able to draw them all providing you keep all four trumps in your hand. You have a certain club loser anyway, so let the defence win the third spade and throw away ♣5 from your hand. If the defence switch to another suit, you win, draw trumps and claim ten tricks, while if they lead a fourth spade *you can ruff in dummy!* By doing that you have not shortened your own trump holding. You can draw the outstanding trumps as before and claim.

♠	2
♡	2
◊	0
♣	1
TLT	5

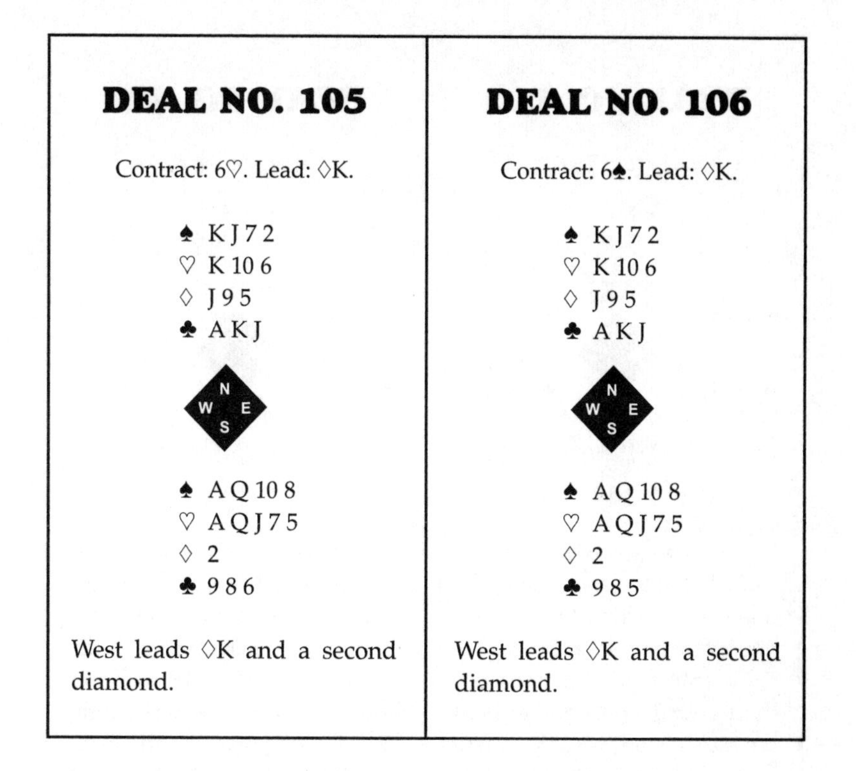

DEAL NO. 105

Contract: 6♡. Lead: ◊K.

♠ K J 7 2
♡ K 10 6
◊ J 9 5
♣ A K J

♠ A Q 10 8
♡ A Q J 7 5
◊ 2
♣ 9 8 6

West leads ◊K and a second diamond.

DEAL NO. 106

Contract: 6♠. Lead: ◊K.

♠ K J 7 2
♡ K 10 6
◊ J 9 5
♣ A K J

♠ A Q 10 8
♡ A Q J 7 5
◊ 2
♣ 9 8 5

West leads ◊K and a second diamond.

DEAL NO. 105

Contract: 6♡. Lead: ♢K.

Don't try to get extra tricks by ruffing diamonds in hand, for this is an illusion. Even if you do ruff two diamonds *you will still only make five trump tricks* – the number you had counted on making anyway. You will have done nothing to tackle the possible club loser predicted by TLT. No, correct play is to draw trumps, cash the top spades and take a club finesse by playing low to ♣J. If you want to be really expert it won't harm to cash ♣A first in case East has ♣Q singleton.

♠	0
♡	0
♢	1
♣	1
TLT	2

DEAL NO. 106

Contract: 6♠. Lead: ♢K.

Surely this is *Deal 105?* Yes, except now the contract is 6♠! Ruff the second diamond, draw trumps and then take five heart tricks and two clubs to bring the total to twelve, discarding ♣J on a long heart. With hearts as trumps you only had four spade tricks. Now you have five. You make extra tricks in a trump contract by *ruffing with the short trumps.* With a 4-4 trump fit a ruff in *either* hand provides an extra trick. We had to put a loser in the trump suit in the TLT table in case trumps broke 5-0.

♠	1
♡	0
♢	1
♣	1
TLT	3

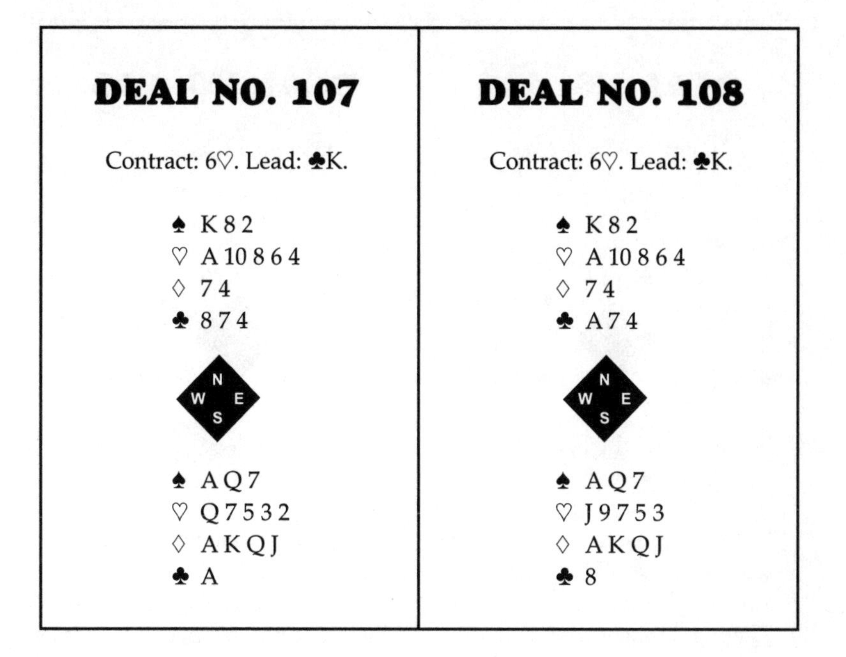
DEAL NO. 107
Contract: 6♡. Lead: ♣K.
♠ K 8 2
♡ A 10 8 6 4
◊ 7 4
♣ 8 7 4
N
W E
S
♠ A Q 7
♡ Q 7 5 3 2
◊ A K Q J
♣ A
DEAL NO. 108
Contract: 6♡. Lead: ♣K.
♠ K 8 2
♡ A 10 8 6 4
◊ 7 4
♣ A 7 4
N
W E
S
♠ A Q 7
♡ J 9 7 5 3
◊ A K Q J
♣ 8

DEAL NO. 107

Contract: 6♡. Lead: ♣K.

With no losers outside the trump suit you must play that suit in the optimal manner. Playing the ace first will lose two tricks if West has both the king and jack, whereas playing the queen first is fatal if East has both those cards. But if you play a low card from hand and insert the *ten* if West plays low you are guaranteed one loser at most. If East wins, your ace will later draw the last trump. If West shows out when you lead low, then you put up the ace and lead low from dummy.

♠	0
♡	2
♢	0
♣	0
TLT	2

DEAL NO. 108

Contract: 6♡. Lead: ♣K.

TLT shows that you have no losers outside trumps, so must play that suit with care. It may look natural to play the ace first, but just suppose that West has all three missing trumps! Then he will make both the king and queen. At trick two play a spade to hand and lead a low trump. If West plays the two play low from dummy! If East wins, the remaining trump will later fall under the ace while if East has all three trumps you are doomed to go one down.

♠	0
♡	2
♢	0
♣	0
TLT	2

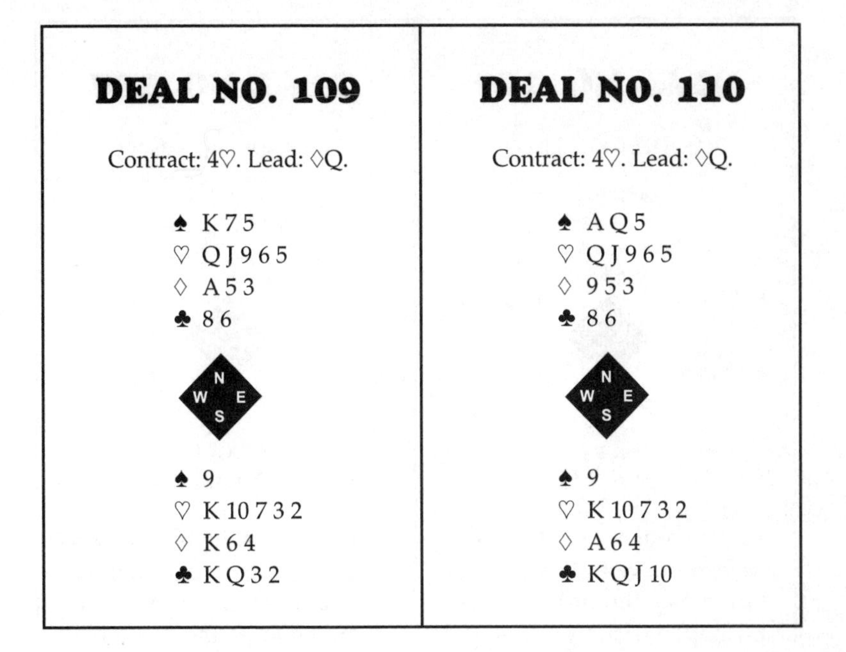

DEAL NO. 109

Contract: 4♡. Lead: ♢Q.

♠ K 7 5
♡ Q J 9 6 5
♢ A 5 3
♣ 8 6

N / W E / S

♠ 9
♡ K 10 7 3 2
♢ K 6 4
♣ K Q 3 2

DEAL NO. 110

Contract: 4♡. Lead: ♢Q.

♠ A Q 5
♡ Q J 9 6 5
♢ 9 5 3
♣ 8 6

N / W E / S

♠ 9
♡ K 10 7 3 2
♢ A 6 4
♣ K Q J 10

DEAL NO. 109

Contract: 4♡. Lead: ◇Q.

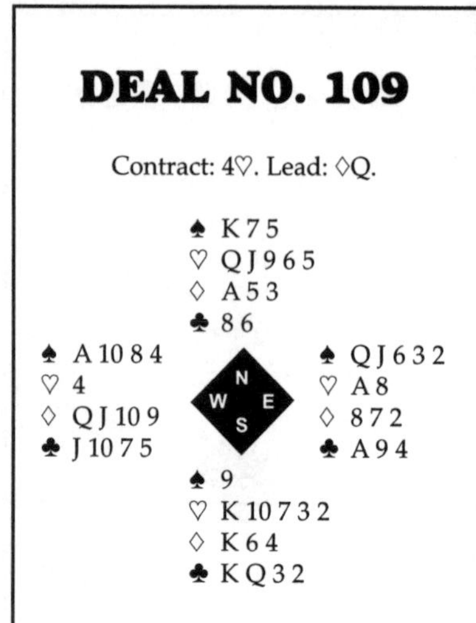

As you must lose the three aces you have to avoid losing a diamond. Suppose you lead a trump at trick two. East will win and return a diamond setting up a winner in that suit. Now when you lead a black suit the defence will cash out for one down. You have to assume that West has ♠A. Win the diamond in hand and lead ♠9. If West ducks, your spade loser will vanish while if he wins and plays another diamond, you will win in dummy and discard your losing diamond on ♠K.

♠	1
♡	1
◇	1
♣	3
TLT	6

DEAL NO. 110

Contract: 4♡. Lead: ◇Q.

This is essentially the same as *Deal 109*. With two certain aces to lose, you have to get rid of a diamond loser and if you play a trump at Trick 2 it will be too soon. The defence will win, and then cash ♣A and two diamonds. Instead, you must play a spade to the queen at Trick 2! If it loses, you will go two down but if it wins, you can throw a diamond loser on ♠A.

♠	0
♡	1
◇	2
♣	1
TLT	4

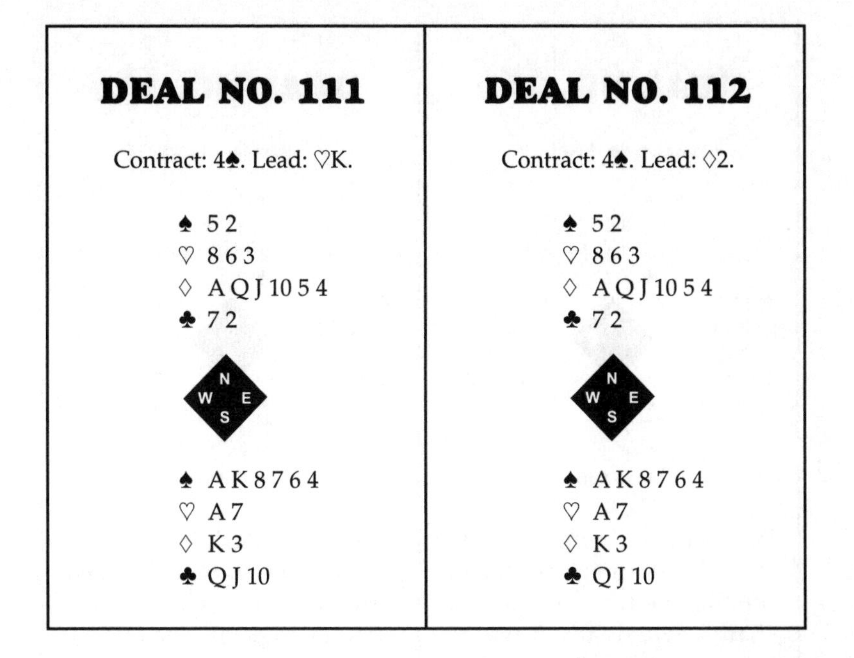
DEAL NO. 111
Contract: 4♠. Lead: ♡K.
♠ 5 2
♡ 8 6 3
♢ A Q J 10 5 4
♣ 7 2
N
W E
S
♠ A K 8 7 6 4
♡ A 7
♢ K 3
♣ Q J 10
DEAL NO. 112
Contract: 4♠. Lead: ♢2.
♠ 5 2
♡ 8 6 3
♢ A Q J 10 5 4
♣ 7 2
N
W E
S
♠ A K 8 7 6 4
♡ A 7
♢ K 3
♣ Q J 10

DEAL NO. 111

Contract: 4♠. Lead: ♡K.

It would be unrealistic to expect a 5-0 trump break and for this contract to stand a chance you really have to hope for a 3-2 split to confine your trump losers to one. Play ♠A-K but not another! If you do the opponents will make one spade, one heart and two clubs. Instead play ♢K-A and if both opponents follow carry on playing diamonds. Discard your heart first of course. West will ruff but he will no longer be able to cash a heart, and you will lose just a trump and two clubs.

♠	3!
♡	1
♢	0
♣	2
TLT	6

DEAL NO. 112

Contract: 4♠. Lead: ♢2.

The same deal but with a different lead! That diamond lead looks like a singleton and now it is imperative to remove all the trumps. Suppose you win in hand, cash ♠A-K, and lead a second diamond. West will ruff and now you can wave good-bye to dummy's long suit. Instead, lead a third trump. The defence can cash ♣A-K now, but that is all.

♠	3!
♡	1
♢	0
♣	2
TLT	6

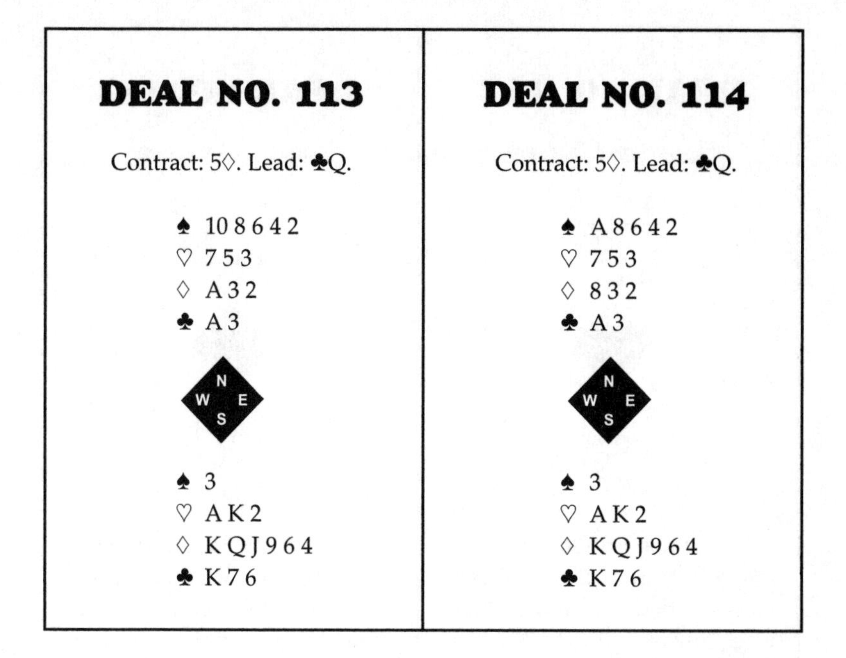

DEAL NO. 113
Contract: 5♢. Lead: ♣Q.
♠ 10 8 6 4 2
♡ 7 5 3
♢ A 3 2
♣ A 3
N
W E
S
♠ 3
♡ A K 2
♢ K Q J 9 6 4
♣ K 7 6
DEAL NO. 114
Contract: 5♢. Lead: ♣Q.
♠ A 8 6 4 2
♡ 7 5 3
♢ 8 3 2
♣ A 3
N
W E
S
♠ 3
♡ A K 2
♢ K Q J 9 6 4
♣ K 7 6

DEAL NO. 113

Contract: 5♢. Lead: ♣Q.

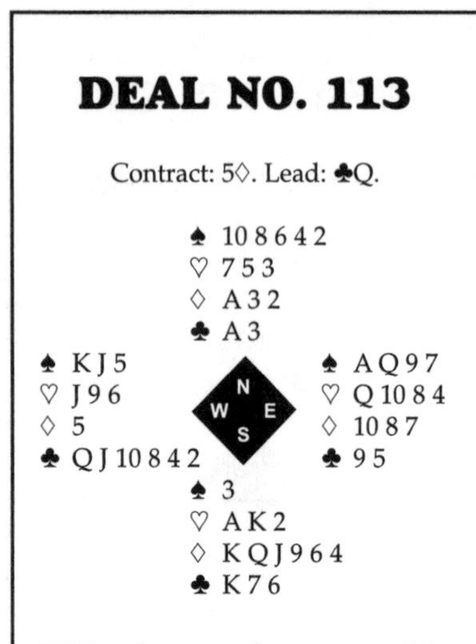

TLT shows three possible losers but surely the club loser can be ruffed in dummy? Take care however in case clubs break badly, so win in dummy and play a low diamond to the king. If all follow, play ♢Q and now, if there is one trump outstanding, you cannot afford to pull it because then you would not be able to ruff the club. Play ♣K-7, ruffing with ♢A, return to hand and pull the last trump. If West shows out on ♢K, ruff the club with ♢A and then take the marked finesse against the ten.

♠	1
♡	1
♢	0
♣	1
TLT	3

DEAL NO. 114

Contract: 5♢. Lead: ♣Q.

North: ♠ A 8 6 4 2 ♡ 7 5 3 ♢ 8 3 2 ♣ A 3

West: ♠ K J 5 ♡ J 9 6 4 ♢ 5 ♣ Q J 10 8 4

East: ♠ Q 10 9 7 ♡ Q 10 8 ♢ A 10 7 ♣ 9 5 2

South: ♠ 3 ♡ A K 2 ♢ K Q J 9 6 4 ♣ K 7 6

As in *Deal 113* you need to ruff a club in dummy. Good technique tells you to draw some trumps before you do that in case clubs break very badly, so it would be in order to play a low diamond to the king at trick two. If the king wins, however, do not play another! Can you see why? A sly defender with three trumps might win and play a third round, denying you your ruff. So, if ♢K does win, abandon trumps and ruff your third club with ♢8. Only later can you knock out ♢A.

♠	0
♡	1
♢	1
♣	1
TLT	3

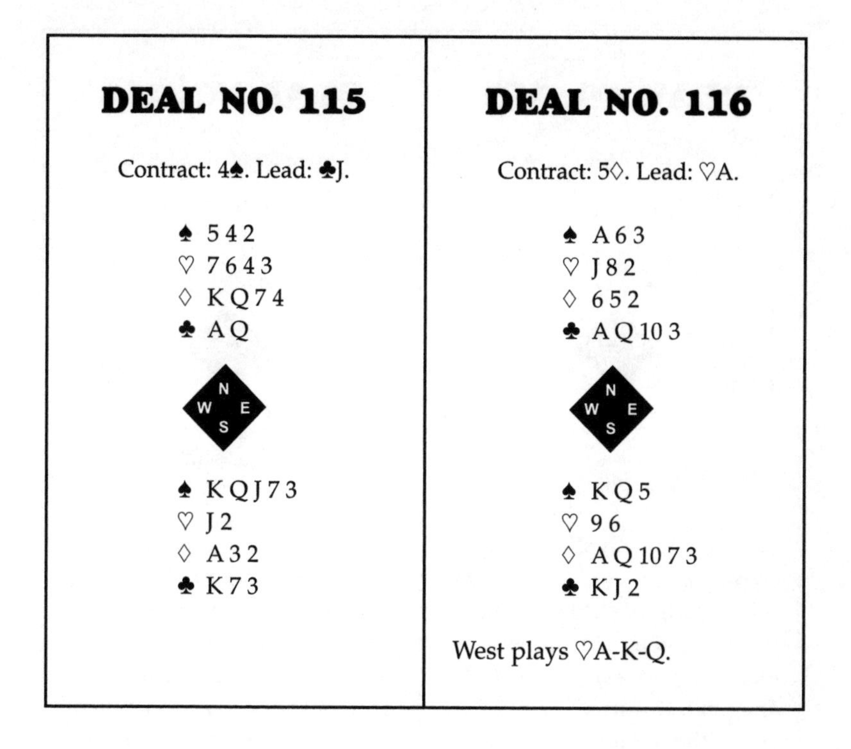

DEAL NO. 115

Contract: 4♠. Lead: ♣J.

♠ 5 4 2
♡ 7 6 4 3
♢ K Q 7 4
♣ A Q

N / W E / S

♠ K Q J 7 3
♡ J 2
♢ A 3 2
♣ K 7 3

DEAL NO. 116

Contract: 5♢. Lead: ♡A.

♠ A 6 3
♡ J 8 2
♢ 6 5 2
♣ A Q 10 3

N / W E / S

♠ K Q 5
♡ 9 6
♢ A Q 10 7 3
♣ K J 2

West plays ♡A-K-Q.

DEAL NO. 115

Contract: 4♠. Lead: ♣J.

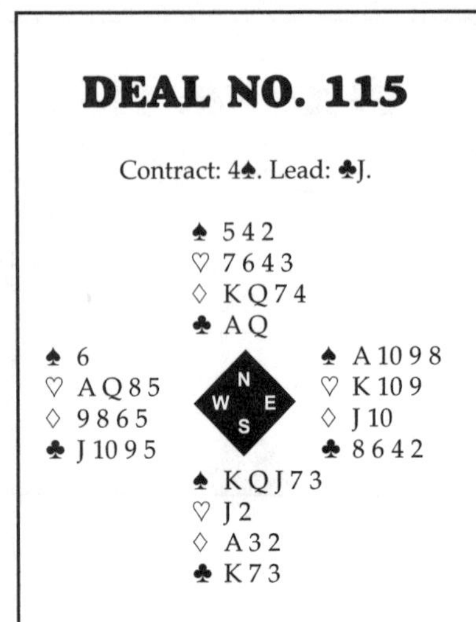

If trumps break 5-0 you are doomed, so you must pay attention to possible 4-1 splits. Suppose you win the club in dummy and lead a spade to the king. If it holds, you must resist the temptation to play the queen next; instead, return to dummy with a club in order to lead another spade. If the queen now wins, but West shows out, return to dummy again to lead a third trump. You will hold your trump losers to just one if they break 3-2 or if East holds four to the ace or the singleton ace.

♠	3!
♡	2
◇	0
♣	0
TLT	5

DEAL NO. 116

Contract: 5◇. Lead: ♡A.

North: ♠ A 6 3 ♡ J 8 2 ◇ 6 5 2 ♣ A Q 10 3

West: ♠ J 9 7 2 ♡ A K Q 5 3 ◇ 9 4 ♣ 7 5

East: ♠ 10 8 4 ♡ 10 7 4 ◇ K J 8 ♣ 9 8 6 4

South: ♠ K Q 5 ♡ 9 6 ◇ A Q 10 7 3 ♣ K J 2

Despite the high point count 5◇ is a dreadful contract! Having lost the first two heart tricks you have to find a way to lose no diamond tricks and you will certainly need a lot of luck. Ruff the third heart and enter dummy with a spade. Lead a diamond to the ten and cross your fingers. If it wins re-enter dummy with a club and lead a second trump, finessing against the king. On a good day trumps will split 3-2 with East holding both the king and jack. On a bad day . . .

♠	0
♡	2
◇	4!
♣	0
TLT	6

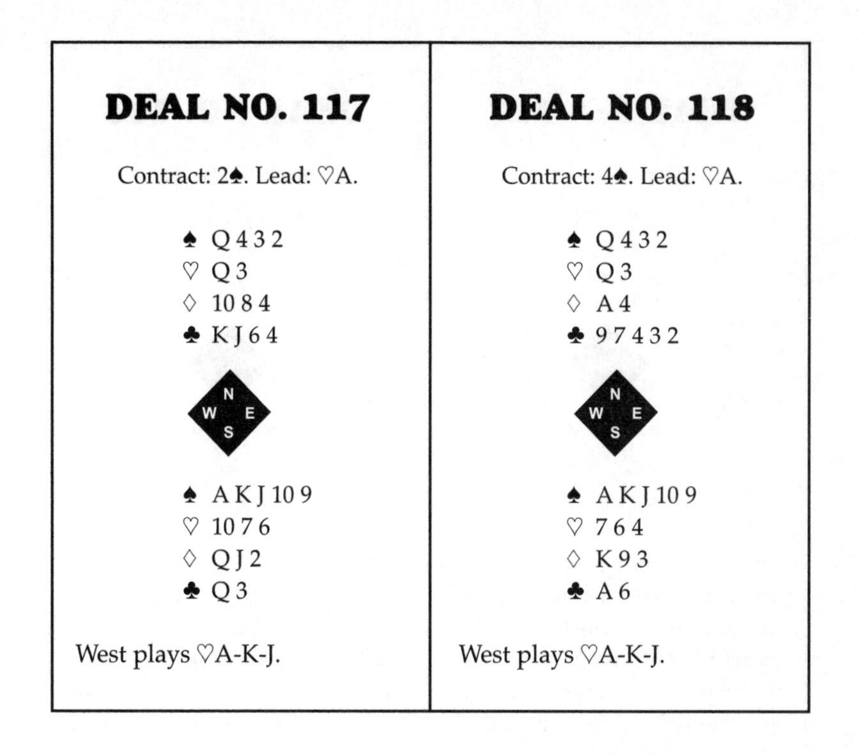

DEAL NO. 117

Contract: 2♠. Lead: ♡A.

♠ Q 4 3 2
♡ Q 3
♢ 10 8 4
♣ K J 6 4

♠ A K J 10 9
♡ 10 7 6
♢ Q J 2
♣ Q 3

West plays ♡A-K-J.

DEAL NO. 118

Contract: 4♠. Lead: ♡A.

♠ Q 4 3 2
♡ Q 3
♢ A 4
♣ 9 7 4 3 2

♠ A K J 10 9
♡ 7 6 4
♢ K 9 3
♣ A 6

West plays ♡A-K-J.

DEAL NO. 117

Contract: 2♠. Lead: ♡A.

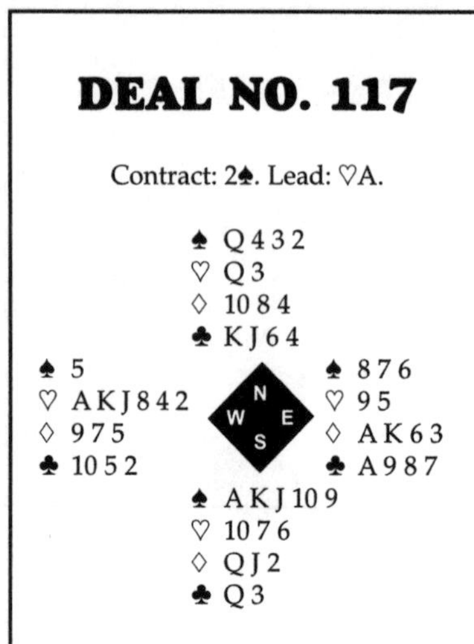

There is nothing you can do about the three losing tricks in the minors so you have to be extra vigilant with regard to the heart suit. It looks as though you can ruff the third round of hearts in dummy, and so you can, but if you ruff low you may live to regret it if East only has two hearts and can over-ruff dummy. Make sure you win the trick by ruffing with the queen. Then draw trumps and knock out ♣A.

♠	0
♡	3
◊	2
♣	1
TLT	6

DEAL NO. 118

Contract: 4♠. Lead: ♡A.

As in *Deal 107* you would be wise to trump the third heart with ♠Q in case East can over-ruff. However, you must not think that you can necessarily draw all the defenders' trumps now. Play two rounds by all means but no more, because you need that last trump in dummy to ruff your losing diamond. Only when you have done that can you return to hand with a club to draw any remaining trumps.

♠	0
♡	3
◊	1
♣	1
TLT	5

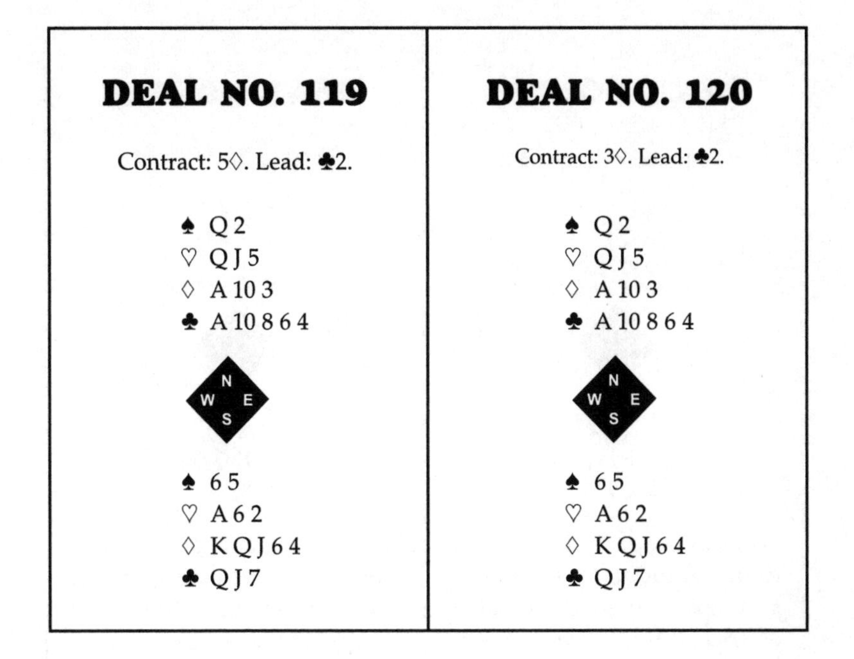
DEAL NO. 119
Contract: 5♢. Lead: ♣2.
♠ Q 2
♡ Q J 5
♢ A 10 3
♣ A 10 8 6 4
N
W E
S
♠ 6 5
♡ A 6 2
♢ K Q J 6 4
♣ Q J 7
DEAL NO. 120
Contract: 3♢. Lead: ♣2.
♠ Q 2
♡ Q J 5
♢ A 10 3
♣ A 10 8 6 4
N
W E
S
♠ 6 5
♡ A 6 2
♢ K Q J 6 4
♣ Q J 7

DEAL NO. 119

Contract: 5♢. Lead: ♣2.

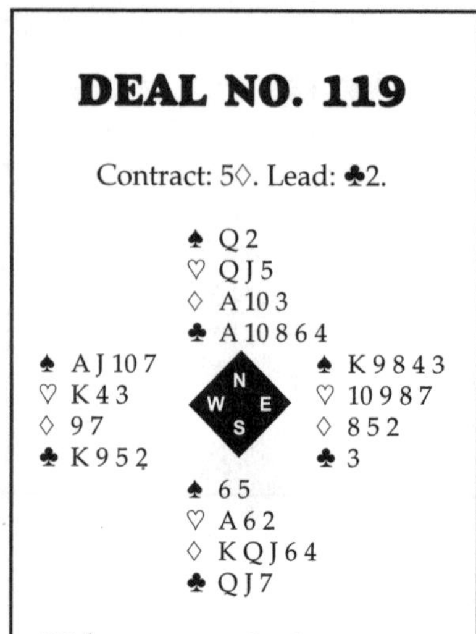

With two spade losers you cannot afford to lose a club so you must play low from table at Trick 1. But be sure to win with the queen or jack! Why? If you win ♣7, draw trumps and then play ♣Q, West will play ♣K. You can win with dummy's ♣A, but then have to play back to ♣J with no way back to dummy. By winning the first club with the queen you can later lead the jack and, if West covers that, you have a finesse against the nine after returning to hand with ♡A. Your two low hearts are thrown on dummy's winning clubs.

♠	2
♡	1
♢	0
♣	1
TLT	4

DEAL NO. 120

Contract: 3♢. Lead: ♣2.

North: ♠ Q 2 ♡ Q J 5 ♢ A 10 3 ♣ A 10 8 6 4

West: ♠ A J 10 7 ♡ K 9 8 4 3 ♢ 9 7 2 ♣ 2

East: ♠ K 9 8 4 3 ♡ 10 7 ♢ 8 5 ♣ K 9 5 3

South: ♠ 6 5 ♡ A 6 2 ♢ K Q J 6 4 ♣ Q J 7

This looks familiar but now you are only in 3♢ and it would be madness to take an early club finesse. Can you see why? West might have led a singleton club so East would win and give his partner a ruff. What is more West might get another ruff if he puts his partner in with ♠K. TLT shows you only have four possible losers, so win ♣A, draw trumps, and lead another club. All the defenders can take are two spades, one heart and a club.

♠	2
♡	1
♢	0
♣	1
TLT	4

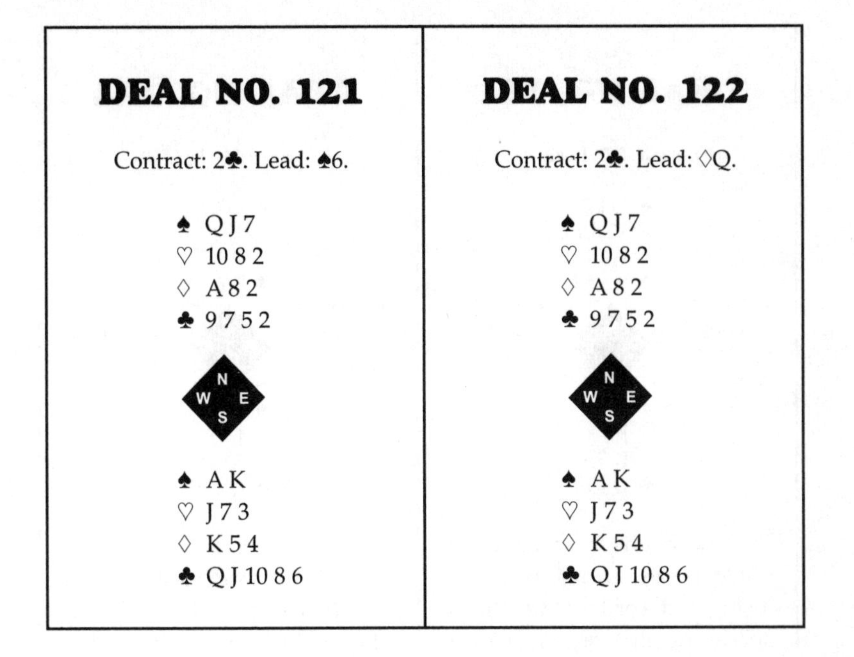
DEAL NO. 121
Contract: 2♣. Lead: ♠6.
♠ Q J 7
♡ 10 8 2
♢ A 8 2
♣ 9 7 5 2
N
W E
S
♠ A K
♡ J 7 3
♢ K 5 4
♣ Q J 10 8 6
DEAL NO. 122
Contract: 2♣. Lead: ♢Q.
♠ Q J 7
♡ 10 8 2
♢ A 8 2
♣ 9 7 5 2
N
W E
S
♠ A K
♡ J 7 3
♢ K 5 4
♣ Q J 10 8 6

DEAL NO. 121

Contract: 2♣. Lead: ♠6.

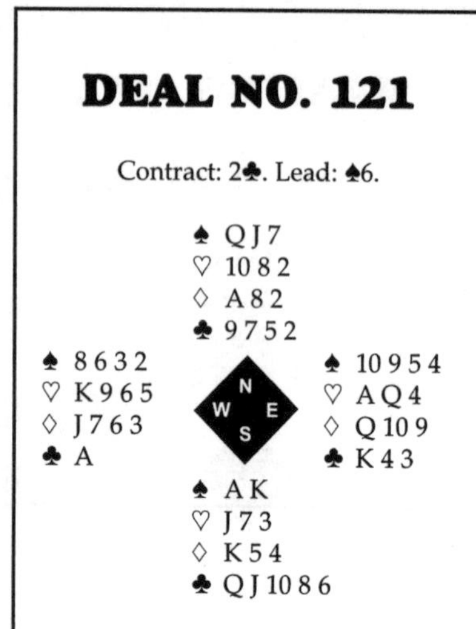

TLT shows one loser too many but you can always discard a losing red card on the third spade in dummy. However there is no need to do this yet. Win the spade and lead a trump and, whatever East-West do now, you will eventually regain the lead. Then knock out the other top trump. Next time in, you cash ♠K, enter dummy either with ◇A or ♣9, and discard any losing red card you may have. Playing spades before drawing trumps would have worked too, but stands the slight chance of an adverse ruff.

♠	0
♡	3
◇	1
♣	2
TLT	6

DEAL NO. 122

Contract: 2♣. Lead: ◇Q.

North: ♠ Q J 7 ♡ 10 8 2 ◇ A 8 2 ♣ 9 7 5 2

West: ♠ 10 8 6 4 ♡ A 9 6 ◇ Q J 10 7 ♣ K 4

East: ♠ 9 5 3 2 ♡ K Q 5 4 ◇ 9 6 3 ♣ A 3

South: ♠ A K ♡ J 7 3 ◇ K 5 4 ♣ Q J 10 8 6

Same contract as *Deal 121* but a different lead! See what a difference it makes. If you start by playing trumps, the defence can knock out your other diamond stopper – and then you would have no entry for that precious ♠Q before it is too late. So win the lead in hand, play ♠A-K, and only then lead a trump. Now you still have ◇A intact for that vital red suit discard.

♠	0
♡	3
◇	1
♣	2
TLT	6

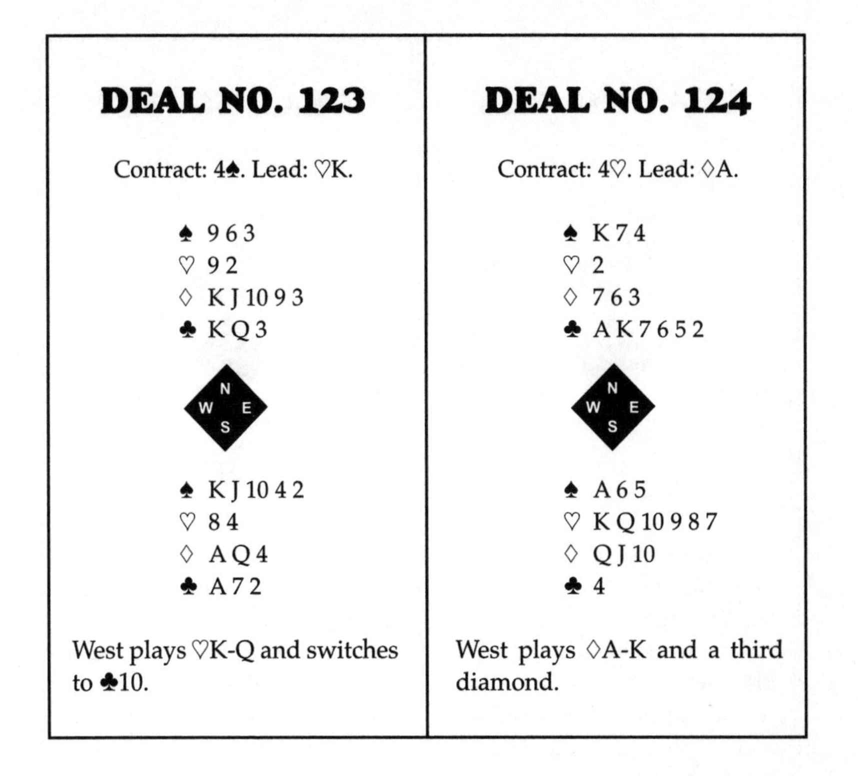

DEAL NO. 123

Contract: 4♠. Lead: ♡K.

♠ 9 6 3
♡ 9 2
♢ K J 10 9 3
♣ K Q 3

♠ K J 10 4 2
♡ 8 4
♢ A Q 4
♣ A 7 2

West plays ♡K-Q and switches to ♣10.

DEAL NO. 124

Contract: 4♡. Lead: ♢A.

♠ K 7 4
♡ 2
♢ 7 6 3
♣ A K 7 6 5 2

♠ A 6 5
♡ K Q 10 9 8 7
♢ Q J 10
♣ 4

West plays ♢A-K and a third diamond.

DEAL NO. 123

Contract: 4♠. Lead: ♡K.

North: ♠ 9 6 3 ♡ 9 2 ♢ K J 10 9 3 ♣ K Q 3

West: ♠ A 8 7 5 ♡ K Q J 3 ♢ 7 6 ♣ 10 9 4

East: ♠ Q ♡ A 10 7 6 5 ♢ 8 5 2 ♣ J 8 6 5

South: ♠ K J 10 4 2 ♡ 8 4 ♢ A Q 4 ♣ A 7 2

With two losers already you must optimise the play in the trump suit. It might look right to win the club in dummy and play ♠9 but imagine what would happen if East had ♠Q bare. Your remaining ♠J-10 is not enough to pick up West's ♠8-7-5 and West's ♠8 will be promoted. Better to lead a low trump from dummy, playing ♠10 if East plays low. If he follows with ♠Q, you cover and, although West can win, your ♠9-10-J will draw the remaining trumps.

♠	3
♡	2
♢	0
♣	0
TLT	5

DEAL NO. 124

Contract: 4♡. Lead: ♢A.

North: ♠ K 7 4 ♡ 2 ♢ 7 6 3 ♣ A K 7 6 5 2

West: ♠ Q 10 8 2 ♡ 6 4 3 ♢ A K 8 2 ♣ 9 3

East: ♠ J 9 3 ♡ A J 5 ♢ 9 5 4 ♣ Q J 10 8

South: ♠ A 6 5 ♡ K Q 10 9 8 7 ♢ Q J 10 ♣ 4

You have lost two tricks already and, although your losing spade can be thrown on a top club in dummy, you must ensure you play the trump suit in the best way possible. You have two choices. You could play ♡K and later the ♡Q hoping to find ♡J singleton or doubleton, but a much superior line is to enter dummy and play a heart to the ten. This line will work whenever East has ♡J singleton, doubleton or trebleton.

♠	1
♡	2
♢	2
♣	0
TLT	5

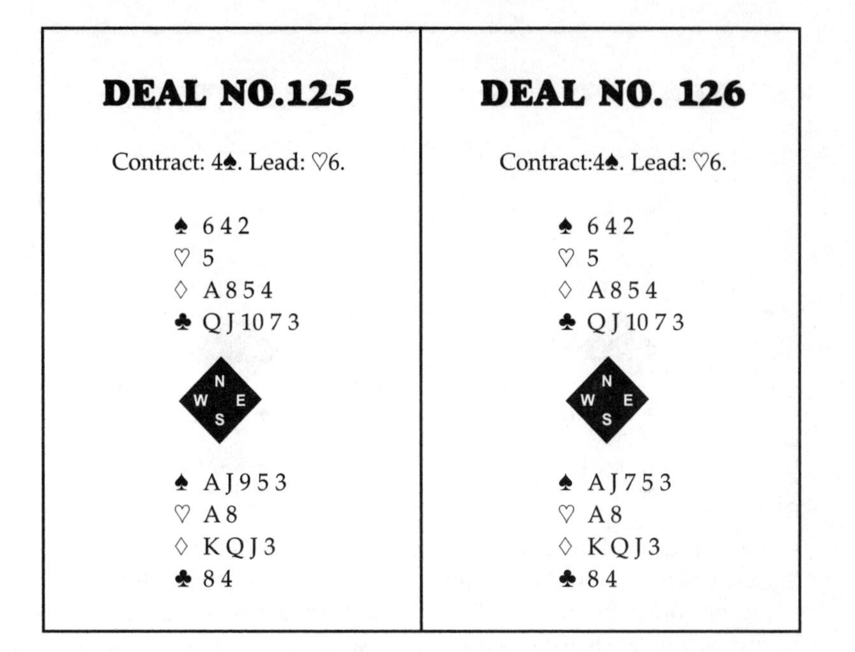
DEAL NO.125
Contract: 4♠. Lead: ♡6.
♠ 6 4 2
♡ 5
◊ A 8 5 4
♣ Q J 10 7 3
N
W E
S
♠ A J 9 5 3
♡ A 8
◊ K Q J 3
♣ 8 4
DEAL NO. 126
Contract:4♠. Lead: ♡6.
♠ 6 4 2
♡ 5
◊ A 8 5 4
♣ Q J 10 7 3
N
W E
S
♠ A J 7 5 3
♡ A 8
◊ K Q J 3
♣ 8 4

DEAL NO.125

Contract: 4♠. Lead: ♡6.

You can do nothing about the club losers but the low heart can be ruffed in dummy. The best way to tackle trumps is to lead low from dummy and play ♠9 if East plays low. If this loses you have to hope it is to ♠K or ♠Q, *not* ♠10. Say it loses to ♠K. Re-enter dummy with ◇A and lead another trump. If East plays ♠10 you cover with ♠J and hope it wins! This plan works whenever East has one top honour, plus the ten, and no more than three trumps.

♠	4!
♡	1
◇	0
♣	2
TLT	7

DEAL NO. 126

Contract:4♠. Lead: ♡6.

What a difference a nine makes! This is a truly dreadful contract and will need a great deal of luck to make because, again, you have to try and limit the trump losers to one but this time with a weaker suit. So ruff the heart loser in dummy and play a trump. If East plays low, insert ♠J and pray: you will need to find East with both king and queen of trumps and no more than three. If East plays a top trump, you must re-enter dummy with ◇A and lead low towards ♠J.

♠	4!
♡	1
◇	0
♣	2
TLT	7

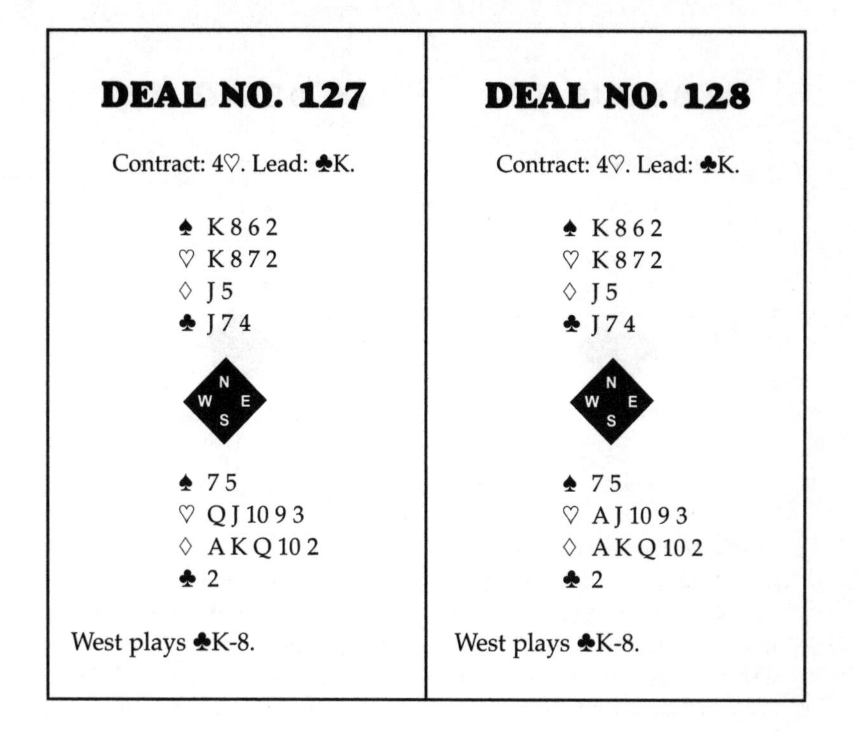
DEAL NO. 127
Contract: 4♡. Lead: ♣K.
♠ K 8 6 2
♡ K 8 7 2
◊ J 5
♣ J 7 4
N
W E
S
♠ 7 5
♡ Q J 10 9 3
◊ A K Q 10 2
♣ 2
West plays ♣K-8.
DEAL NO. 128
Contract: 4♡. Lead: ♣K.
♠ K 8 6 2
♡ K 8 7 2
◊ J 5
♣ J 7 4
N
W E
S
♠ 7 5
♡ A J 10 9 3
◊ A K Q 10 2
♣ 2
West plays ♣K-8.

DEAL NO. 127

Contract: 4♡. Lead: ♣K.

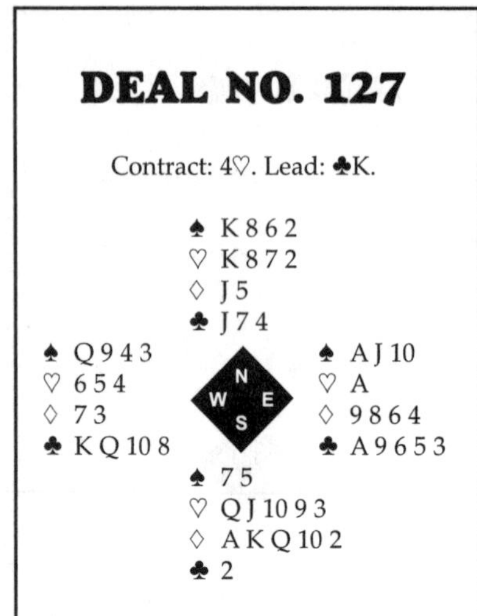

With a certain trump and club loser it looks as if you have to find ♠A with West in order to make a spade trick. But if you discard three spades from table on your long diamonds, you can eventually ruff a spade. Can anything go wrong? Yes, after ruffing ♣8 you must draw trumps and if West wins and plays a low spade you might end up with the losers you feared. Nothing you can do about that – so hope East has ♡A so that your ♠K cannot be attacked, and you later get your discards.

♠	2
♡	1
◇	0
♣	1
TLT	4

DEAL NO. 128

Contract: 4♡. Lead: ♣K.

Same as *Deal 127* but better trumps, and this time you can arrange it so that if you lose a trump you lose it to the safe hand, namely East. So ruff ♣8, cash ♡A and lead ♡J, letting it run if West plays low. You may lose to a doubleton queen in the East hand but your contract is now assured as you can obtain three spade discards on your diamonds. If ♡J wins you can pull the remaining trump and make an overtrick!

♠	2
♡	1
◇	0
♣	1
TLT	4

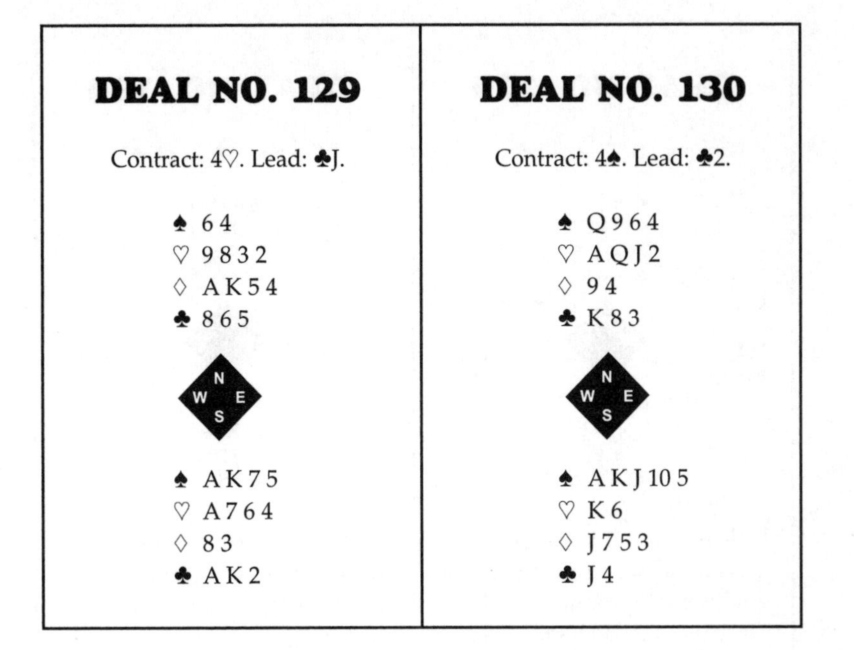

DEAL NO. 129

Contract: 4♡. Lead: ♣J.

North:
♠ 6 4
♡ 9 8 3 2
♢ A K 5 4
♣ 8 6 5

South:
♠ A K 7 5
♡ A 7 6 4
♢ 8 3
♣ A K 2

DEAL NO. 130

Contract: 4♠. Lead: ♣2.

North:
♠ Q 9 6 4
♡ A Q J 2
♢ 9 4
♣ K 8 3

South:
♠ A K J 10 5
♡ K 6
♢ J 7 5 3
♣ J 4

DEAL NO. 129

Contract: 4♡. Lead: ♣J.

Unless trumps break 3-2 you are bound to be defeated, so you mentally reduce TLT to 5. The club loser is inescapable, so you have to ruff the two losing spades in dummy. If you play ♡A and another, an unkind defender might play a third round, reducing your ruffing ability, while if you ruff a spade without touching trumps, you might run into an overruff from a defender with only two trumps. The answer is to play a *low* trump from both hands. Win the return, play ♡A and then cross-ruff spades and diamonds.

♠	2
♡	4!
◇	0
♣	1
TLT	7

DEAL NO. 130

Contract: 4♠. Lead: ♣2.

After trumps have been drawn you can discard two losing diamonds on dummy's hearts so you have to try to avoid losing two clubs. If East has both club honours there is nothing you can do so you must assume he has only one – but is it the ace or the queen? While it is reasonable to lead away from an ace against a no-trump contract it is rarely done against a suit contract because it is all too likely to give away a trick without any gain. So playing *low* from dummy is likely to be the winning action.

♠	0
♡	0
◇	4
♣	2
TLT	6

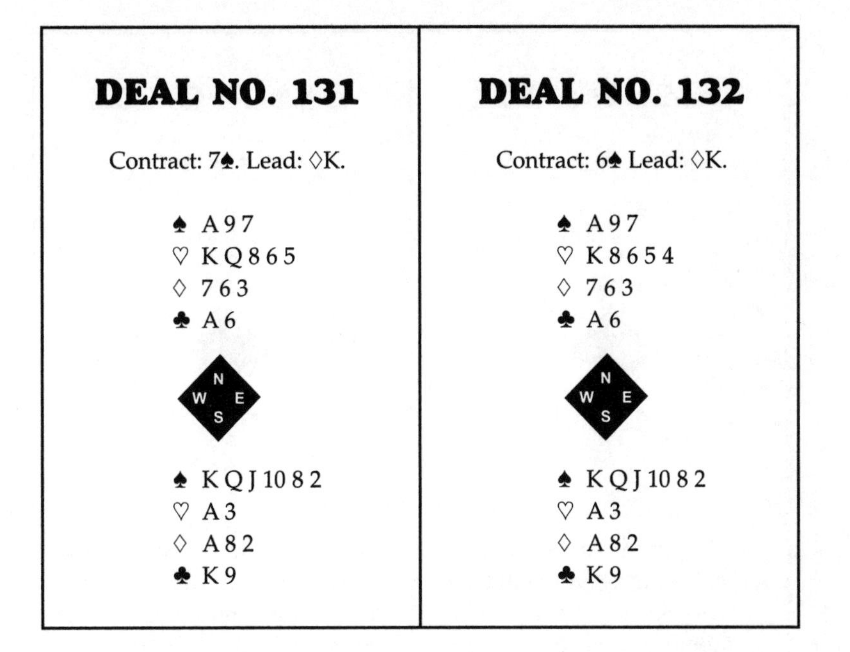
DEAL NO. 131
Contract: 7♠. Lead: ♢K.
♠ A 9 7
♡ K Q 8 6 5
♢ 7 6 3
♣ A 6
N
W E
S
♠ K Q J 10 8 2
♡ A 3
♢ A 8 2
♣ K 9
DEAL NO. 132
Contract: 6♠ Lead: ♢K.
♠ A 9 7
♡ K 8 6 5 4
♢ 7 6 3
♣ A 6
N
W E
S
♠ K Q J 10 8 2
♡ A 3
♢ A 8 2
♣ K 9

DEAL NO. 131

Contract: 7♠. Lead: ♢K.

Two losers are far too many in a grand slam, so you will have to dispose of the two low diamonds and the heart suit is the obvious place to look for discards. Draw trumps and then play ♡A-K-Q, discarding a diamond from hand. If both opponents follow three times the two remaining hearts in dummy are masters but, if one hand has four hearts, then you must ruff a low heart in hand, return to dummy with ♣A and discard your last diamond on the last remaining heart.

♠	0
♡	0
♢	2
♣	0
TLT	2

DEAL NO. 132

Contract: 6♠ Lead: ♢K.

Again you must set up the heart suit in dummy for discards but now you cannot afford to draw all the trumps if they break 3-1. Why? Because you need the ♠A in dummy as a vital entry. So play ♠K-Q, then ♡A-K and ruff a heart high. If they break 3-3 enter dummy with ♠A and claim thirteen tricks but, if not, re-enter dummy with ♠A in order to ruff yet another heart. The remaining heart in dummy will be a master now, on which you can discard a diamond, and dummy can be reached via ♣A.

♠	0
♡	0
♢	2
♣	0
TLT	2

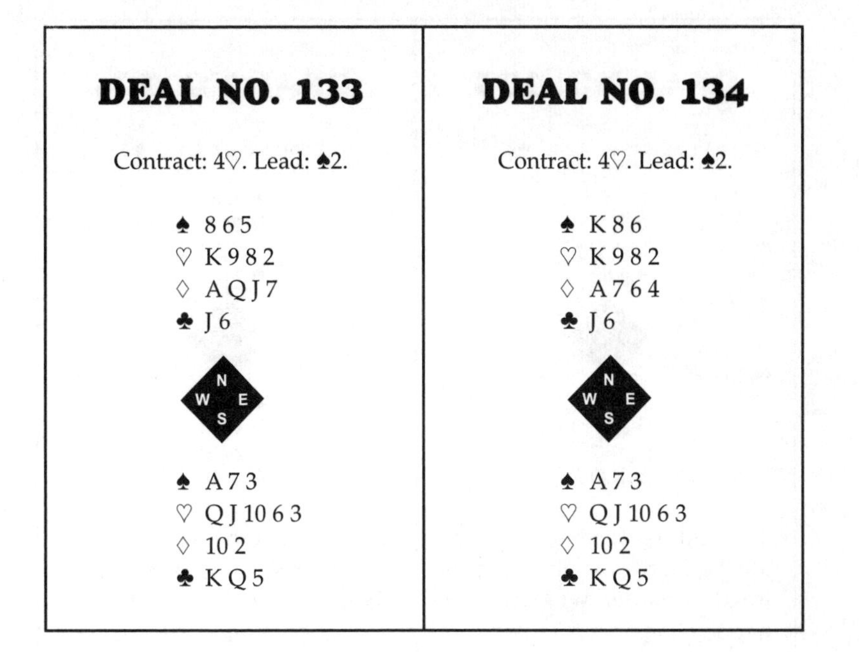
DEAL NO. 133
Contract: 4♡. Lead: ♠2.
♠ 8 6 5
♡ K 9 8 2
◊ A Q J 7
♣ J 6
N
W
E
S
♠ A 7 3
♡ Q J 10 6 3
◊ 10 2
♣ K Q 5
DEAL NO. 134
Contract: 4♡. Lead: ♠2.
♠ K 8 6
♡ K 9 8 2
◊ A 7 6 4
♣ J 6
N
W
E
S
♠ A 7 3
♡ Q J 10 6 3
◊ 10 2
♣ K Q 5

DEAL NO. 133

Contract: 4♡. Lead: ♠2.

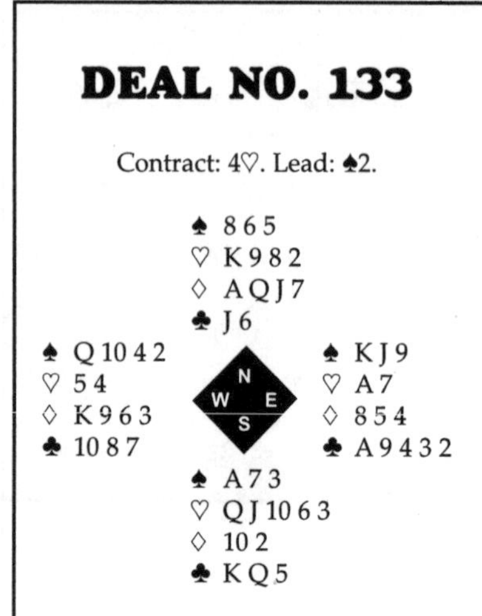

The lead indicates that spades are breaking evenly, so you must consider what would happen if you won and played a trump at trick two. After taking ♡A the defence would now cash two spades and ♣A – one down! You must hope the diamond finesse is right, and you have to take it at once. At trick two lead ◇10 because you want to remain in your hand if it wins. If West plays low, let the ten run, then play low to ◇J. Finally, pitch a spade loser on ◇A. Only now tackle trumps.

♠	2
♡	1
◇	1
♣	1
TLT	5

DEAL NO. 134

Contract: 4♡. Lead: ♠2.

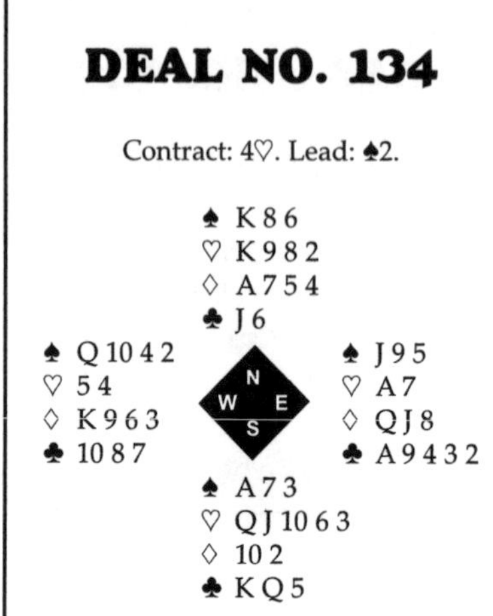

It may seem that holding both ♠A and ♠K you are safe to play trumps at trick two, but that would be wrong. The defence would win, knock out your other spade stopper and now, when in with ♣A, they would have a spade trick established. And the diamond loser is inescapable. You must win the first trick in dummy and knock out ♣A. If the defence now lead another spade, you win in hand and throw dummy's third spade on a club. Only then can you tackle trumps. Later your low spade can be ruffed in dummy.

♠	1
♡	1
◇	1
♣	1
TLT	4

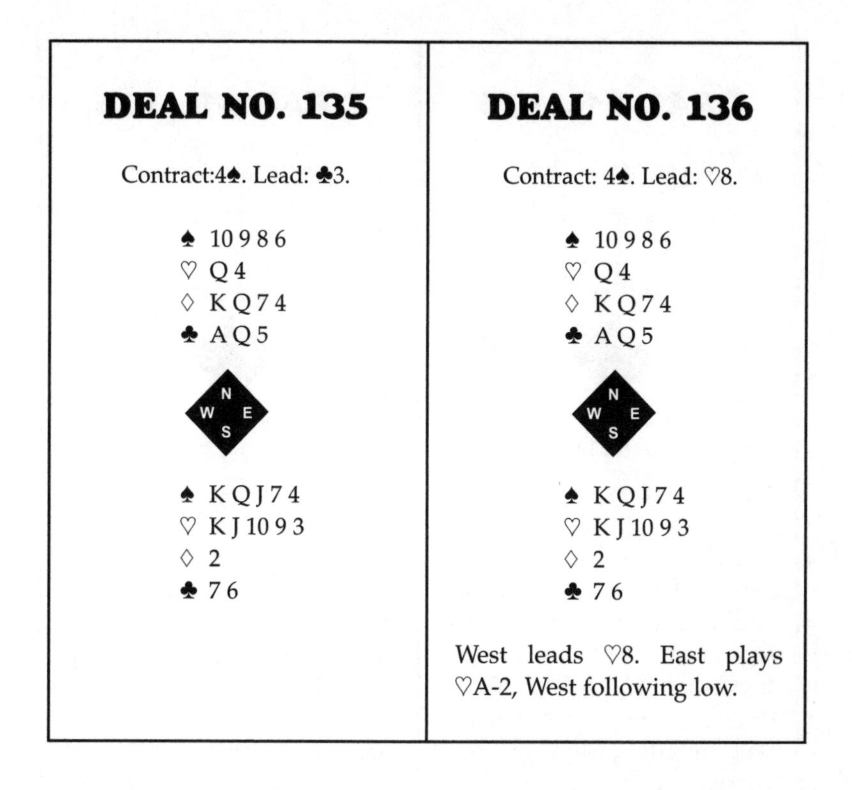

DEAL NO. 135

Contract:4♠. Lead: ♣3.

♠ 10 9 8 6
♡ Q 4
♢ K Q 7 4
♣ A Q 5

♠ K Q J 7 4
♡ K J 10 9 3
♢ 2
♣ 7 6

DEAL NO. 136

Contract: 4♠. Lead: ♡8.

♠ 10 9 8 6
♡ Q 4
♢ K Q 7 4
♣ A Q 5

♠ K Q J 7 4
♡ K J 10 9 3
♢ 2
♣ 7 6

West leads ♡8. East plays ♡A-2, West following low.

DEAL NO. 135

Contract:4♠. Lead: ♣3.

TLT shows four losers and as three of them are inescapable aces you have to try and not lose a club. If you win the first trick with ♣A and set about drawing trumps, the defence will smartly cash their four winners, so you have to hope West has ♣K, making the play of ♣Q from dummy at Trick 1 the smart move. Half the time you will be lucky and the ♣Q will win. Now you set about drawing trumps.

♠ 1
♡ 1
◇ 1
♣ 1
TLT 4

DEAL NO. 136

Contract: 4♠. Lead: ♡8.

North: ♠ 10 9 8 6 ♡ Q 4 ◇ K Q 7 4 ♣ A Q 5

West: ♠ A 3 2 ♡ 8 5 ◇ J 9 6 5 ♣ J 9 4 2

East: ♠ 5 ♡ A 7 6 2 ◇ A 10 8 3 ♣ K 10 8 3

South: ♠ K Q J 7 4 ♡ K J 10 9 3 ◇ 2 ♣ 7 6

Same hands as *Deal 135* but a more friendly lead. When you win the second trick, it might look right to play a trump immediately but in the worst case scenario West could win and play a club. You would win ♣A and hope to discard clubs from dummy on good hearts in hand, but this plan fails if trumps are 4-0. Much better to play a diamond at Trick 3, forcing out the ace, and enabling your losing club to be discarded on dummy's master diamond. Only then would it be safe for you to tackle trumps.

♠ 1
♡ 1
◇ 1
♣ 1
TLT 4

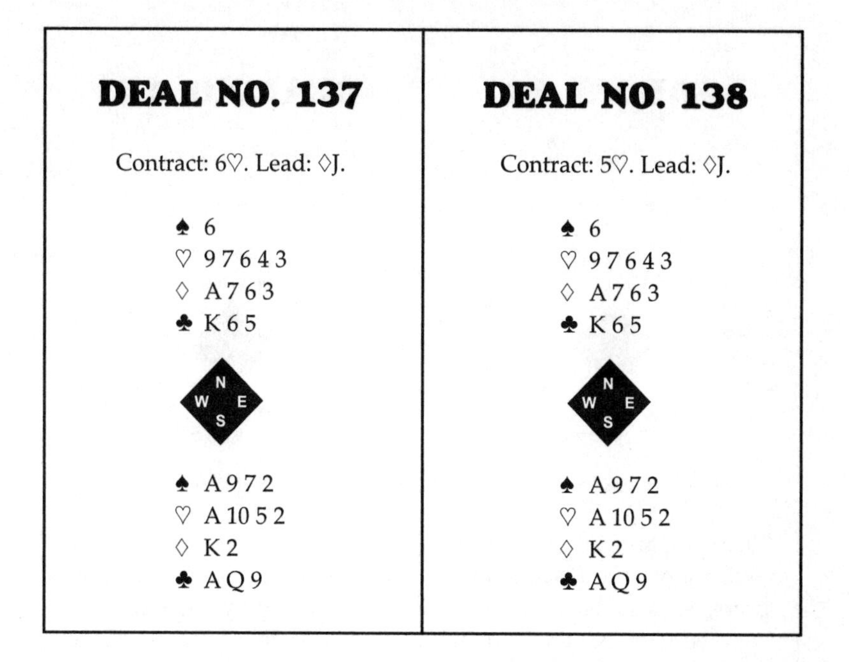

DEAL NO. 137

Contract: 6♡. Lead: ♢J.

♠ 6
♡ 9 7 6 4 3
♢ A 7 6 3
♣ K 6 5

♠ A 9 7 2
♡ A 10 5 2
♢ K 2
♣ A Q 9

DEAL NO. 138

Contract: 5♡. Lead: ♢J.

♠ 6
♡ 9 7 6 4 3
♢ A 7 6 3
♣ K 6 5

♠ A 9 7 2
♡ A 10 5 2
♢ K 2
♣ A Q 9

DEAL NO. 137

Contract: 6♡. Lead: ♢J.

When you are in a small slam, you cannot afford two trump losers, so you have to hope from the start that the adverse trumps split 2-2. Accordingly, win the opening lead and play ace and a low heart, and if this draws all the outstanding trumps you will find that you can ruff your three losing spades in dummy.

♠	3
♡	3
♢	0
♣	0
TLT	6

DEAL NO. 138

Contract: 5♡. Lead: ♢J.

North: ♠ 6 ♡ 9 7 6 4 3 ♢ A 7 6 3 ♣ K 6 5

West: ♠ Q 10 8 4 ♡ K Q 8 ♢ J 10 8 ♣ J 7 2

East: ♠ K J 5 3 ♡ J ♢ Q 9 5 4 ♣ 10 8 4 3

South: ♠ A 9 7 2 ♡ A 10 5 2 ♢ K 2 ♣ A Q 9

The same deal as 137 but a different contract. Can you see that if you play ace and a low heart this time a defender with three trumps might play a third round leaving only two trumps in dummy to cater for three spade ruffs? The safe way is to play just ♡A and set about ruffing spades at once, using club entries back to the closed hand. At some stage the defenders might make two trumps, but that is all.

♠	3
♡	3
♢	0
♣	0
TLT	6

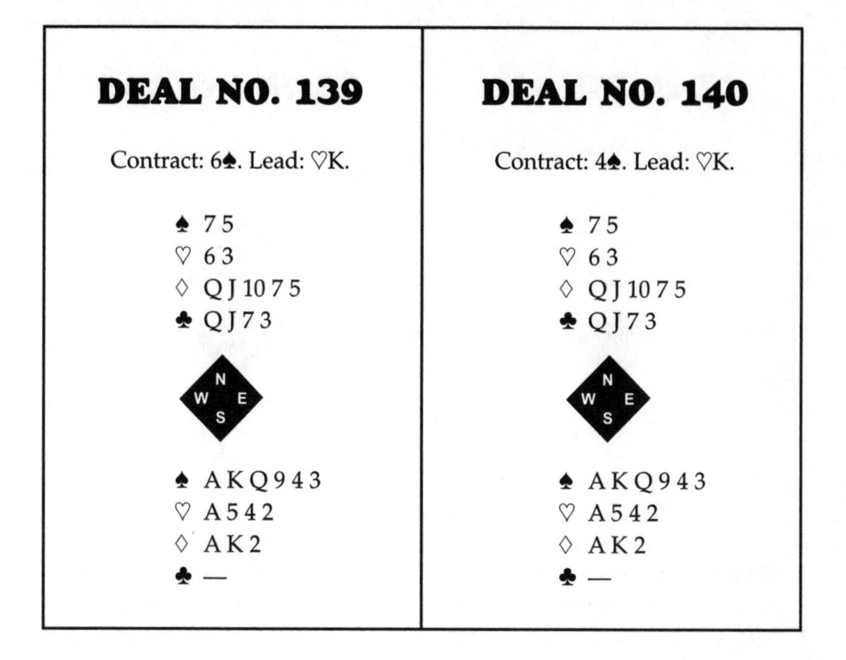
DEAL NO. 139
Contract: 6♠. Lead: ♡K.
♠ 7 5
♡ 6 3
◇ Q J 10 7 5
♣ Q J 7 3
N
W E
S
♠ A K Q 9 4 3
♡ A 5 4 2
◇ A K 2
♣ —
DEAL NO. 140
Contract: 4♠. Lead: ♡K.
♠ 7 5
♡ 6 3
◇ Q J 10 7 5
♣ Q J 7 3
N
W E
S
♠ A K Q 9 4 3
♡ A 5 4 2
◇ A K 2
♣ —

DEAL NO. 139

Contract: 6♠. Lead: ♡K.

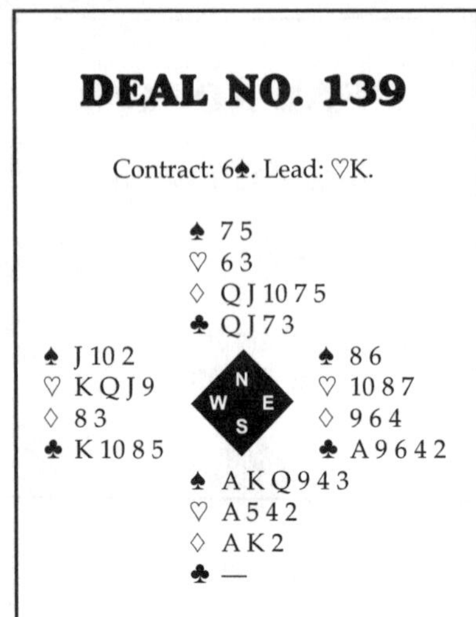

Two of your losing hearts can eventually be discarded on dummy's diamonds, but you will still be left with one heart loser. Therefore you cannot afford a trump loser and must assume that the adverse trumps break 3-2. Just win the first trick and draw trumps before playing ◊A-K-2.

Couldn't be easier!

♠	2
♡	3
◊	0
♣	0
TLT	5

DEAL NO. 140

Contract: 4♠. Lead: ♡K.

With twelve tricks likely it would be a shame not to make ten! Imagine trumps break 4-1. You would be in difficulty if you won the first trick and played ♠A-K-Q. If you play a fourth trump, the defence wins and cashes three hearts, while if you abandon trumps and play on diamonds, the defence ruff early and again cash three hearts. To cater for this you have to play a low trump at trick two. The defenders can cash one heart but dummy can ruff the next one. When you regain the lead, draw the remaining trumps and play on diamonds.

♠	2
♡	3
◊	0
♣	0
TLT	5

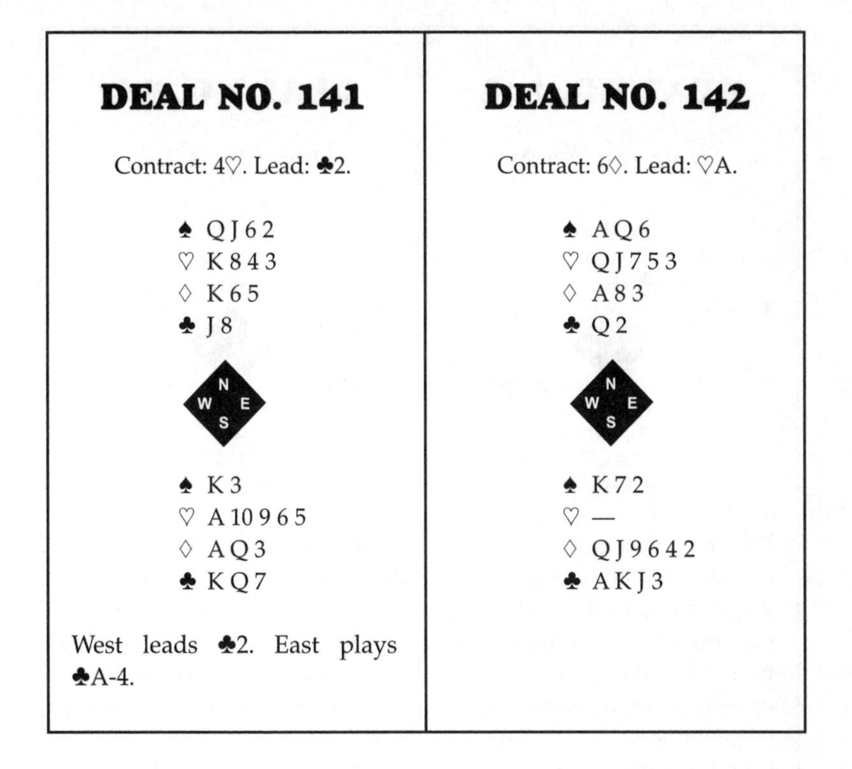

DEAL NO. 141

Contract: 4♡. Lead: ♣2.

♠ Q J 6 2
♡ K 8 4 3
♢ K 6 5
♣ J 8

N / W E / S

♠ K 3
♡ A 10 9 6 5
♢ A Q 3
♣ K Q 7

West leads ♣2. East plays ♣A-4.

DEAL NO. 142

Contract: 6♢. Lead: ♡A.

♠ A Q 6
♡ Q J 7 5 3
♢ A 8 3
♣ Q 2

N / W E / S

♠ K 7 2
♡ —
♢ Q J 9 6 4 2
♣ A K J 3

DEAL NO. 141

Contract: 4♡. Lead: ♣2.

With two black aces to lose the contract is only in danger if you lose two trump tricks and, superficially, this might seem possible. However, you have a sure-fire way to restrict your losers in hearts to just one. At trick three play ♡5 from hand and if West plays low play ♡8 from dummy! If it wins you have just one loser, and if East wins you can later draw the remaining trumps with ♡A-K. If West shows out on the first round play the ♡K and finesse on the way back.

♠	1
♡	1
◇	0
♣	1
TLT	3

DEAL NO. 142

Contract: 6◇. Lead: ♡A.

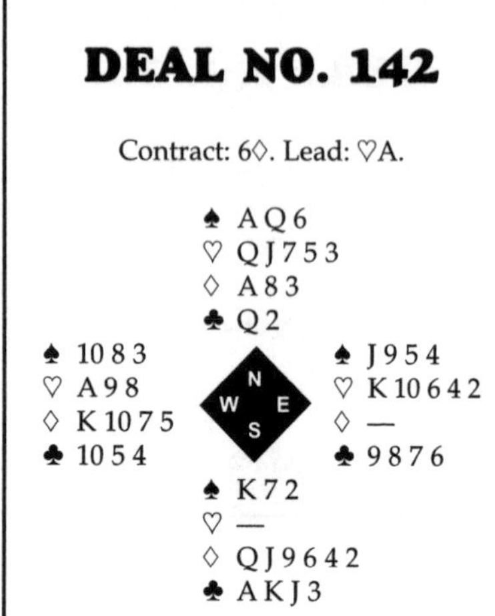

With no losers outside the trump suit it might seem that you should draw as many trumps as possible by playing ◇A first. But consider what would happen if West started with all four missing trumps – you would lose to the king and the ten. So play ◇Q from hand at trick two and play low from dummy if West plays low. If ◇Q loses to ◇K in the East hand, ◇A-J will pull the remaining trumps. If West shows out you later have a finesse against ◇10 in the East hand.

♠	0
♡	0
◇	1
♣	0
TLT	1

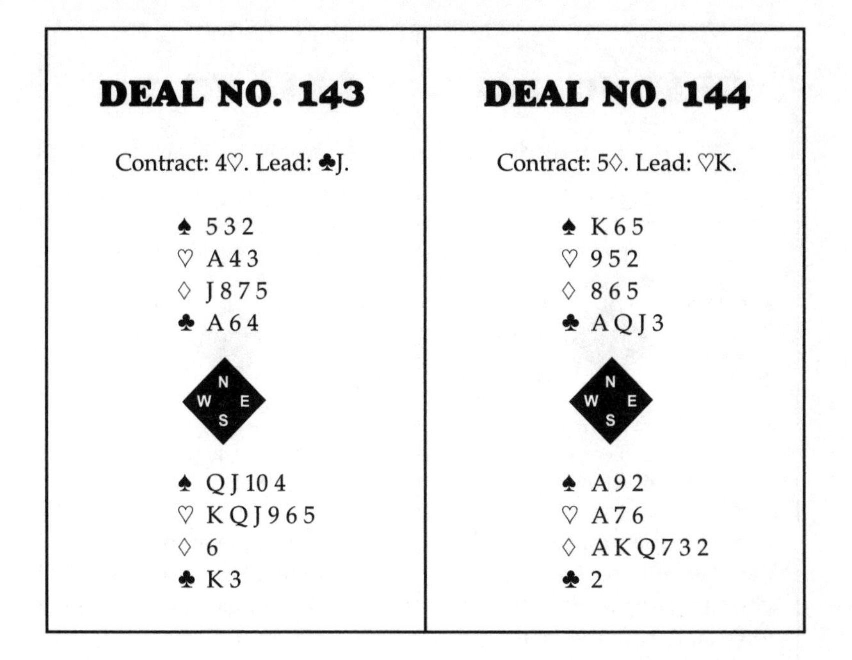

DEAL NO. 143

Contract: 4♡. Lead: ♣J.

North:
♠ 5 3 2
♡ A 4 3
♢ J 8 7 5
♣ A 6 4

South:
♠ Q J 10 4
♡ K Q J 9 6 5
♢ 6
♣ K 3

DEAL NO. 144

Contract: 5♢. Lead: ♡K.

North:
♠ K 6 5
♡ 9 5 2
♢ 8 6 5
♣ A Q J 3

South:
♠ A 9 2
♡ A 7 6
♢ A K Q 7 3 2
♣ 2

DEAL NO. 143

Contract: 4♡. Lead: ♣J.

North: ♠ 5 3 2 ♡ A 4 3 ◇ J 8 7 5 ♣ A 6 4

West: ♠ A 9 8 6 ♡ 10 ◇ K 9 3 2 ♣ J 10 8 7

East: ♠ K 7 ♡ J 7 2 ◇ A Q 10 4 ♣ Q 9 5 2

South: ♠ Q J 10 4 ♡ K Q 9 8 6 5 ◇ 6 ♣ K 3

If the missing trumps break 2-2 there is no problem because you can set up a spade trick by force and ruff the remaining one in dummy if necessary. But if trumps break 3-1 there might be three spade losers unless you play carefully. Win the lead in hand and play ♡K-Q. If there is still a trump outstanding draw it. Now in dummy, play a spade to the queen. This will probably lose to West but win the next club in dummy and lead another spade. Your contract is now assured if East started with K-x or K-x-x.

♠	3
♡	1
◇	1
♣	0
TLT	5

DEAL NO. 144

Contract: 5◇. Lead: ♡K.

North: ♠ K 6 5 ♡ 9 5 2 ◇ 8 6 5 ♣ A Q J 3

West: ♠ Q 10 4 3 ♡ K Q 10 4 ◇ 4 ♣ 10 7 6 5

East: ♠ J 8 7 ♡ J 8 3 ◇ J 10 9 ♣ K 9 8 4

South: ♠ A 9 2 ♡ A 7 6 ◇ A K Q 7 3 2 ♣ 2

3NT would have been easy but it's too late to worry about that. You must assume you have no trump loser, which means that one major-suit loser has to disappear. Superficially it looks as though you need a successful club finesse after drawing trumps but try the effect of playing to ♣A, then leading ♣Q. If East plays low you discard a heart and later your spade loser is thrown on ♣J. If East covers with ♣K you can ruff, enter dummy with ♠K and discard a loser once more on ♣J.

♠	1
♡	2
◇	1
♣	0
TLT	4

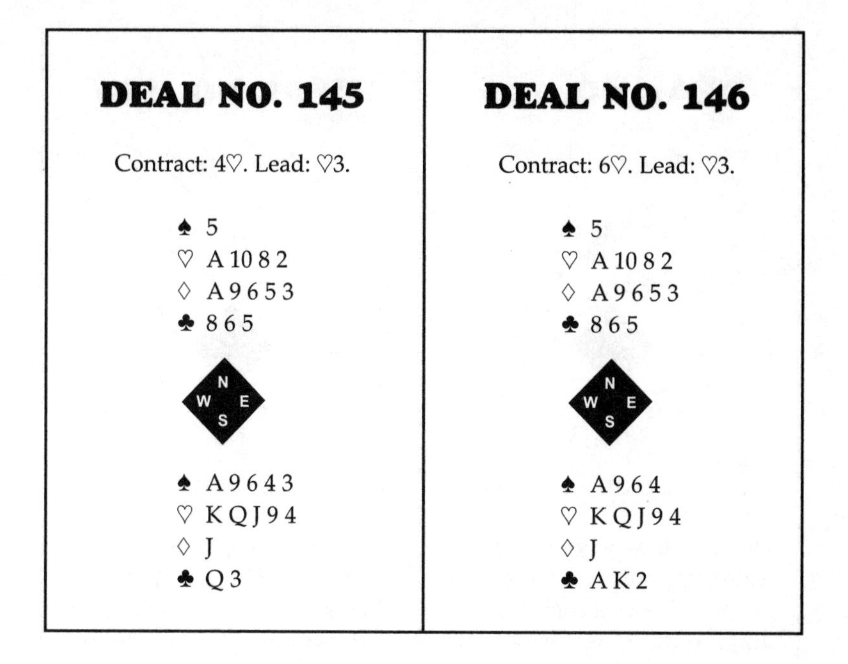
DEAL NO. 145
Contract: 4♡. Lead: ♡3.
♠ 5
♡ A 10 8 2
◊ A 9 6 5 3
♣ 8 6 5
N
W E
S
♠ A 9 6 4 3
♡ K Q J 9 4
◊ J
♣ Q 3
DEAL NO. 146
Contract: 6♡. Lead: ♡3.
♠ 5
♡ A 10 8 2
◊ A 9 6 5 3
♣ 8 6 5
N
W E
S
♠ A 9 6 4
♡ K Q J 9 4
◊ J
♣ A K 2

DEAL NO. 145

Contract: 4♡. Lead: ♡3.

The TLT is worrying but not realistic, because obviously lots of spades can be ruffed in the dummy. But the defence have found a good lead and it would be fatal to draw just one more round of trumps. Instead play ♠A at trick two and ruff a spade. Play ◇A, ruff a diamond and then continue this plan of alternating between spade and diamond ruffs. Effectively, you will now make *eight* trump tricks plus the two outside aces. This happy procedure is called a *cross-ruff*.

♠	4
♡	0
◇	0
♣	2
TLT	6

DEAL NO. 146

Contract: 6♡. Lead: ♡3.

North: ♠ 5 ♡ A 10 8 2 ◇ A 9 6 5 3 ♣ 8 6 5

West: ♠ Q 10 8 7 3 ♡ 7 6 3 ◇ 10 2 ♣ 10 7 3

East: ♠ K J 2 ♡ 5 ◇ K Q 8 7 4 ♣ Q J 9 4

South: ♠ A 9 6 4 ♡ K Q J 9 4 ◇ J ♣ A K 2

It looks as though all you have to do is ruff three spades in dummy and lose a club at the end, but it is more complicated than that. If you return to hand each time by ruffing diamonds – as in *Deal 145* – you will find that West will throw his clubs away and will end up winning a trump and a long spade. Much better to return to hand each time via clubs when you will make twelve tricks in some comfort.

♠	3
♡	0
◇	0
♣	1
TLT	4

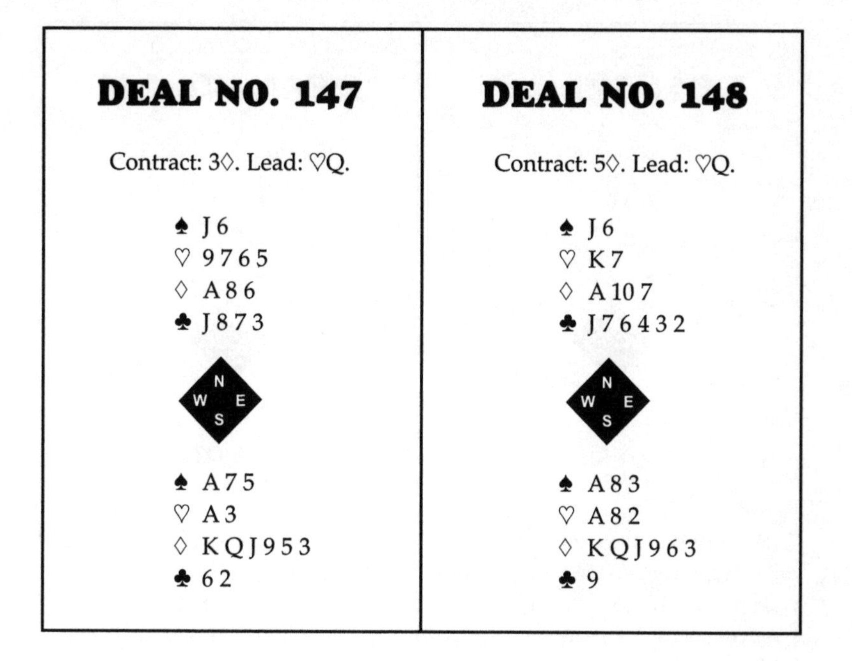
DEAL NO. 147
Contract: 3♢. Lead: ♡Q.
♠ J 6
♡ 9 7 6 5
♢ A 8 6
♣ J 8 7 3
N
W E
S
♠ A 7 5
♡ A 3
♢ K Q J 9 5 3
♣ 6 2
DEAL NO. 148
Contract: 5♢. Lead: ♡Q.
♠ J 6
♡ K 7
♢ A 10 7
♣ J 7 6 4 3 2
N
W E
S
♠ A 8 3
♡ A 8 2
♢ K Q J 9 6 3
♣ 9

DEAL NO. 147

Contract: 3♢. Lead: ♡Q.

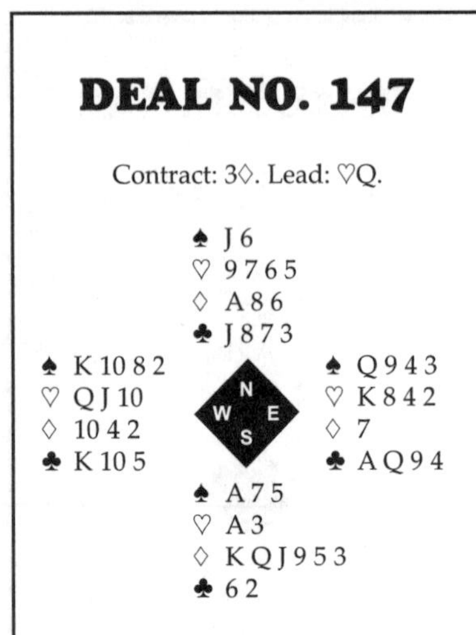

With two clubs and a heart as unavoidable losers, you must aim to do something about your second spade loser and the answer, of course, is to ruff it in dummy. But you have to be careful. If you were to draw two rounds of trumps before playing ♠A-5, then a defender might well win and play a third round of trumps, denying you your ruff. You can play ♢K at Trick 2 to see if East started with all four, but that is all.

♠	2
♡	1
♢	0
♣	2
TLT	5

DEAL NO. 148

Contract: 5♢. Lead: ♡Q.

North: ♠ J 6 ♡ K 7 ♢ A 10 7 ♣ J 7 6 4 3 2
West: ♠ Q 10 7 4 ♡ Q J 10 9 ♢ 8 ♣ K 10 8 5
East: ♠ K 9 5 2 ♡ 6 5 4 3 ♢ 5 4 2 ♣ A Q
South: ♠ A 8 3 ♡ A 8 2 ♢ K Q J 9 6 3 ♣ 9

A trump lead would have defeated you, but now you have a chance to ruff both your losing spade and heart. Clearly you cannot afford even one round of trumps because the defence would play a second round when in with a spade. So play ♡K-A and ruff a heart high. Now play ♠A-3. The defence will probably return a trump, but win in hand and ruff your last spade. All you will lose are a spade and a club.

♠	2
♡	1
♢	0
♣	1
TLT	4

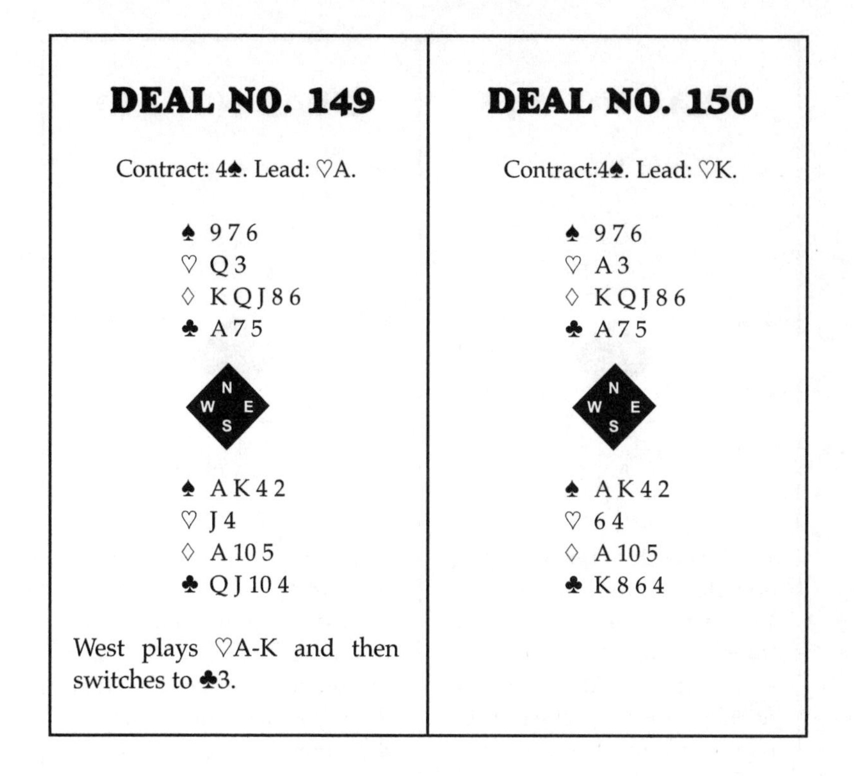

DEAL NO. 149

Contract: 4♠. Lead: ♡A.

♠ 9 7 6
♡ Q 3
♢ K Q J 8 6
♣ A 7 5

N / W E / S

♠ A K 4 2
♡ J 4
♢ A 10 5
♣ Q J 10 4

West plays ♡A-K and then switches to ♣3.

DEAL NO. 150

Contract:4♠. Lead: ♡K.

♠ 9 7 6
♡ A 3
♢ K Q J 8 6
♣ A 7 5

N / W E / S

♠ A K 4 2
♡ 6 4
♢ A 10 5
♣ K 8 6 4

DEAL NO. 149

Contract: 4♠ Lead: ♡A.

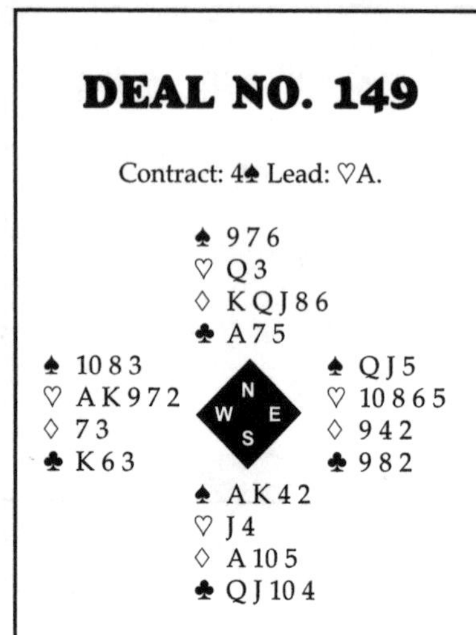

TLT makes depressing reading and clearly you have to hope that you only have one trump loser as you have lost two tricks already. Also, you can only throw two clubs from hand on dummy's diamonds so you have to hope the club finesse is working as well. Accordingly, play low from dummy at trick three and win – hopefully – in hand. Play ♠A-K-2 and if everyone follows you are home. Not a good contract but you have loads of points in the two hands and nothing is much better.

♠	4!
♡	2
◊	0
♣	1
TLT	7

DEAL NO. 150

Contract:4♠. Lead: ♡K.

North: ♠ 976 ♡ A3 ◊ KQJ86 ♣ A75

West: ♠ 105 ♡ KQJ97 ◊ 942 ♣ Q102

East: ♠ QJ83 ♡ 10852 ◊ 73 ♣ J93

South: ♠ AK42 ♡ 64 ◊ A105 ♣ K864

Here it would be a tragic mistake to play three rounds of trumps after winning the first trick. If they broke 4-2, a mean defender might then draw your last trump, enabling the defence to cash loads of hearts. So just cash ♠A-K and play on diamonds – but do remember to cash ◊A first! A defender will eventually ruff and cash a heart, but you can win any club continuation in hand and play your last trump. You will find your eventual tally comes to ten tricks!

♠	4!
♡	1
◊	0
♣	2
TLT	7

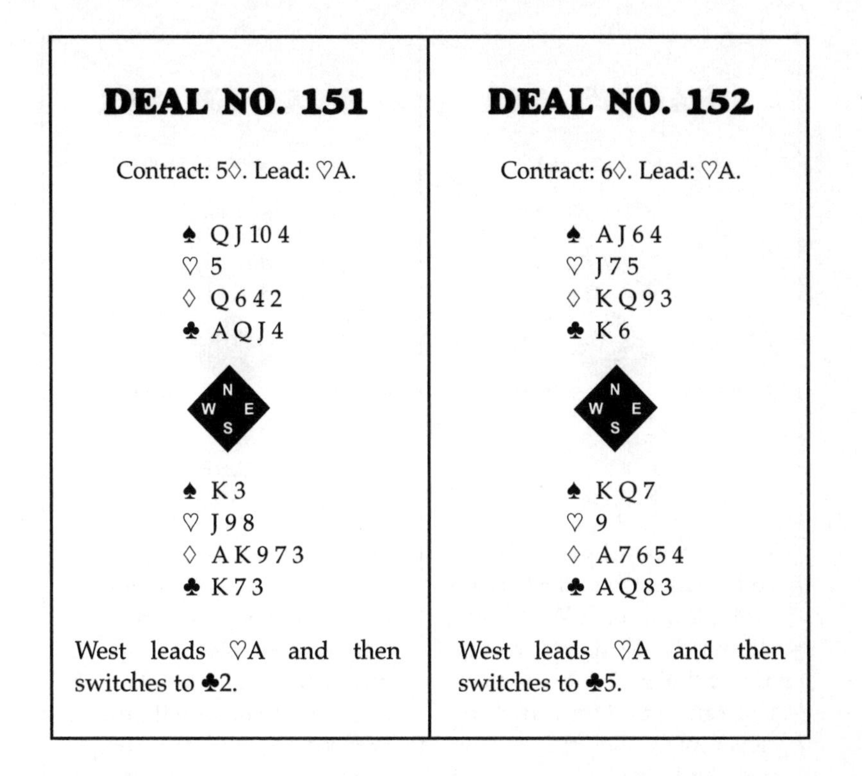

DEAL NO. 151

Contract: 5♢. Lead: ♡A.

North:
♠ Q J 10 4
♡ 5
♢ Q 6 4 2
♣ A Q J 4

South:
♠ K 3
♡ J 9 8
♢ A K 9 7 3
♣ K 7 3

West leads ♡A and then switches to ♣2.

DEAL NO. 152

Contract: 6♢. Lead: ♡A.

North:
♠ A J 6 4
♡ J 7 5
♢ K Q 9 3
♣ K 6

South:
♠ K Q 7
♡ 9
♢ A 7 6 5 4
♣ A Q 8 3

West leads ♡A and then switches to ♣5.

DEAL NO. 151

Contract: 5♢. Lead: ♡A.

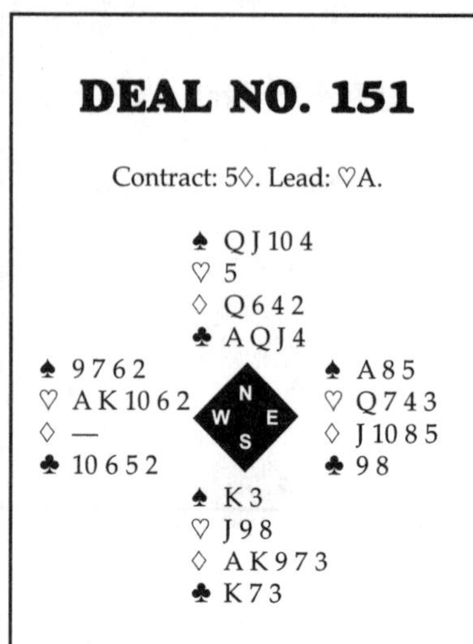

With a certain loser in hearts and spades you must avoid losing a trump. If West holds all four diamonds you will go down, but if East holds them you can deny him a trick by clever play. Win the club in hand and play a low diamond to the queen. If all follow, you can draw trumps, ruff one heart in dummy and throw the other on a long club. But if West shows out you can catch all of East's trumps by leading from dummy and covering whatever he plays. You return to dummy by ruffing a heart.

♠	1
♡	3
♢	1
♣	0
TLT	5

DEAL NO. 152

Contract: 6♢. Lead: ♡A.

North: ♠ A J 6 4 ♡ J 7 5 ♢ K Q 9 3 ♣ K 6

West: ♠ 10 8 ♡ A K 8 4 ♢ J 10 7 2 ♣ 10 7 5

East: ♠ 9 5 3 2 ♡ Q 10 6 3 2 ♢ — ♣ J 9 4 2

South: ♠ K Q 7 ♡ 9 ♢ A 8 6 5 4 ♣ A Q 8 3

The losing club can eventually be thrown on a long spade, so attention must be given to the best way to play trumps. It might feel right to play ♢K first, but that would lose if West started with four trumps. Just as in *Deal 151* you can pick up four trumps, but only if they are in the West hand. Win the club in dummy and play a low diamond to the ace. If everyone follows you have twelve top tricks, but if East shows out you just play trumps through West, coming back to hand with a spade.

♠	0
♡	1
♢	1
♣	1
TLT	3

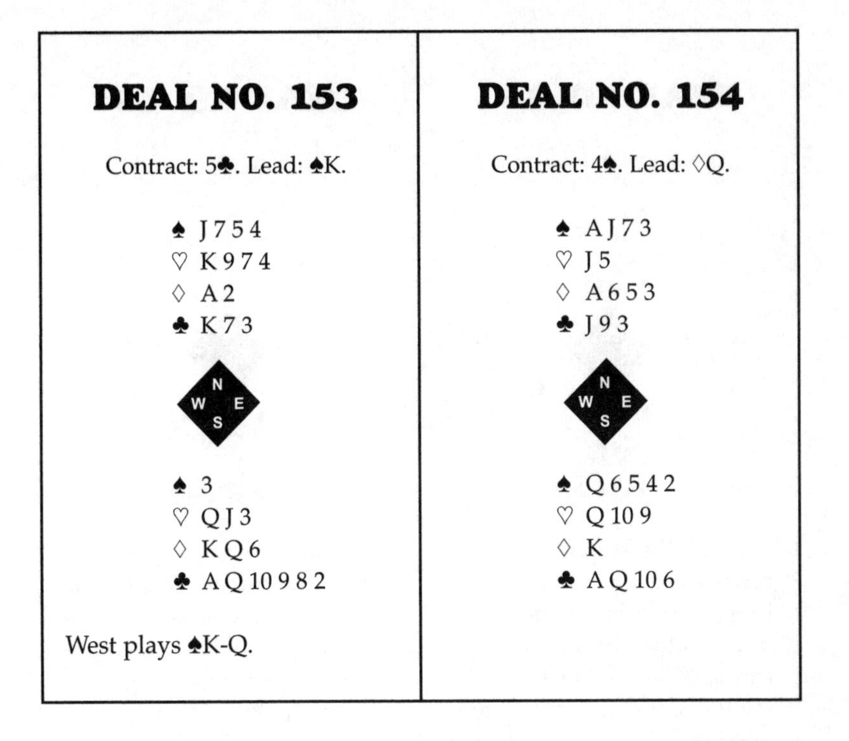

DEAL NO. 153

Contract: 5♣. Lead: ♠K.

♠ J 7 5 4
♡ K 9 7 4
◊ A 2
♣ K 7 3

♠ 3
♡ Q J 3
◊ K Q 6
♣ A Q 10 9 8 2

West plays ♠K-Q.

DEAL NO. 154

Contract: 4♠. Lead: ◊Q.

♠ A J 7 3
♡ J 5
◊ A 6 5 3
♣ J 9 3

♠ Q 6 5 4 2
♡ Q 10 9
◊ K
♣ A Q 10 6

DEAL NO. 153

Contract: 5♣. Lead: ♠K.

North: ♠ J 7 5 4 ♡ K 9 7 4 ♢ A 2 ♣ K 7 3

West: ♠ K Q 8 ♡ A 2 ♢ 10 9 5 4 ♣ J 6 5 4

East: ♠ A 10 9 6 2 ♡ 10 8 6 5 ♢ J 8 7 3 ♣ —

South: ♠ 3 ♡ Q J 3 ♢ K Q 6 ♣ A Q 10 9 8 2

You ruff the second spade, of course, and notice that with an inescapable heart loser you must endeavour not to lose a trump. You would be unlucky if either defender held all four missing trumps but, in fact, it doesn't really matter if one of them does. Cash ♣A (or ♣Q) first. If either side shows out, you now have a marked finesse against ♣J one way or the other. Note that if you made the mistake of cashing ♣K first, you might lose a trick to West.

♠	1
♡	1
♢	0
♣	0
TLT	2

DEAL NO. 154

Contract: 4♠. Lead: ♢Q.

North: ♠ A J 7 3 ♡ J 5 ♢ A 6 5 3 ♣ J 9 3

West: ♠ K ♡ 8 7 4 2 ♢ Q J 10 8 ♣ K 8 5 2

East: ♠ 10 9 8 ♡ A K 6 3 ♢ 9 7 4 2 ♣ 7 4

South: ♠ Q 6 5 4 2 ♡ Q 10 9 ♢ K ♣ A Q 10 6

TLT shows five possible losers; while there may be no club loser if the finesse is right, if it is wrong you have to make sure you maximise the play in the trump suit. Many players would lead ♠Q from hand at trick two but that is wrong. If West has the king, he will cover irrespective of how many trumps he holds and, if he has the king singleton, you will generate one more trump loser. So lead low from hand, playing ♠J if West contributes a low card.

♠	2
♡	2
♢	0
♣	1
TLT	5

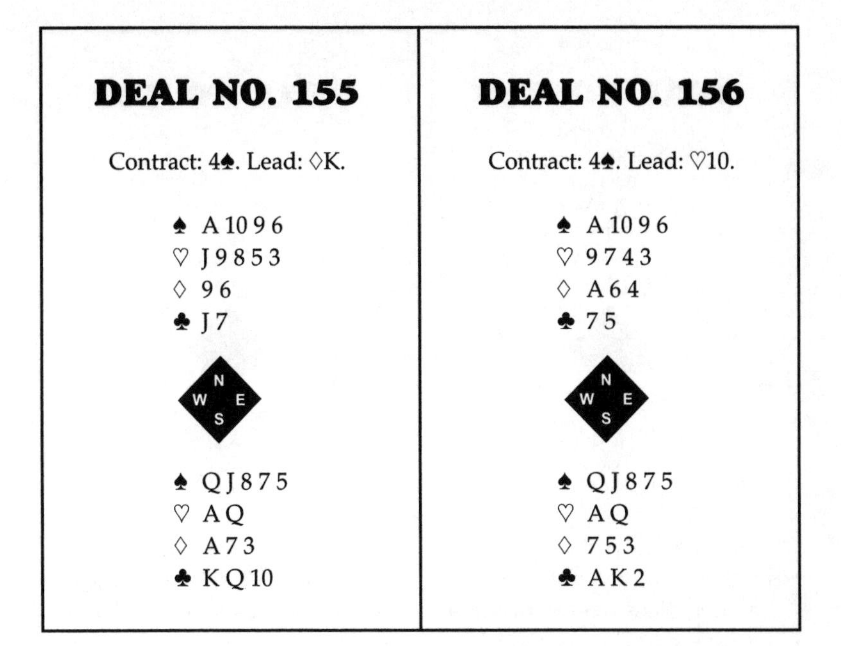

DEAL NO. 155
Contract: 4♠. Lead: ◊K.
♠ A 10 9 6
♡ J 9 8 5 3
◊ 9 6
♣ J 7
N
W E
S
♠ Q J 8 7 5
♡ A Q
◊ A 7 3
♣ K Q 10
DEAL NO. 156
Contract: 4♠. Lead: ♡10.
♠ A 10 9 6
♡ 9 7 4 3
◊ A 6 4
♣ 7 5
N
W E
S
♠ Q J 8 7 5
♡ A Q
◊ 7 5 3
♣ A K 2

DEAL NO. 155

Contract: 4♠. Lead: ◊K.

You hope to ruff a diamond loser in dummy, but one club and one diamond loser cannot be escaped. The contract is a sound one, however, for all you need is a successful finesse in either spades or hearts. Win ◊A and lead ♠Q, letting it run if West plays low. Should the finesse lose you will later have to take what you hope is a winning heart finesse.

♠	1
♡	1
◊	2
♣	1
TLT	5

DEAL NO. 156

Contract: 4♠. Lead: ♡10.

Things are more complicated this time. TLT shows no heart losers because the lead has come up to your tenace, but you have to wonder about that ♡10 lead! It is not top of a sequence and must be from shortage and the last thing you want is for your ♡A to be ruffed. Consequently it is best to play ♠A first, followed by a low one. By doing this, you will avoid East winning ♠K and giving his partner a heart ruff. Your losing club is ruffed in dummy and you will later lose two diamonds.

♠	1
♡	0
◊	2
♣	1
TLT	4

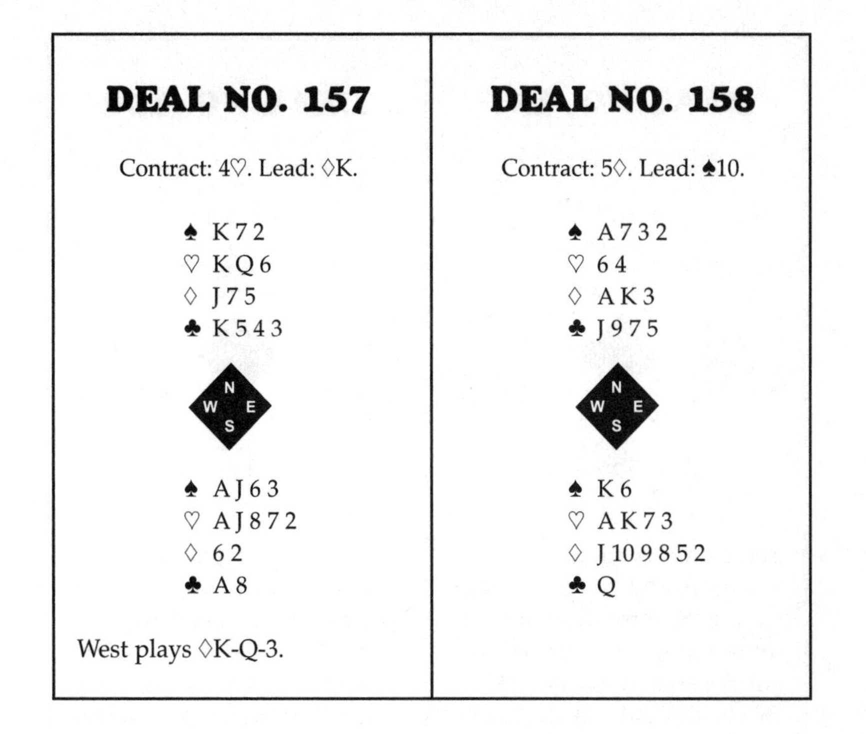

DEAL NO. 157

Contract: 4♡. Lead: ◊K.

♠ K 7 2
♡ K Q 6
◊ J 7 5
♣ K 5 4 3

♠ A J 6 3
♡ A J 8 7 2
◊ 6 2
♣ A 8

West plays ◊K-Q-3.

DEAL NO. 158

Contract: 5◊. Lead: ♠10.

♠ A 7 3 2
♡ 6 4
◊ A K 3
♣ J 9 7 5

♠ K 6
♡ A K 7 3
◊ J 10 9 8 5 2
♣ Q

DEAL NO. 157

Contract: 4♡. Lead: ◊K.

You would be unlucky to lose a trump and, in fact, after ruffing the third diamond you draw trumps in three rounds. All depends upon not losing two spades and initially it looks as if you either need the suit to break 3-3 or the finesse to work. But you can do better than that. Play ♠A first and then low to ♠K. A significant amount of the time West will have started with ♠Q-x but if he has not, then you can lead towards the jack. This plan of action still works, of course, if West started with ♠Q trebleton.

♠	2
♡	1
◊	2
♣	0
TLT	5

DEAL NO. 158

Contract: 5◊. Lead: ♠10.

It seems a simple matter to ruff two hearts in dummy but you have to be careful. Suppose you win the lead in dummy and cash ♡A-K. If you then ruff a third heart *low* it might be possible for East to overruff and return a trump, leaving you with a heart loser if you draw trumps, or another trump loser if you ruff your last heart. The answer is to ruff the third heart *high,* return to ♠K and ruff the fourth heart *high.* In the end you will lose just a trump and a club.

♠	0
♡	2
◊	1
♣	1
TLT	4

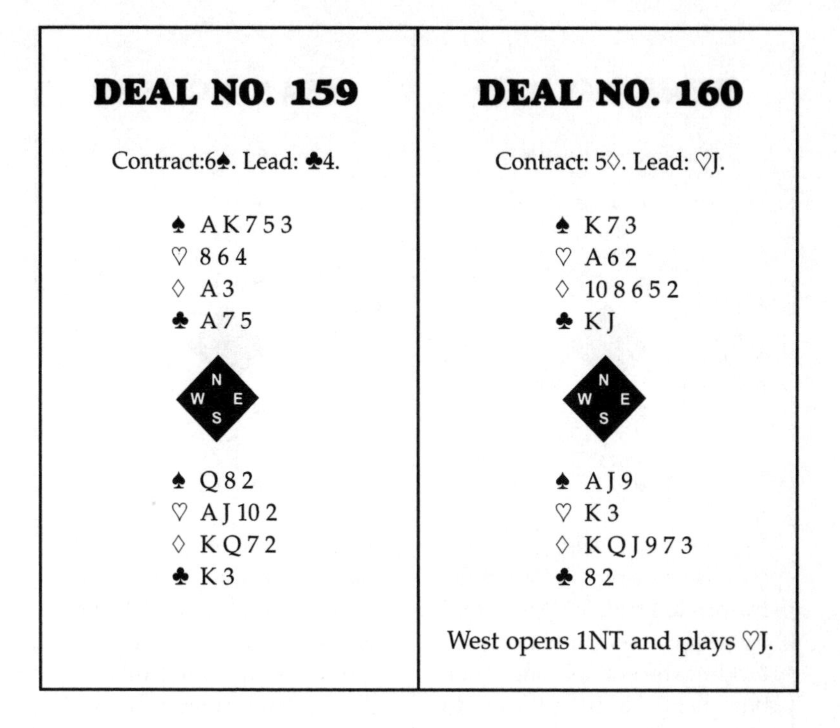

DEAL NO. 159

Contract:6♠. Lead: ♣4.

North
♠ A K 7 5 3
♡ 8 6 4
♢ A 3
♣ A 7 5

South
♠ Q 8 2
♡ A J 10 2
♢ K Q 7 2
♣ K 3

DEAL NO. 160

Contract: 5♢. Lead: ♡J.

North
♠ K 7 3
♡ A 6 2
♢ 10 8 6 5 2
♣ K J

South
♠ A J 9
♡ K 3
♢ K Q J 9 7 3
♣ 8 2

West opens 1NT and plays ♡J.

DEAL NO. 159

Contract:6♠. Lead: ♣4.

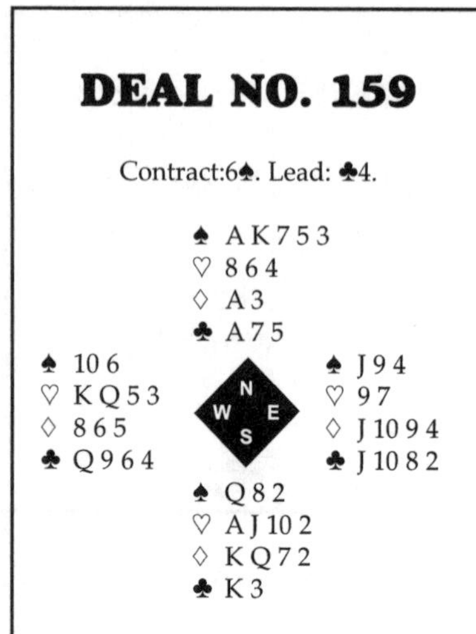

You are playing in 6♠ after a *transfer* sequence and need the trumps to break 3-2. You could try ruffing a diamond and then tackling hearts for one loser, but there's a better way to manage this deal. Played this way round it's harder to see but all you really have to do is ruff a club in hand, after drawing two rounds of trumps with the ace and the queen. The last trump can be drawn and one heart is thrown on a top diamond.

♠	2
♡	2
◇	1
♣	0
TLT	5

DEAL NO. 160

Contract: 5◇. Lead: ♡J.

With two minor-suit aces to lose for sure, this looks like you need a slice of luck in dealing with the black suits. But have you noticed something we haven't mentioned before? That 'something' can totally change the way we go about forming our strategy! The introduction to Part 3 of this book will make everything clear . . .

♠	1
♡	0
◇	1
♣	2
TLT	4

SECTION 3
MORE PRACTICE

MORE PRACTICE

If you are still with us, you have worked diligently through 160 deals and should now be quite confident that you can apply the fundamental techniques of no-trump and suit declarer play. We hope you are also burning with curiosity on how to play the last deal in each of the preceding sections. All will be revealed shortly.

In this last section we drop the TTA and TLT tables, on the grounds that you should now be able to calculate them mentally for yourself. These last 80 deals are made up of more confidence-building practice. We make no apologies for repeating many of the themes you have already met, albeit often in different guise, for practice makes perfect. However, we will introduce one new and important factor.

At the table, the pesky opponents are seldom silent. This can interfere with your smooth bidding sequences but, once you have become declarer, you can glean vital inferences from the opponents' bidding, or lack of it. Whole books have been written about this aspect of declarer play, but we intend only to introduce a few of the basic ideas in this publication. Deals 80 and 160 are examples we sneaked in early to pique your interest.

In *Deal 80* (repeated on the next page), East opens 1♢, you end up in 3NT and, not surprisingly, West leads ♢10. TTA = 7. You might hold up ♢A for two rounds, hoping that West has to win ♡A once he is exhausted of diamonds. That would be reasonable play if the opponents had not bid. But East did bid 1♢ and the defenders do have only 12 points between them, so it would be surprising if West had so much as a jack, never mind an ace. When you play a heart, East will win and cash as many diamonds as he can find.

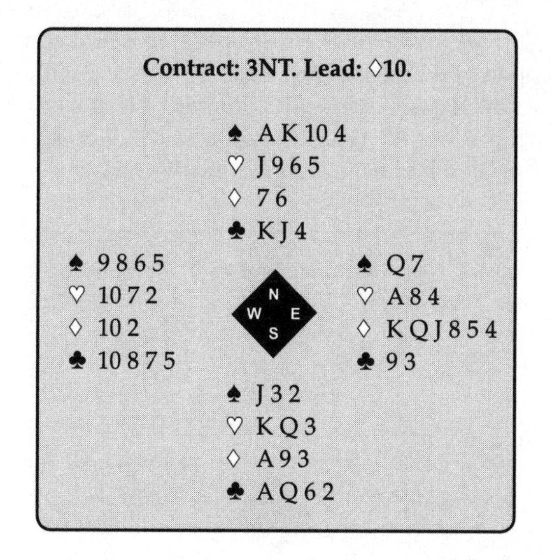

What about the spade finesse? Forget it. East must also have ♠Q to justify his bid. If you finesse, East will win, cash diamonds and ♡A. No, your only hope is to play off ♠A-K, hoping that East has no more than two spades. As you can see, ♠Q falls and you can enjoy two more spade tricks for the contract, leaving the opposition to marvel that you did not make the 'obvious' play of knocking out ♡A.

On *Deal 160* (repeated below), West opens 1NT and some optimistic bidding propels you into 5♢. West leads ♡J. You win with ♡K and lead a diamond which West wins with the ace. He cashes the ♣A and continues with the ♡10. What now? If East holds ♠Q a successful finesse will see you home, but can that really work?

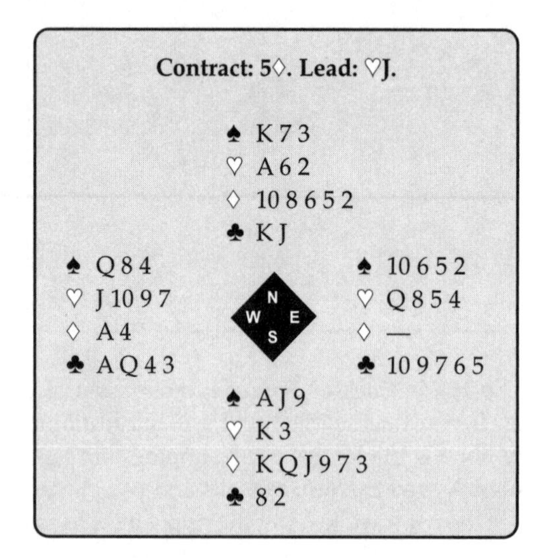

Remember, West opened 1NT, showing 12-14 points, and the ♡J lead denies the queen (because people lead the top card of a sequence). West must hold every outstanding high card! Your best chance is to hope East holds ♠10. Draw the remaining trump and lead ♠J. If West covers, win with ♠K and finesse against ♠10 on the way back!

We do not intend to take this notion of counting the opposition hands much further than these two examples. If you have not long started the game, keeping track of your own cards and dummy's, and trying to recall which cards have been played, is quite enough! We know, we have been there. But on the odd occasion where a defender does bid, remember to make a quick tally of the outstanding points to see whether that helps you to decide how to play a hand. You will be surprised how often it does!

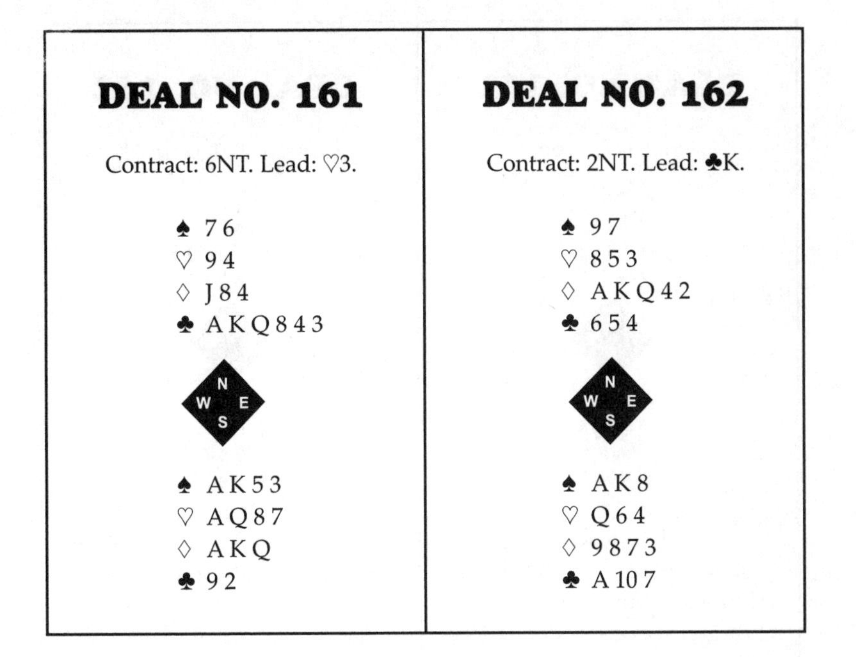
DEAL NO. 161
Contract: 6NT. Lead: ♡3.
♠ 7 6
♡ 9 4
♢ J 8 4
♣ A K Q 8 4 3
N
W E
S
♠ A K 5 3
♡ A Q 8 7
♢ A K Q
♣ 9 2
DEAL NO. 162
Contract: 2NT. Lead: ♣K.
♠ 9 7
♡ 8 5 3
♢ A K Q 4 2
♣ 6 5 4
N
W E
S
♠ A K 8
♡ Q 6 4
♢ 9 8 7 3
♣ A 10 7

DEAL NO. 161

Contract: 6NT. Lead: ♡3.

The opening lead has given you a welcome extra heart trick. Now you only need five club tricks, not six. Play a low club from both hands at Trick 2. Win the next trick and then play ♣A-K-Q. If clubs were 3-2, you have given up an unnecessary trick, but if they were 4-1 you have saved your contract. Why? Because, if clubs are 4-1 and you play ♣A-K-Q immediately, the defence will win the fourth club trick and you have no entry to dummy for the remaining club winners.

DEAL NO. 162

Contract: 2NT. Lead: ♣K.

Win ♣A and then play on diamonds. But be careful how you do that. When you cash ♢A-K-Q, you must play ♢9-8-7 from hand. Then you can play ♢4 from dummy and ♢3 from hand, and at last win ♢2. You will find that if you play ♢3 on any of the first three rounds, you will have to win the fourth diamond in your own hand. You will 'block' the diamond suit: ♢2 will be a winner in dummy but there will be no entry to it.

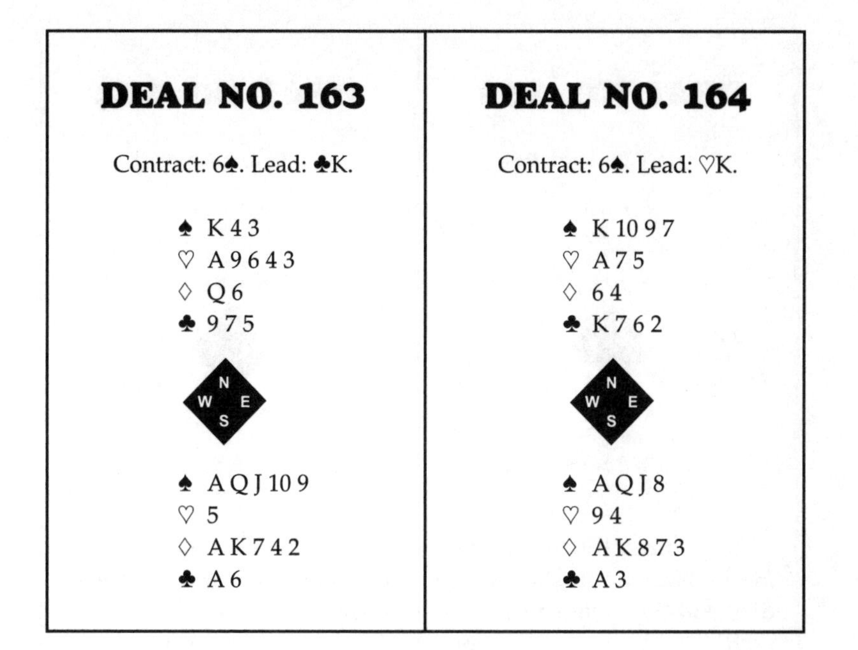

DEAL NO. 163

Contract: 6♠. Lead: ♣K.

♠ K 4 3
♡ A 9 6 4 3
◊ Q 6
♣ 9 7 5

♠ A Q J 10 9
♡ 5
◊ A K 7 4 2
♣ A 6

DEAL NO. 164

Contract: 6♠. Lead: ♡K.

♠ K 10 9 7
♡ A 7 5
◊ 6 4
♣ K 7 6 2

♠ A Q J 8
♡ 9 4
◊ A K 8 7 3
♣ A 3

DEAL NO. 163

Contract: 6♠. Lead: ♣K.

With a sure club loser you must find a way of establishing diamonds. If you knew that each defender had three, you could just draw trumps and play ♢Q followed by ♢A-K, but it is likely that one defender will have four diamonds and that you will need to ruff one in dummy. So win ♣A, play two top trumps from hand, and then play a diamond to the queen and one back to the ace. Then lead a low diamond and ruff in dummy with ♠K. Finally, return to your hand by cashing ♡A, ruff a heart, draw any remaining trumps, and play diamonds from the top. Note that you needed to keep a top trump in dummy so that neither defender could over-ruff.

DEAL NO. 164

Contract: 6♠. Lead: ♡K.

North: ♠ K 10 9 7 ♡ A 7 5 ♢ 6 4 ♣ K 7 6 2

West: ♠ 6 4 2 ♡ K Q J 8 ♢ J 9 5 2 ♣ Q 5

East: ♠ 5 3 ♡ 10 6 3 2 ♢ Q 10 ♣ J 10 9 8 4

South: ♠ A Q J 8 ♡ 9 4 ♢ A K 8 7 3 ♣ A 3

Again, you need to establish the diamonds and you need them to break no worse than 4-2. So win ♡A, cash both top diamonds and ruff a diamond in dummy. If both defenders follow to three rounds, your troubles are over; if not, return to hand with a trump and ruff the diamond suit good. Now overtake dummy's last trump in hand, draw any remaining trumps, cash the established diamonds and concede a heart.

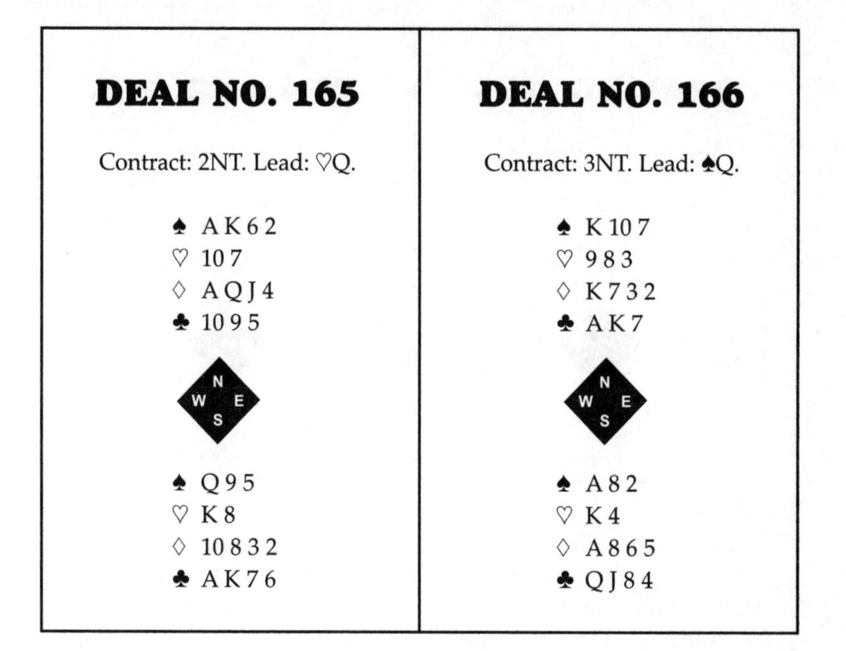

DEAL NO. 165	DEAL NO. 166
Contract: 2NT. Lead: ♡Q.	Contract: 3NT. Lead: ♠Q.
♠ A K 6 2 ♡ 10 7 ♢ A Q J 4 ♣ 10 9 5	♠ K 10 7 ♡ 9 8 3 ♢ K 7 3 2 ♣ A K 7
N / W E / S	N / W E / S
♠ Q 9 5 ♡ K 8 ♢ 10 8 3 2 ♣ A K 7 6	♠ A 8 2 ♡ K 4 ♢ A 8 6 5 ♣ Q J 8 4

DEAL NO. 165

Contract: 2NT. Lead: ♡Q.

You win with ♡K at Trick 1, but now you are wide open in hearts and cannot afford to lose the lead. If the diamond finesse works, you will have plenty of tricks. But if you take the finesse and it loses, the defence might be able to cash enough heart tricks to defeat you. Play on spades first. If they break 3-3, you have enough tricks without having to take the risky diamond finesse. If spades are 4-2, or worse, you will have to take the diamond finesse after all, but at least it is the second string to your bow.

DEAL NO. 166

Contract: 3NT. Lead: ♠Q.

North: ♠ K 10 7 / ♡ 9 8 3 / ◇ K 7 3 2 / ♣ A K 7

West: ♠ Q J 9 5 3 / ♡ A 6 5 / ◇ 9 4 / ♣ 9 6 5

East: ♠ 6 4 / ♡ Q J 10 7 2 / ◇ Q J 10 / ♣ 10 3 2

South: ♠ A 8 2 / ♡ K 4 / ◇ A 8 6 5 / ♣ Q J 8 4

You have four clubs, two diamonds and two spades, so you need one more trick. Yes, you could try to make a third diamond trick but East may win and play a heart through your ♡K to defeat you. Instead, win ♠A in hand and finesse dummy's ♠10 immediately for your ninth trick. This should be completely safe, as West's lead of ♠Q promises possession of ♠J too.

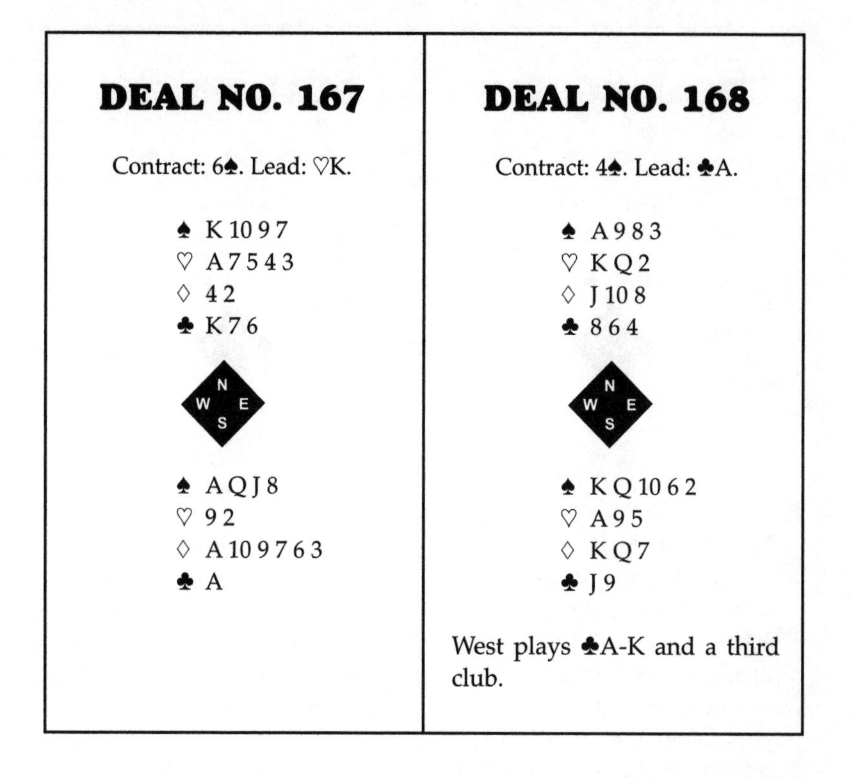

DEAL NO. 167

Contract: 6♠. Lead: ♡K.

♠ K 10 9 7
♡ A 7 5 4 3
◊ 4 2
♣ K 7 6

♠ A Q J 8
♡ 9 2
◊ A 10 9 7 6 3
♣ A

DEAL NO. 168

Contract: 4♠. Lead: ♣A.

♠ A 9 8 3
♡ K Q 2
◊ J 10 8
♣ 8 6 4

♠ K Q 10 6 2
♡ A 9 5
◊ K Q 7
♣ J 9

West plays ♣A-K and a third club.

DEAL NO. 167

Contract: 6♠. Lead: ♡K.

The heart lead sets up a winner for the defence, but win ♡A, return to hand with ♣A, and play ◇A and trump a diamond. Discard your losing heart on ♣K and ruff hearts in your hand and diamonds in dummy. Nobody can overruff because all your trumps are high. You will make one heart, one diamond, two clubs and *eight* trumps because you will make them all separately. In the end-game, one defender will make a trump trick!

DEAL NO. 168

Contract: 4♠. Lead: ♣A.

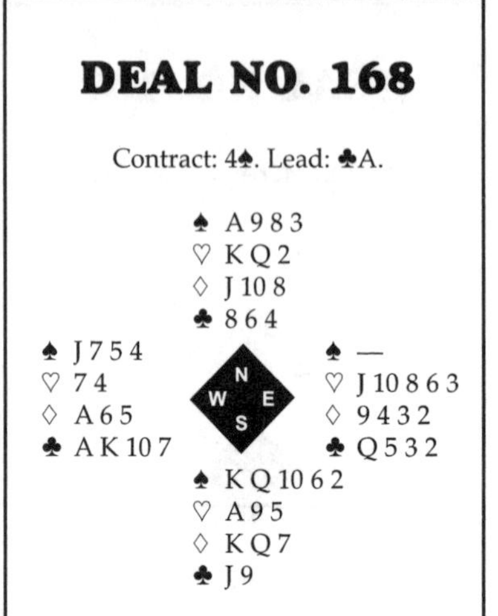

It looks as though you only have two clubs and ◇A to lose, but there may be a problem. Suppose one opponent has all four missing trumps? You must be careful not to lose one, and can guarantee this by ruffing the third club and playing the ♠K. If both opponents follow, just draw trumps and concede ◇A. If either shows out, you finesse against ♠J, whichever opponent holds it. However there is a further problem! If trumps *do* break 4-0, you must knock out ◇A before drawing all the trumps, otherwise the defenders will have clubs to cash which you cannot ruff.

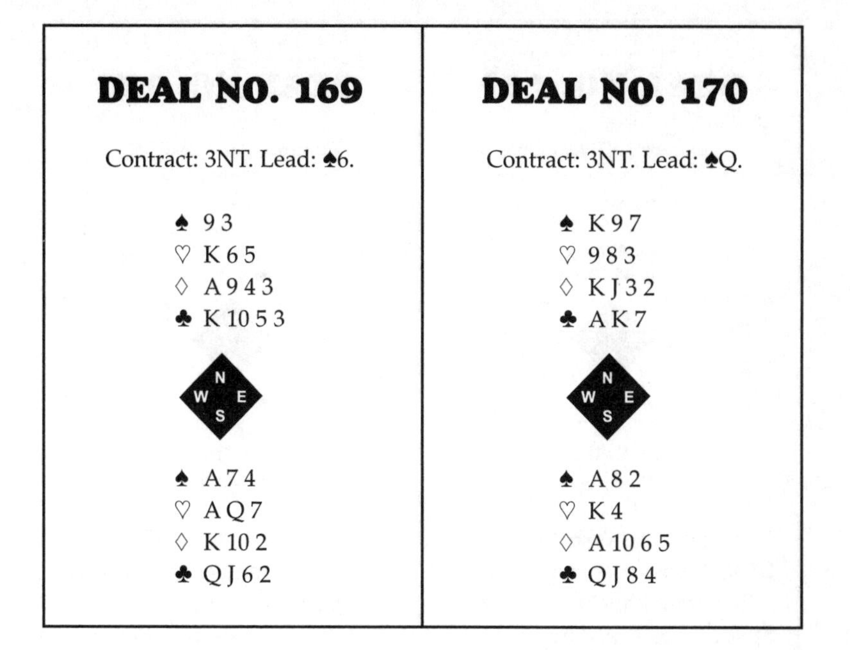

DEAL NO. 169

Contract: 3NT. Lead: ♠6.

♠ 9 3
♡ K 6 5
◊ A 9 4 3
♣ K 10 5 3

♠ A 7 4
♡ A Q 7
◊ K 10 2
♣ Q J 6 2

DEAL NO. 170

Contract: 3NT. Lead: ♠Q.

♠ K 9 7
♡ 9 8 3
◊ K J 3 2
♣ A K 7

♠ A 8 2
♡ K 4
◊ A 10 6 5
♣ Q J 8 4

DEAL NO. 169

Contract: 3NT. Lead: ♠6.

You have to make three club tricks for your contract, which will entail knocking out ♣A. Spades are the danger. Hold up ♠A till the third round. If the spades were 4-4, you were never in danger, but if they were 5-3 you have given yourself the chance that the defender with only three spades (presumably East) has ♣A. If that is the case, when East wins ♣A, he will be out of spades and you will make the contract. If a defender holds five spades and ♣A, you cannot make the contract. Be honest – would you have spotted this routine hold-up play before picking up this book?

DEAL NO. 170

Contract: 3NT. Lead: ♠Q.

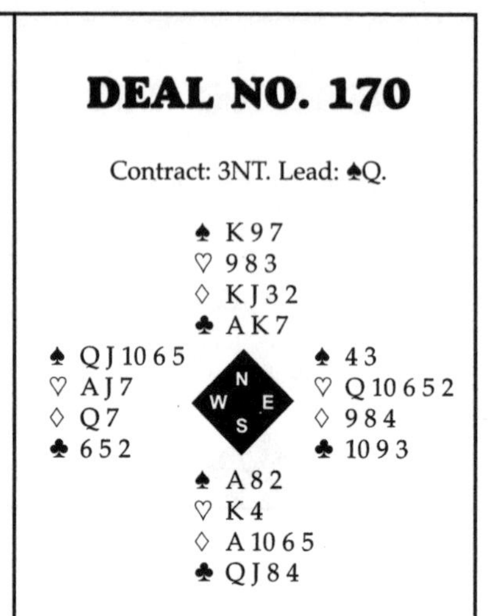

Almost the same as *Deal 166* . . . This time you don't have the ♠10 for your safe ninth trick but because the diamond pips are different, you have an equally safe play. Just win in dummy with ♠K, cash ◊K, and finesse ◊10. If it wins, you will have at least nine tricks. If West is able to win with ◊Q, he is not be able attack hearts profitably and ◊J becomes your ninth trick instead.

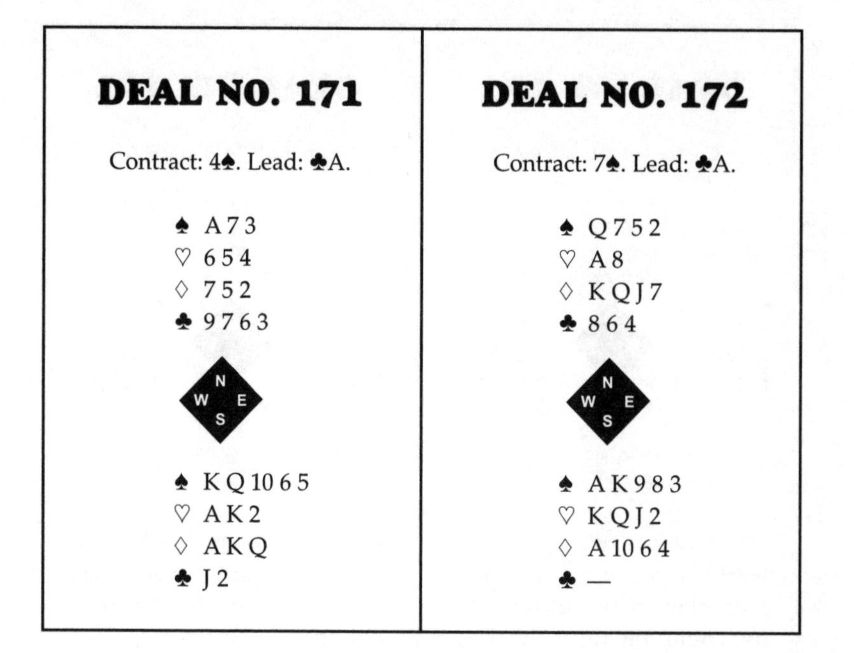
DEAL NO. 171
Contract: 4♠. Lead: ♣A.
♠ A 7 3
♡ 6 5 4
◊ 7 5 2
♣ 9 7 6 3
N
W E
S
♠ K Q 10 6 5
♡ A K 2
◊ A K Q
♣ J 2
DEAL NO. 172
Contract: 7♠. Lead: ♣A.
♠ Q 7 5 2
♡ A 8
◊ K Q J 7
♣ 8 6 4
N
W E
S
♠ A K 9 8 3
♡ K Q J 2
◊ A 10 6 4
♣ —

DEAL NO. 171

Contract: 4♠. Lead: ♣A.

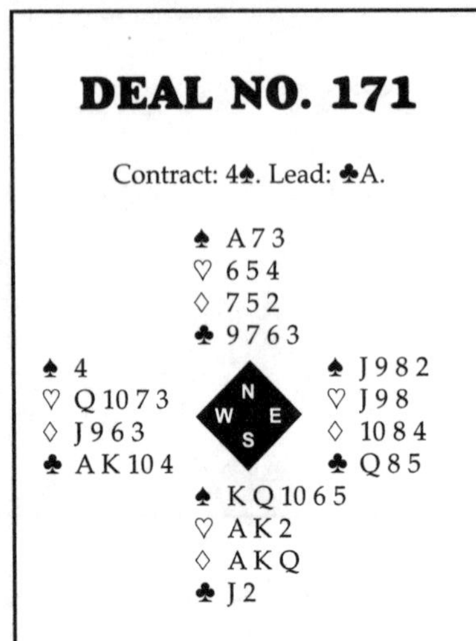

You must lose two clubs and a heart, so you must maximise your play in the trump suit. You trump the third club and, suppose, you start to draw trumps by playing small to the ace. You would follow up by playing small to the king, but the contract would fail if West showed out on the second round. Although you have a marked finesse against the jack, *you have no way of getting to dummy.* This problem can be remedied by cashing ♠K first, and then playing low to ♠A. If West shows out you are in dummy for a finesse against the jack of trumps.

DEAL NO. 172

Contract: 7♠. Lead: ♣A.

You have reached a brilliant grand slam and it would be a shame if you misplayed it! You trump the opening lead, of course, and must consider any possible danger. Only a 4-0 trump break will cause an anxious moment and if West holds all four trumps you are bound to lose one. But not if East has that holding *as long as you play the ♠Q first.* If West shows out, lead a trump from dummy and watch carefully what East does. Probably he will play the jack or the ten, but you win, return to dummy with a red card, and then lead another trump. You now have a marked finesse against his remaining honour. Well done!

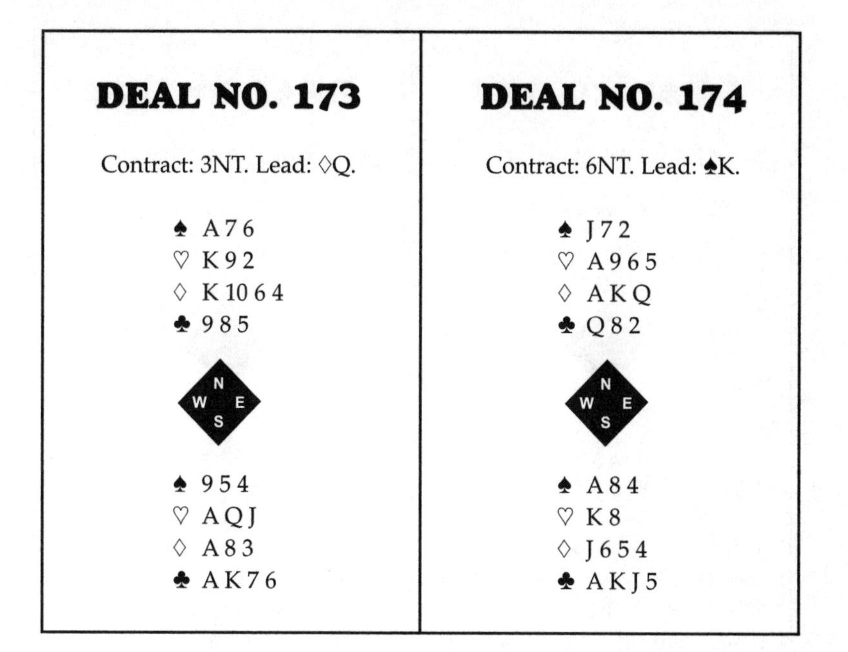

DEAL NO. 173

Contract: 3NT. Lead: ♢Q.

North:
♠ A 7 6
♡ K 9 2
♢ K 10 6 4
♣ 9 8 5

South:
♠ 9 5 4
♡ A Q J
♢ A 8 3
♣ A K 7 6

DEAL NO. 174

Contract: 6NT. Lead: ♠K.

North:
♠ J 7 2
♡ A 9 6 5
♢ A K Q
♣ Q 8 2

South:
♠ A 8 4
♡ K 8
♢ J 6 5 4
♣ A K J 5

DEAL NO. 173

Contract: 3NT. Lead: ♢Q.

You have eight top tricks and can thank your lucky stars West did not find a spade lead, which would have left you with no real chance. As it is, West has made a disastrous lead for the defence. Do you see why? The ♢Q lead promises possession of ♢J as well, so all you have to do is win ♢A in hand, and finesse dummy's ♢10 for your ninth trick. West will look glum but there was nothing wrong with the lead – it was just unlucky.

DEAL NO. 174

Contract: 6NT. Lead: ♠K.

North: ♠ J 7 2 ♡ A 9 6 5 ♢ A K Q ♣ Q 8 2

West: ♠ K Q 10 9 6 ♡ J 7 ♢ 8 7 3 ♣ 9 6 4

East: ♠ 5 3 ♡ Q 10 4 3 2 ♢ 10 9 2 ♣ 10 7 3

South: ♠ A 8 4 ♡ K 8 ♢ J 6 5 4 ♣ A K J 5

You have only eleven top tricks and West has attacked what appears to be your most fragile suit. And yet . . . If you thought the lead on *Deal 173* was disastrous, this is even worse! Because the lead of ♠K guarantees ♠Q as well, you can secure your extra trick by winning with ♠A and leading towards ♠J in dummy. What can West do? Whether or not he plays ♠Q, you are destined to make your twelfth trick with that lowly ♠J.

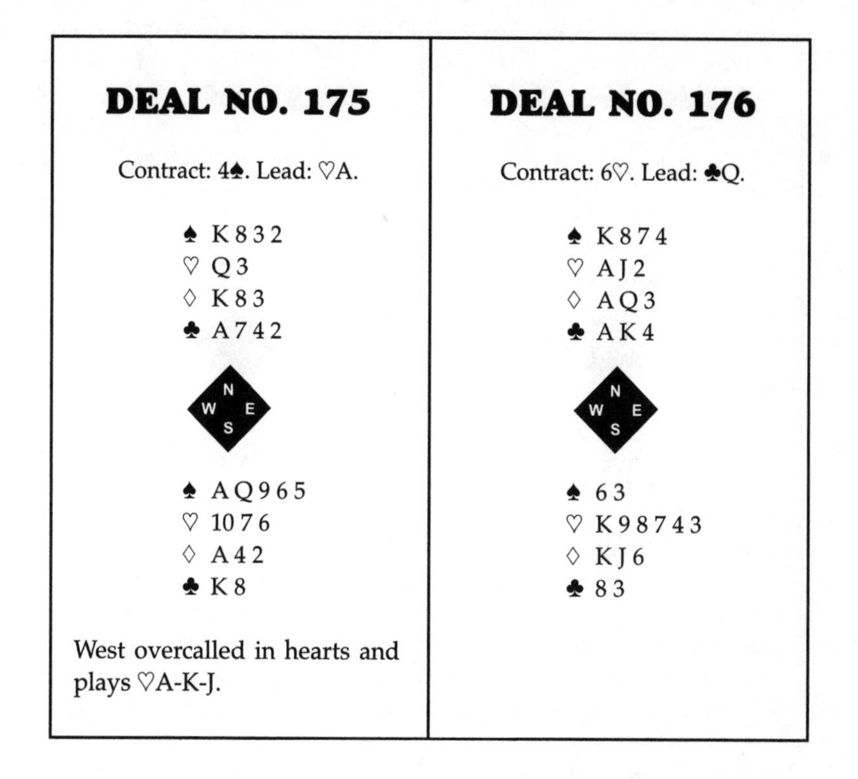

DEAL NO. 175

Contract: 4♠. Lead: ♡A.

♠ K 8 3 2
♡ Q 3
♢ K 8 3
♣ A 7 4 2

♠ A Q 9 6 5
♡ 10 7 6
♢ A 4 2
♣ K 8

West overcalled in hearts and plays ♡A-K-J.

DEAL NO. 176

Contract: 6♡. Lead: ♣Q.

♠ K 8 7 4
♡ A J 2
♢ A Q 3
♣ A K 4

♠ 6 3
♡ K 9 8 7 4 3
♢ K J 6
♣ 8 3

DEAL NO. 175

Contract: 4♠. Lead: ♡A.

It would be unlucky to lose a spade, which means you have to reduce the red-suit losers by one. It might appear natural to ruff the third heart in dummy – but which trump would you use? If you ruff low East might over-ruff, and if you ruff with the king then you might lose a trump trick later. Can you see why you should throw a low diamond from dummy on the third heart? On a fourth round of hearts you can ruff in hand, draw trumps, and then you ruff the losing diamond in dummy. In effect you swap a diamond loser for a heart loser.

DEAL NO. 176

Contract: 6♡. Lead: ♣Q.

North: ♠ K 8 7 4 ♡ A J 2 ◇ A Q 3 ♣ A K 4

West: ♠ A J 9 ♡ 6 5 ◇ 10 8 7 5 ♣ Q J 9 7

East: ♠ Q 10 5 2 ♡ Q 10 ◇ 9 4 2 ♣ 10 6 5 2

South: ♠ 6 3 ♡ K 9 8 7 4 3 ◇ K J 6 ♣ 8 3

The slam is not a good one because of the duplication in diamonds. With nowhere to park your low spades, you have to hope that West has the ace of that suit so that leading up to the king will restrict your losers to one. The ♡Q is a worry too but the odds just about favour playing out the ♡A-K in the hope that the queen will be either singleton or doubleton. The chances of success are only about 26% but if you are having a good day . . .

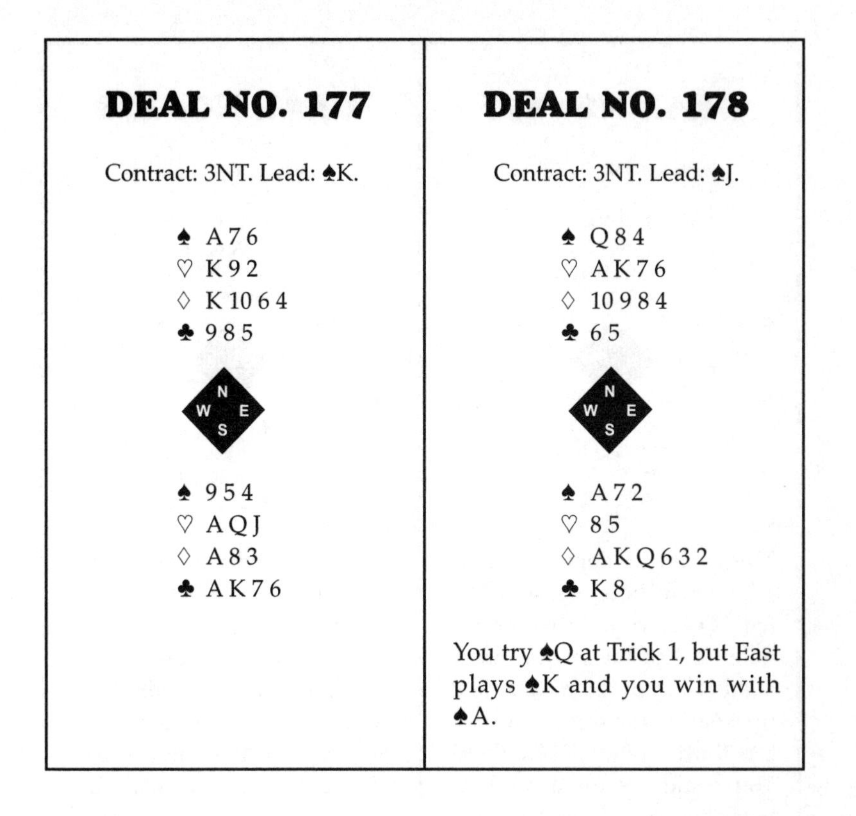

DEAL NO. 177

Contract: 3NT. Lead: ♠K.

♠ A 7 6
♡ K 9 2
♢ K 10 6 4
♣ 9 8 5

♠ 9 5 4
♡ A Q J
♢ A 8 3
♣ A K 7 6

DEAL NO. 178

Contract: 3NT. Lead: ♠J.

♠ Q 8 4
♡ A K 7 6
♢ 10 9 8 4
♣ 6 5

♠ A 7 2
♡ 8 5
♢ A K Q 6 3 2
♣ K 8

You try ♠Q at Trick 1, but East plays ♠K and you win with ♠A.

DEAL NO. 177

Contract: 3NT. Lead: ♠K.

This is almost identical to *Deal 173,* when the defence kindly led ◊Q for you. This time the defence has hit on the nasty spade lead. By all means hold up ♠A until the second or even the third round. What then? You could try for a 3-3 club break but, apart from that being against the odds, East would have to win the third round otherwise West will cash some spades. Your only other hope is that West holds ◊Q and ◊J, in which case a finesse of ◊10 brings in your ninth trick. The chances of this working are only 25%, although we have been kind in the layout above! You see just how useful that diamond lead was on *Deal 173?*

DEAL NO. 178

Contract: 3NT. Lead: ♠J.

Be honest, did you notice that you have to play ◊10-9-8 from dummy as you cash ◊A-K-Q? This theme has appeared in previous deals, so really there is no excuse! If you played ◊4 on any of the first three rounds of diamonds, you will find that you have no way back to dummy except by hazarding the club finesse – which as you can see is doomed to fail. If you did play ◊10-9-8, you can go ahead and cash ◊6-3-2 and claim a well-played contract.

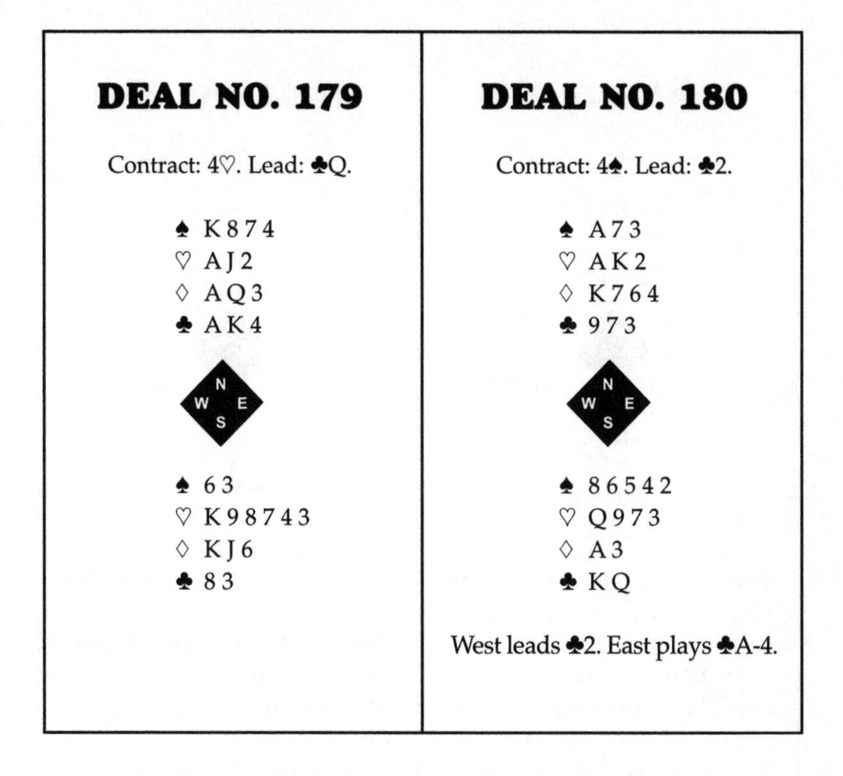

DEAL NO. 179

Contract: 4♡. Lead: ♣Q.

♠ K 8 7 4
♡ A J 2
◊ A Q 3
♣ A K 4

♠ 6 3
♡ K 9 8 7 4 3
◊ K J 6
♣ 8 3

DEAL NO. 180

Contract: 4♠. Lead: ♣2.

♠ A 7 3
♡ A K 2
◊ K 7 6 4
♣ 9 7 3

♠ 8 6 5 4 2
♡ Q 9 7 3
◊ A 3
♣ K Q

West leads ♣2. East plays ♣A-4.

DEAL NO. 179

Contract: 4♡. Lead: ♣Q.

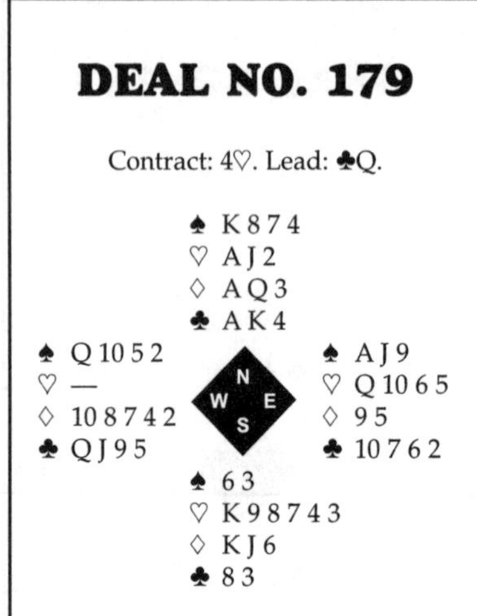

This is *Deal 176* again, but now you are only in 4♡. Before, you had to hope for an ideal layout. Now things looks easy, so assume the worst and do everything to safeguard the success of your contract. You will lose two spades if East has the ace, but you can restrict your trump losers to one even if they break 4-0. Win the club and play ♡A. If West shows out you follow up with the ♡J forcing East to cover and you will just lose to ♡10. If East shows out you come to hand with a diamond and lead ♡9, and West is similarly trapped. What you must not do is play a low heart to the king at trick two.

DEAL NO. 180

Contract: 4♠. Lead: ♣2.

West	North / South	East
	♠ A 7 3 ♡ A K 2 ◊ K 7 6 4 ♣ 9 7 3	
♠ K 10 9 ♡ J 8 6 5 ◊ Q 2 ♣ J 8 6 2	N W E S	♠ Q J ♡ 10 4 ◊ J 10 9 8 5 ♣ A 10 5 4
	♠ 8 6 5 4 2 ♡ Q 9 7 3 ◊ A 3 ♣ K Q	

If trumps break badly this contract is not going to make, so assume they are 3-2 – but there is still a potential heart loser to worry about. If you play ace and another spade, a defender might then play a third round, denying you the chance to ruff your low heart in dummy. If, on the other hand, you play out ♡A-K-Q, a defender might ruff from a doubleton trump holding. The answer is to play a low trump at trick three. Win the return, play ♠A, and now play hearts from the top. If they break 3-3 you simply concede a trump loser while if they break 4-2 a defender can either ruff with a master trump or you ruff the last heart.

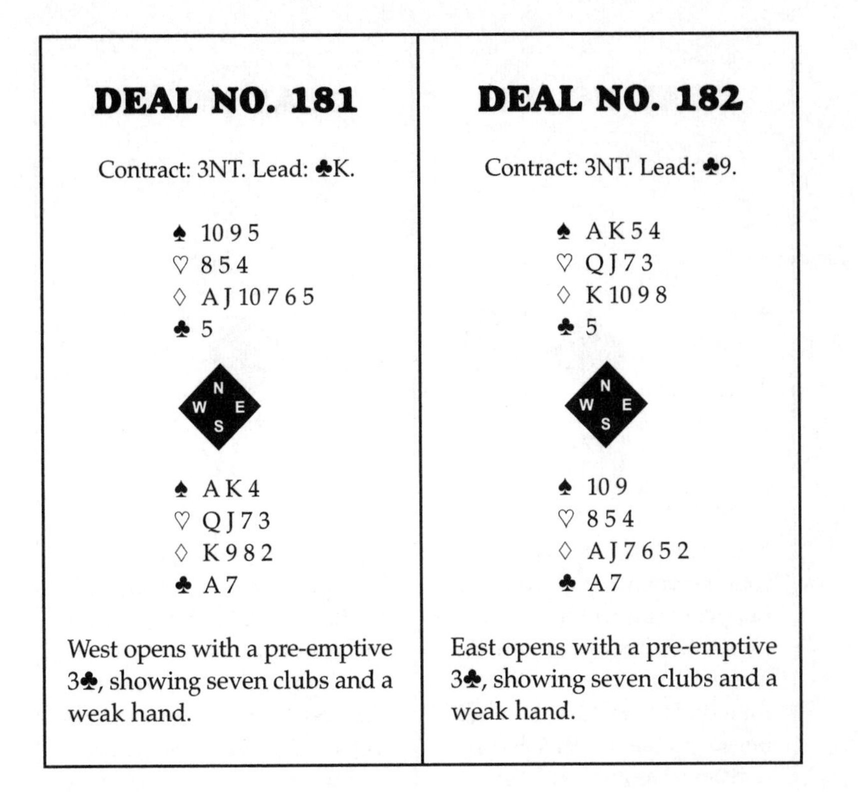

DEAL NO. 181

Contract: 3NT. Lead: ♣K.

♠ 10 9 5
♡ 8 5 4
♢ A J 10 7 6 5
♣ 5

♠ A K 4
♡ Q J 7 3
♢ K 9 8 2
♣ A 7

West opens with a pre-emptive 3♣, showing seven clubs and a weak hand.

DEAL NO. 182

Contract: 3NT. Lead: ♣9.

♠ A K 5 4
♡ Q J 7 3
♢ K 10 9 8
♣ 5

♠ 10 9
♡ 8 5 4
♢ A J 7 6 5 2
♣ A 7

East opens with a pre-emptive 3♣, showing seven clubs and a weak hand.

DEAL NO. 181

Contract: 3NT. Lead: ♣K.

You can hold up ♣A for a round if you like but, whatever happens, you will have to take six diamond tricks to fulfil this rather ambitious contract. If diamonds break 2-1 there will be no problem, but what if a defender has all three? You can take a finesse against either opponent, but you have to decide right now whether you are going to start with ◇A or ◇K, because you cannot afford to lose the lead. Well, nothing is certain, but if anyone is going to hold all three diamonds, it is likely to be East. Why? Simply because he has ten unknown cards and West only six. So the correct play is to cash ◇A first, and then finesse against East's proven ◇Q-4-3. Easy!

DEAL NO. 182

Contract: 3NT. Lead: ♣9.

North: ♠ A K 5 4 · ♡ Q J 7 3 · ◇ K 10 9 8 · ♣ 5

West: ♠ Q J 7 6 · ♡ A 10 6 · ◇ Q 4 3 · ♣ 9 4 2

East: ♠ 8 3 2 · ♡ K 9 2 · ◇ — · ♣ K Q J 10 8 6 3

South: ♠ 10 9 · ♡ 8 5 4 · ◇ A J 7 6 5 2 · ♣ A 7

West obediently leads ♣9 and here you are, in a remarkably similar position to that of the previous deal. You have to win six diamond tricks and this time West is more likely to hold ◇Q-4-3. So, win ♣A, cash ◇A and when East shows out, play ◇J to finesse against West's ◇Q? Right? Almost. Do you see the snag?

Whether or not West covers, dummy's diamonds will all be higher than any left in your hand. The suit will be blocked. The answer is not to play ◇J for a finesse, but lead low to dummy's ◇10. In due course ◇J is then an entry back to your hand.

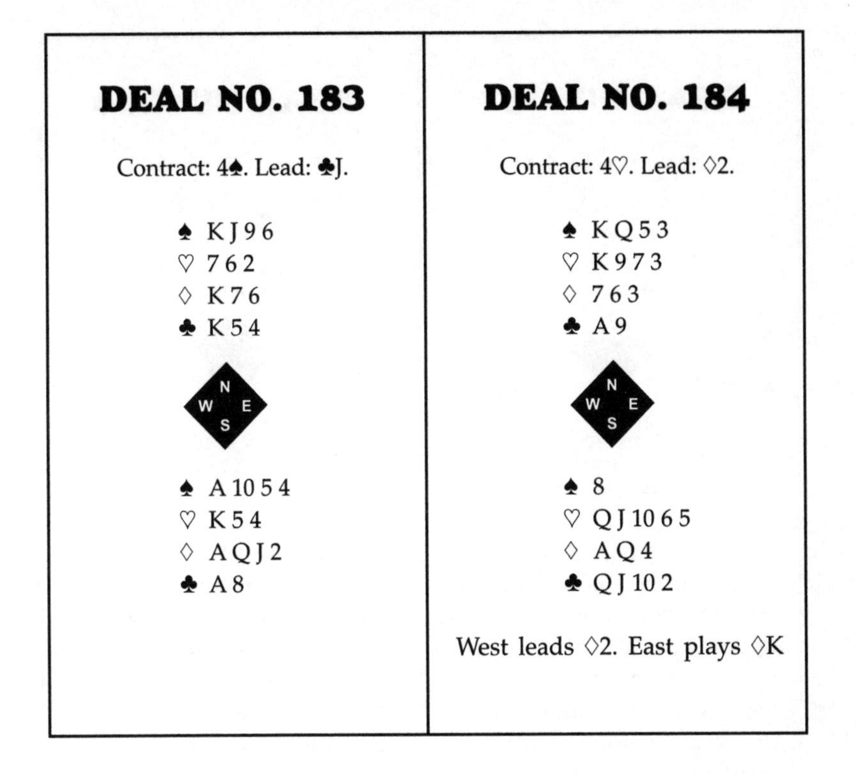
DEAL NO. 183
Contract: 4♠. Lead: ♣J.
♠ K J 9 6
♡ 7 6 2
◊ K 7 6
♣ K 5 4
N
W E
S
♠ A 10 5 4
♡ K 5 4
◊ A Q J 2
♣ A 8
DEAL NO. 184
Contract: 4♡. Lead: ◊2.
♠ K Q 5 3
♡ K 9 7 3
◊ 7 6 3
♣ A 9
N
W E
S
♠ 8
♡ Q J 10 6 5
◊ A Q 4
♣ Q J 10 2
West leads ◊2. East plays ◊K

DEAL NO. 183

Contract: 4♠. Lead: ♣J.

3NT would have been much better but there is nothing you can do about that now. You hope to be able to draw trumps in three rounds and throw a heart loser from dummy on a diamond, ultimately ruffing a heart in dummy. But there is more to it than that. Suppose you win the club in hand and play ♠A followed by a finesse against the queen. On a bad day East would win and then play back a heart through your king and, if West holds the ace twice-guarded, you will go down. Instead you must take the trump finesse through *East*. Even if it loses, your ♡K is protected from attack.

DEAL NO. 184

Contract: 4♡. Lead: ◊2.

The diamond lead has done you no harm but you must realise that there is a potential loser in the suit. Suppose you lead a trump immediately. A defender will win, play another diamond and now, when you lead a spade, the defence can win and cash a diamond, so that your contract will depend on a successful club finesse. Instead, play a spade at trick two. The defence will win – if they don't, there is no spade loser – and then play another diamond. You can win, cross to dummy with ♣A, spurning the finesse, and discard your last diamond on the dummy's master spade. Now you attack trumps and will lose just a spade, a heart and a club.

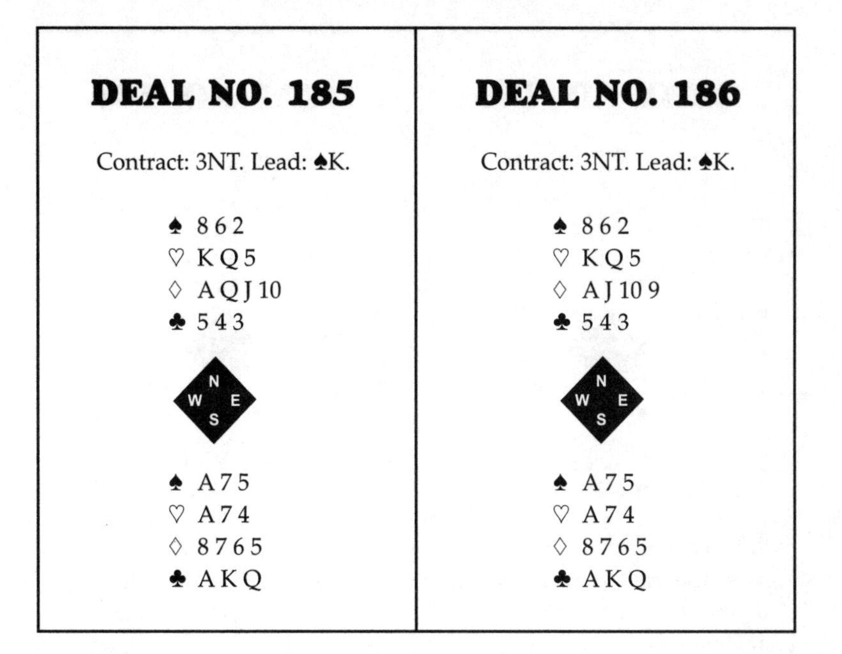

DEAL NO. 185

Contract: 3NT. Lead: ♠K.

♠ 8 6 2
♡ K Q 5
♢ A Q J 10
♣ 5 4 3

♠ A 7 5
♡ A 7 4
♢ 8 7 6 5
♣ A K Q

DEAL NO. 186

Contract: 3NT. Lead: ♠K.

♠ 8 6 2
♡ K Q 5
♢ A J 10 9
♣ 5 4 3

♠ A 7 5
♡ A 7 4
♢ 8 7 6 5
♣ A K Q

DEAL NO. 185

Contract: 3NT. Lead: ♠K.

You have eight top tricks and two more can be established in diamonds even if the finesse against ◇K loses. It is just a matter of making sure that East can do no mischief in spades if he does hold ◇K. This kind of arithmetic should be second nature to you by now. If West has a troublesome five-card spade holding, then East has only two spades. Therefore hold up ♠A until the second round, and take the diamond finesse: now your contract will succeed whether or not East can find another spade.

DEAL NO. 186

Contract: 3NT. Lead: ♠K.

West		East
	♠ 8 6 2 ♡ K Q 5 ◇ A J 10 9 ♣ 5 4 3	
♠ K Q J 9 ♡ 10 9 6 ◇ 4 3 ♣ 9 7 6 2	N W E S	♠ 10 4 3 ♡ J 8 3 2 ◇ K Q 2 ♣ J 10 8
	♠ A 7 5 ♡ A 7 4 ◇ 8 7 6 5 ♣ A K Q	

Very similar to the previous deal, but here you have to cater for the possibility of losing the lead twice to East in diamonds. If that happens, you can afford to lose only two spades, not three. So even a four-card spade suit with West is troublesome. If you hold up ♠A until the second round, East may put West back in to cash his two spades and you still have the other top diamond to lose. The answer is to hold up ♠A until the *third* round. Now East is welcome to both ◇K and ◇Q, because he is out of spades and the defence can come to only four tricks in all.

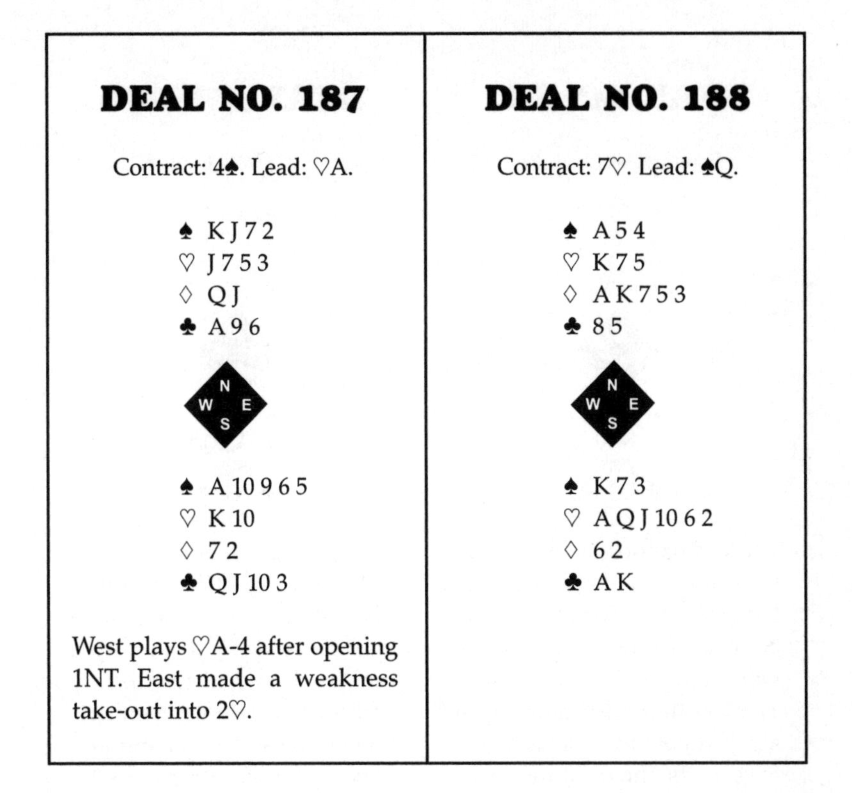

DEAL NO. 187

Contract: 4♠. Lead: ♡A.

♠ K J 7 2
♡ J 7 5 3
♢ Q J
♣ A 9 6

♠ A 10 9 6 5
♡ K 10
♢ 7 2
♣ Q J 10 3

West plays ♡A-4 after opening 1NT. East made a weakness take-out into 2♡.

DEAL NO. 188

Contract: 7♡. Lead: ♠Q.

♠ A 5 4
♡ K 7 5
♢ A K 7 5 3
♣ 8 5

♠ K 7 3
♡ A Q J 10 6 2
♢ 6 2
♣ A K

DEAL NO. 187

Contract: 4♠. Lead: ♡A.

The lead has done you no harm but even so you must hope that the club finesse is working because, if it fails, the defence will surely cash two diamonds. The fact that West didn't lead a top diamond is a sign that East holds one of those cards, indicating that West must have ♣Q. Also, as West is known to have a doubleton heart from the auction, the chances are that he must hold at least three spades – otherwise he might not have opened 1NT. While the normal play might be to play off ♠A-K, here it must be right to play ♠A first and then take a finesse of ♠Q through West.

DEAL NO. 188

Contract: 7♡. Lead: ♠Q.

The grand slam is a good one but you can't afford to relax. The only way you can avoid a spade loser is by setting up a master diamond in dummy and for that you need entries. So win the spade in hand and play ♡A-Q. If trumps are 3-1 you can't afford to play a third round. Instead, play ◊A-K and ruff a diamond high. If both defenders follow, you draw the last trump and have tricks to burn, but more likely one opponent will still have a diamond. That's fine, because you enter dummy with ♡K drawing the last trump, ruff another diamond and by now you'll have a master diamond in dummy, which you can reach via ♠A.

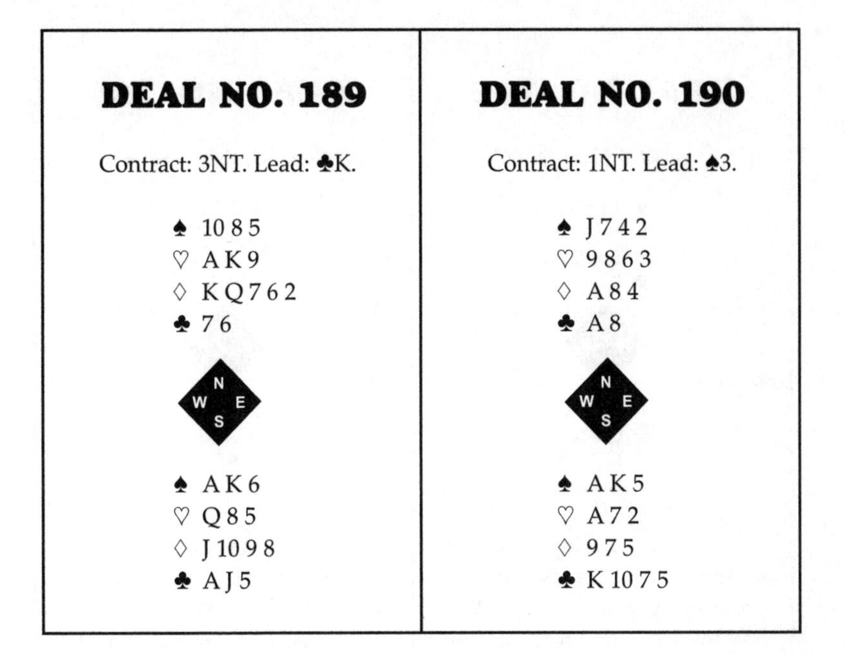
DEAL NO. 189
Contract: 3NT. Lead: ♣K.
♠ 10 8 5
♡ A K 9
◊ K Q 7 6 2
♣ 7 6
N
W E
S
♠ A K 6
♡ Q 8 5
◊ J 10 9 8
♣ A J 5
DEAL NO. 190
Contract: 1NT. Lead: ♠3.
♠ J 7 4 2
♡ 9 8 6 3
◊ A 8 4
♣ A 8
N
W E
S
♠ A K 5
♡ A 7 2
◊ 9 7 5
♣ K 10 7 5

DEAL NO. 189

Contract: 3NT. Lead: ♣K.

With six top tricks, you plan to knock out ◊A as soon as possible. Unfortunately, West has found your weakest spot and you might stare at the diagram of all four hands for some time without spotting the winning line. If you win with ♣A at Trick 1 and then play on diamonds, East will win with the ace and fire back a club through your ♣J-5 to defeat you. So don't win ♣A at Trick 1! What can West do? If he plays another club, your ♣J suddenly becomes a second stopper and it will be perfectly safe for you to knock out ◊A. If West does anything else, you win and go after the diamonds anyway.

DEAL NO. 190

Contract: 1NT. Lead: ♠3.

North: ♠ J 7 4 2 ♡ 9 8 6 3 ◊ A 8 4 ♣ A 8

West: ♠ 10 9 6 3 ♡ K J 4 ◊ K Q 3 ♣ 6 4 3

East: ♠ Q 8 ♡ Q 10 5 ◊ J 10 6 2 ♣ Q J 9 2

South: ♠ A K 5 ♡ A 7 2 ◊ 9 7 5 ♣ K 10 7 5

There is an awful temptation to play ♠J at Trick 1, on the grounds that West has most likely led from ♠Q. But, if the cards are as in the diagram, ♠J is headed by ♠Q and now you are going to struggle to come to seven tricks. Why struggle? Assuming West has led from a four-card suit (dummy has ♠2, so ♠3 must be the lowest from four cards), East can only have two spades. Simply cash ♠A-K and, even if ♠Q doesn't appear, you can then lead towards ♠J secure in the knowledge that West must have the queen.

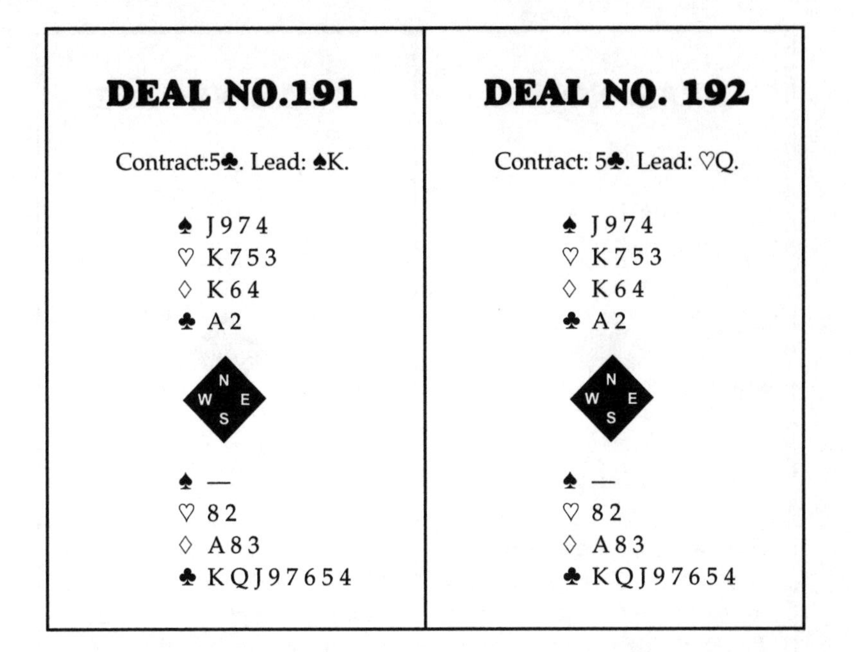
DEAL NO.191
Contract:5♣. Lead: ♠K.
♠ J 9 7 4
♡ K 7 5 3
◊ K 6 4
♣ A 2
N
W E
S
♠ —
♡ 8 2
◊ A 8 3
♣ K Q J 9 7 6 5 4
DEAL NO. 192
Contract: 5♣. Lead: ♡Q.
♠ J 9 7 4
♡ K 7 5 3
◊ K 6 4
♣ A 2
N
W E
S
♠ —
♡ 8 2
◊ A 8 3
♣ K Q J 9 7 6 5 4

DEAL NO.191

Contract:5♣. Lead: ♠K.

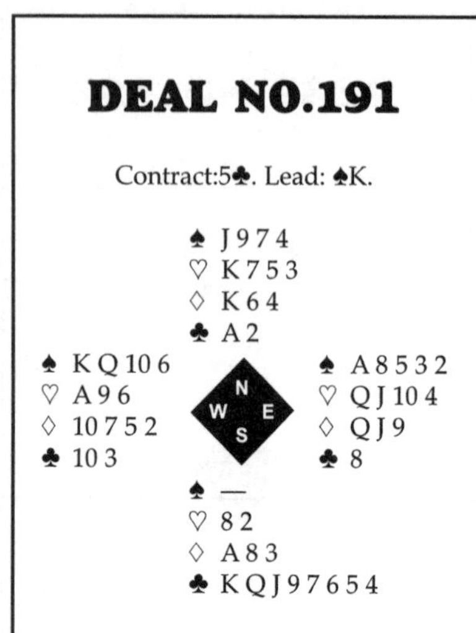

This is not the most taxing of hands, because your options are so limited. With a certain diamond loser you have to keep your heart losers to just one, which means you need ♡K to score a trick. So ruff the spade, draw trumps and lead a heart towards the king. If West has the ace you will make your contract. If East has it, you won't.

DEAL NO. 192

Contract: 5♣. Lead: ♡Q.

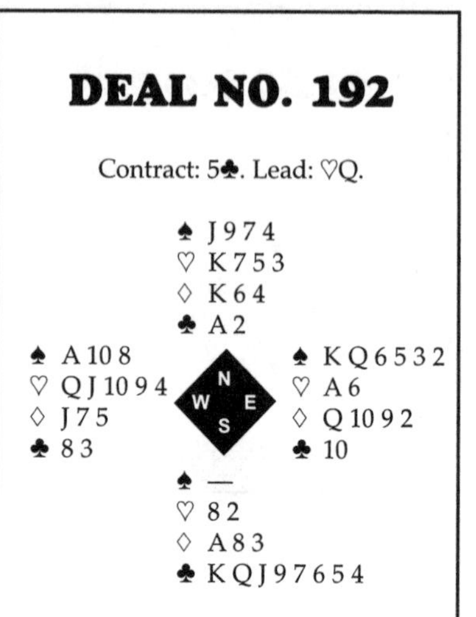

Same contract as *Deal 191* but the ♡Q lead puts an entirely different complexion on things. It's inconceivable that West has lead the queen from a holding headed by the ace, so your only real hope is that East started with just two hearts, one of them being the ace. So play low from dummy at trick one. If West shifts to a diamond, win in hand, draw trumps and duck a heart. If your plan works, East will have to win with the now-bare ace and you can reach dummy with ◇K to discard your losing diamond on ♡K.

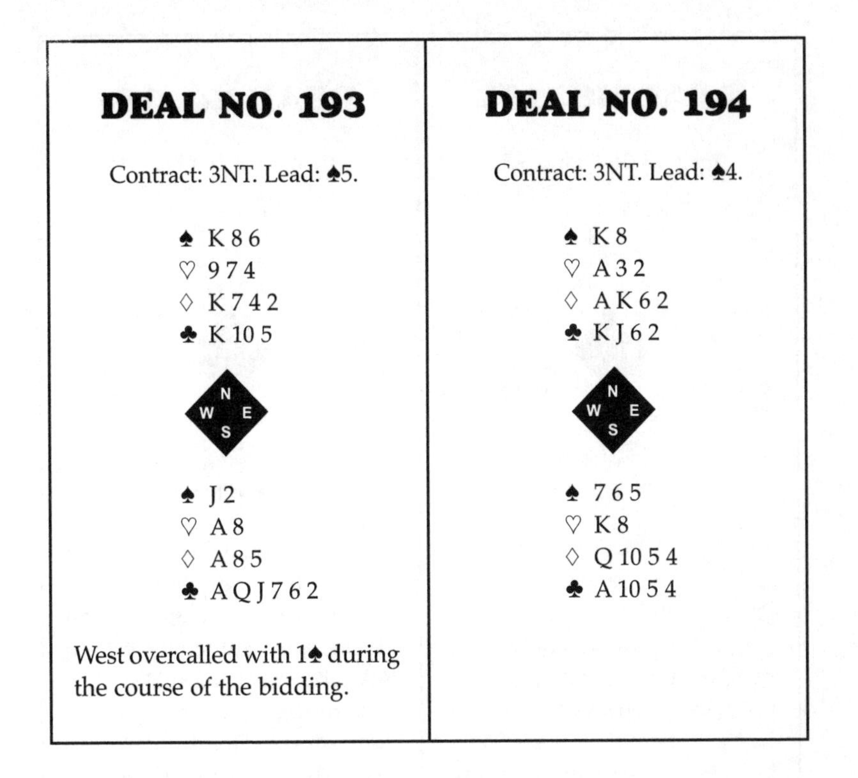

DEAL NO. 193

Contract: 3NT. Lead: ♠5.

♠ K 8 6
♡ 9 7 4
♢ K 7 4 2
♣ K 10 5

♠ J 2
♡ A 8
♢ A 8 5
♣ A Q J 7 6 2

West overcalled with 1♠ during the course of the bidding.

DEAL NO. 194

Contract: 3NT. Lead: ♠4.

♠ K 8
♡ A 3 2
♢ A K 6 2
♣ K J 6 2

♠ 7 6 5
♡ K 8
♢ Q 10 5 4
♣ A 10 5 4

DEAL NO. 193

Contract: 3NT. Lead: ♠5.

North: ♠ K 8 6 ♡ 9 7 4 ♢ K 7 4 2 ♣ K 10 5

West: ♠ Q 10 7 5 4 ♡ K Q J ♢ Q J 6 3 ♣ 3

East: ♠ A 9 3 ♡ 10 6 5 3 2 ♢ 10 9 ♣ 9 8 4

South: ♠ J 2 ♡ A 8 ♢ A 8 5 ♣ A Q J 7 6 2

You have nine tricks waiting just as soon as you gain the lead: six clubs, two diamonds and a heart. But you have to be careful that the defenders do not take five tricks before you can get started! Because West bid 1♠, it is awfully tempting to play ♠K at Trick 1 – but, as you can see, that way lies disaster. East will win ♠A, fire back another spade and . . . curtains. Instead, you should recognise the combination of K-x-x opposite J-x, guaranteed to gain a trick if you just play low in dummy. Look back to *Deal 74* if you've forgotten. Now the defence can't take more than two spade tricks and you make the contract easily.

DEAL NO. 194

Contract: 3NT. Lead: ♠4.

North: ♠ K 8 ♡ A 3 2 ♢ A K 6 2 ♣ K J 6 2

West: ♠ A J 9 4 3 ♡ Q 9 7 4 ♢ 7 ♣ 9 8 3

East: ♠ Q 10 2 ♡ J 10 6 5 ♢ J 9 8 3 ♣ Q 7

South: ♠ 7 6 5 ♡ K 8 ♢ Q 10 5 4 ♣ A 10 5 4

This time you must play ♠K at Trick 1. If you don't, it will sit in dummy, a singleton for all to see, and will surely lose to ♠A. You must hope West has led from ♠A and that ♠K will win Trick 1. That hurdle over, play ♢A-K, since you can only cope with East having four diamonds (assuming they do not break 3-2). As it happens, East shows up with ♢J-x-x-x so you can finesse ♢10 safely. If you count up your tricks, you will find that you have enough tricks now without having to hazard the club finesse.

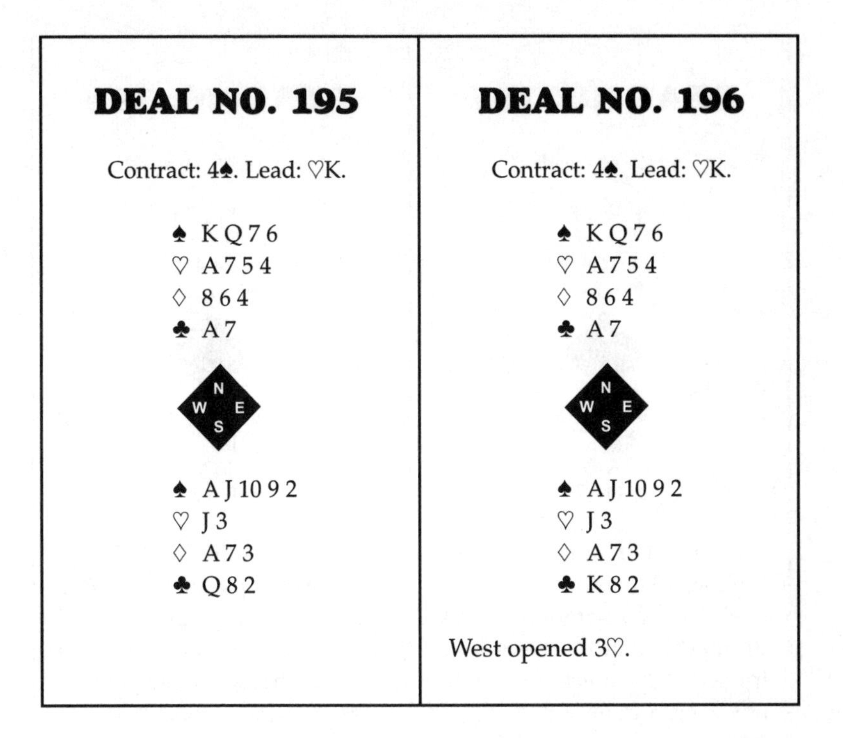

DEAL NO. 195

Contract: 4♠. Lead: ♡K.

♠ K Q 7 6
♡ A 7 5 4
♢ 8 6 4
♣ A 7

N / W E / S

♠ A J 10 9 2
♡ J 3
♢ A 7 3
♣ Q 8 2

DEAL NO. 196

Contract: 4♠. Lead: ♡K.

♠ K Q 7 6
♡ A 7 5 4
♢ 8 6 4
♣ A 7

N / W E / S

♠ A J 10 9 2
♡ J 3
♢ A 7 3
♣ K 8 2

West opened 3♡.

DEAL NO. 195

Contract: 4♠. Lead: ♡K.

With a certain club and heart loser you have to try to make one of the diamond losers disappear. Win the heart lead immediately – because you do not want a diamond switch – draw trumps, hopefully in two or three rounds, and play ♣A-7. If East has ♣K and plays it you can throw a low diamond from dummy on the established ♣Q and later ruff your last diamond in dummy. If East doesn't play the ♣K then you do not lose a club and the last club is ruffed in dummy instead.

DEAL NO. 196

Contract: 4♠. Lead: ♡K.

This is the same as *Deal 195* with ♣Q replaced with ♣K. Does that make things better? Yes, in a way, but have you noticed that West pre-empted with 3♡ which probably shows a seven card suit which in turn means that East has – none! So it would be folly to play ♡A at Trick 1, because East would ruff it. Instead play low from both hands and do so again if West carries on leading hearts. Ruff a third heart lead, draw trumps, play ♣A-K and ruff the low club in dummy, and then finally throw a low diamond from hand on the carefully preserved ♡A. In all you lose two hearts and one diamond.

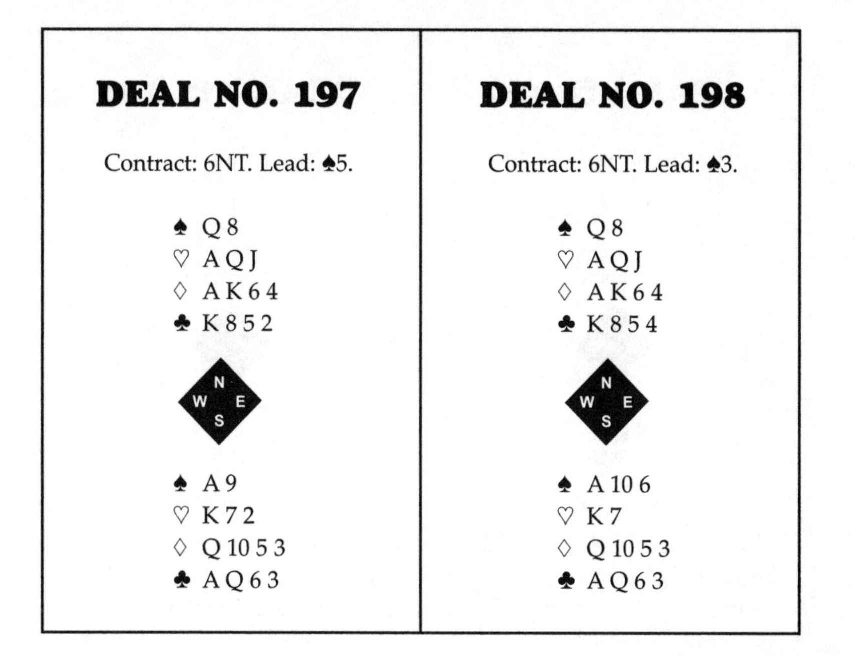

DEAL NO. 197

Contract: 6NT. Lead: ♠5.

North:
♠ Q 8
♡ A Q J
◇ A K 6 4
♣ K 8 5 2

South:
♠ A 9
♡ K 7 2
◇ Q 10 5 3
♣ A Q 6 3

DEAL NO. 198

Contract: 6NT. Lead: ♠3.

North:
♠ Q 8
♡ A Q J
◇ A K 6 4
♣ K 8 5 4

South:
♠ A 10 6
♡ K 7
◇ Q 10 5 3
♣ A Q 6 3

DEAL NO. 197

Contract: 6NT. Lead: ♠5.

You must play ♠Q at Trick 1, because that is surely your only chance to take a trick with it. Fortunately West has led from ♠K, so dummy's ♠Q holds. Now play ◊A-K in case East has four diamonds to the jack. As it happens, the diamonds break and there is no further problem. But notice that if you did not play ♠Q, you would be looking to make four club tricks – and, as the cards lie, you would go down.

DEAL NO. 198

Contract: 6NT. Lead: ♠3.

Almost the same as the previous deal, but now South has ♠A-10-6 instead of ♠A-9. This is a big difference, because you can now guarantee making two spade tricks. Can you see how? Play low in dummy. If East plays low, you win with ♠10. If East plays ♠J, you win with ♠A and have ♠Q-10 as equals against ♠K. And if East plays ♠K, you win ♠A and can cash ♠Q in dummy. Note that if South had only ♠A-6-5, say, it would have been right to play ♠Q at Trick 1, just as in the previous deal. What a difference one card can make!

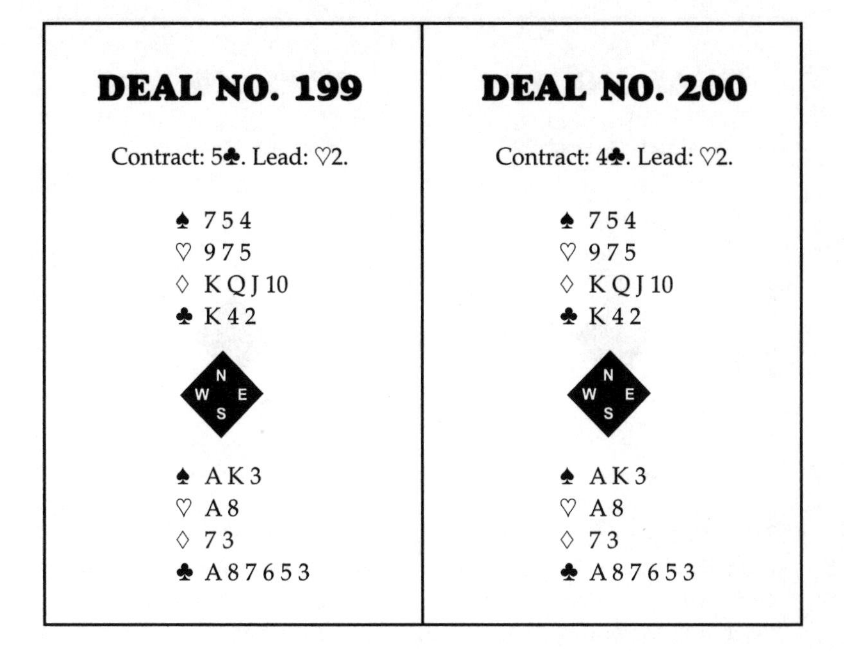
DEAL NO. 199
Contract: 5♣. Lead: ♡2.
♠ 7 5 4
♡ 9 7 5
♢ K Q J 10
♣ K 4 2
N
W E
S
♠ A K 3
♡ A 8
♢ 7 3
♣ A 8 7 6 5 3
DEAL NO. 200
Contract: 4♣. Lead: ♡2.
♠ 7 5 4
♡ 9 7 5
♢ K Q J 10
♣ K 4 2
N
W E
S
♠ A K 3
♡ A 8
♢ 7 3
♣ A 8 7 6 5 3

DEAL NO. 199

Contract: 5♣. Lead: ♡2.

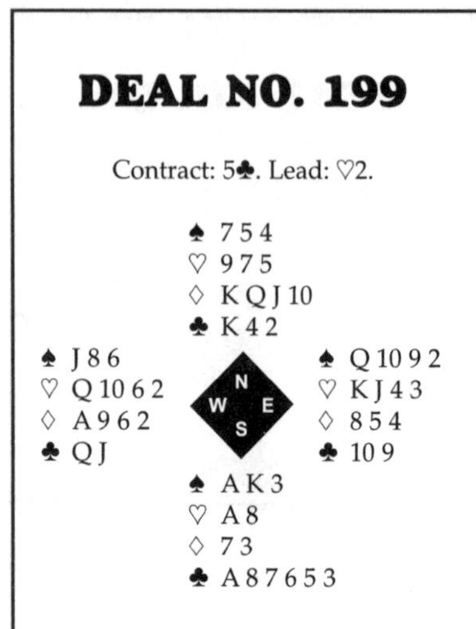

The heart lead has set up an immediate loser in that suit and, with ◊A also a certain loser, it is imperative that you do not lose a trump. The only hope is that the suit breaks 2-2, so win the first trick, draw trumps in two rounds and play on diamonds. The defence may cash a heart when in with ◊A but you can enter dummy with a trump and throw your losing spade on a master diamond. Is that too easy? Well if you think it is I am sure you will have retained ♣3 in your hand as that is the only card that will let you get to dummy!

DEAL NO. 200

Contract: 4♣. Lead: ♡2.

With more breathing space this time (you are only in 4♣), you can cater for the probable 3-1 trump break. If you cash ♣A-K and then play on diamonds, an astute defender will win the second round, draw dummy's last trump and play major suits. With no entry to dummy, you will lose a trick in every suit. Much better to play a low trump from both hands at trick two. The defence can play hearts, but you ruff the third round, play ♣A and, even if there is another trump outstanding, knock out ◊A. The defence can win the second round, as before, but you win any return and enter dummy with ♣K. Your losing spade is pitched on a master diamond.

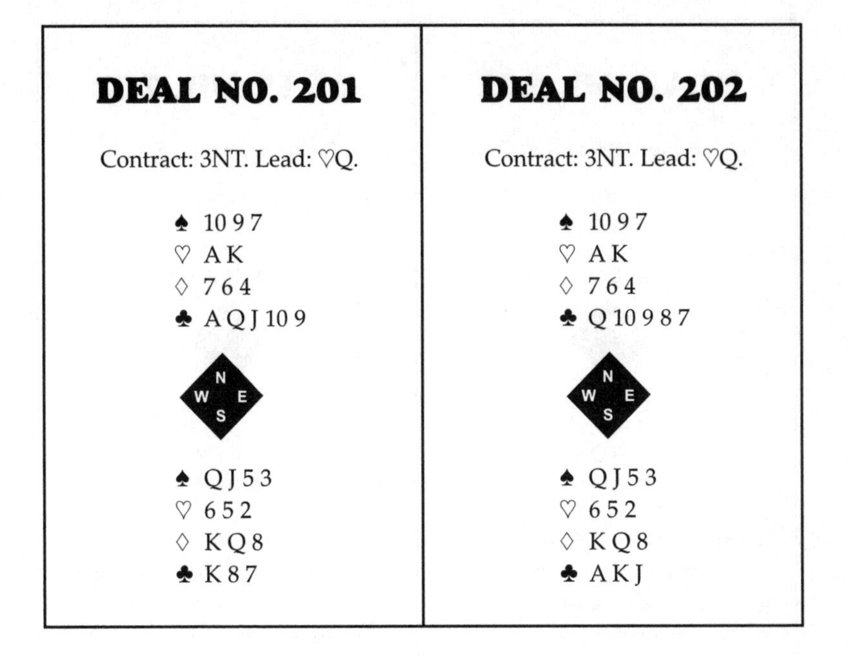
DEAL NO. 201
Contract: 3NT. Lead: ♡Q.
♠ 10 9 7
♡ A K
◊ 7 6 4
♣ A Q J 10 9
N
W E
S
♠ Q J 5 3
♡ 6 5 2
◊ K Q 8
♣ K 8 7
DEAL NO. 202
Contract: 3NT. Lead: ♡Q.
♠ 10 9 7
♡ A K
◊ 7 6 4
♣ Q 10 9 8 7
N
W E
S
♠ Q J 5 3
♡ 6 5 2
◊ K Q 8
♣ A K J

DEAL NO. 201

Contract: 3NT. Lead: ♡Q.

Given time, you could develop two spade tricks for your contract. Unfortunately, West's lead denies you that time. Work it out. Win heart, drive out ♠A, win next heart, drive out ♠K . . . but with no heart stop remaining, you can be sure the defence will cash heart tricks when in with ♠K. Your best chance is to hope East has ◇A. Play a diamond to the king and, assuming it holds, cross back to dummy with a club to play another diamond towards ◇Q. If East does hold ◇A (a 50% chance), he can do nothing to stop you.

DEAL NO. 202

Contract: 3NT. Lead: ♡Q.

Almost the same as *Deal 201*, but the clubs are arranged differently. You still have to lead twice towards ◇K-Q, but be careful how you manage the entries back and forth. Suppose you win Trick 1, play to your ◇K, cross to dummy by playing ♣J to ♣Q and play another diamond. East will hop up with ◇A and knock out dummy's ♡A. Now, in theory, you have enough tricks but your ♣A-K block the suit and you will never get to make dummy's ♣10 and ♣9. The answer is to play all the clubs (♣A-K-Q-10-9) before playing the second diamond. If you work it through, you will find this untangles your entries and lets you make nine tricks.

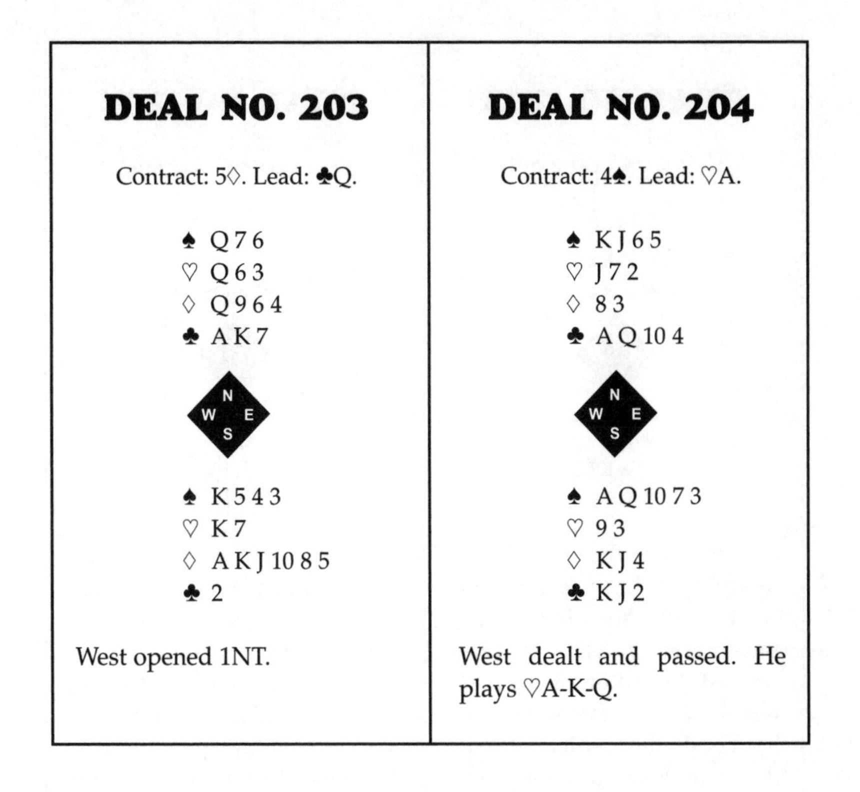

DEAL NO. 203

Contract: 5♢. Lead: ♣Q.

North:
♠ Q 7 6
♡ Q 6 3
♢ Q 9 6 4
♣ A K 7

South:
♠ K 5 4 3
♡ K 7
♢ A K J 10 8 5
♣ 2

West opened 1NT.

DEAL NO. 204

Contract: 4♠. Lead: ♡A.

North:
♠ K J 6 5
♡ J 7 2
♢ 8 3
♣ A Q 10 4

South:
♠ A Q 10 7 3
♡ 9 3
♢ K J 4
♣ K J 2

West dealt and passed. He plays ♡A-K-Q.

DEAL NO. 203

Contract: 5♢. Lead: ♣Q.

North: ♠ Q 7 6 ♡ Q 6 3 ♢ Q 9 6 4 ♣ A K 7

West: ♠ A J 10 ♡ A 10 8 4 ♢ 7 3 ♣ Q J 10 3

East: ♠ 9 8 2 ♡ J 9 5 2 ♢ 2 ♣ 9 8 6 5 4

South: ♠ K 5 4 3 ♡ K 7 ♢ A K J 10 8 5 ♣ 2

It looks on the surface as though you have to lose two spades and a heart but, in fact, the contract is cast-iron. West opened the bidding with 1NT, remember, and therefore must hold both major suit aces. Win the club lead, draw trumps ending in hand and lead ♡7. What can West do? If he ducks you win with ♡Q, discard your ♡K on ♣K and play a top spade to knock out the ace. You will lose another spade but that is all. If West rises with ♡A, you can eventually throw one spade from hand on ♣K and another on ♡Q. West is caught between the devil and the deep blue sea!

DEAL NO. 204

Contract: 4♠. Lead: ♡A.

North: ♠ K J 6 5 ♡ J 7 2 ♢ 8 3 ♣ A Q 10 4

West: ♠ 9 4 ♡ A K Q 5 ♢ Q 9 6 2 ♣ 7 6 3

East: ♠ 8 2 ♡ 10 8 6 4 ♢ A 10 7 5 ♣ 9 8 5

South: ♠ A Q 10 7 3 ♡ 9 3 ♢ K J 4 ♣ K J 2

At times what *hasn't* happened can be informative and that is very much the case here. It might look as though the contract depends on not losing two diamond tricks. Obviously you ruff the third heart, draw trumps, discard a diamond from hand on the fourth club if you wish – and lead a diamond from dummy. It would be poor play for East to rush in with an honour, so it seems as if you have to guess whether to play East for the ace or the queen. But think what *didn't* happen in the bidding: West passed originally, and has by now shown up with 9 points. He *may* have ♢Q but he certainly won't have ♢A.

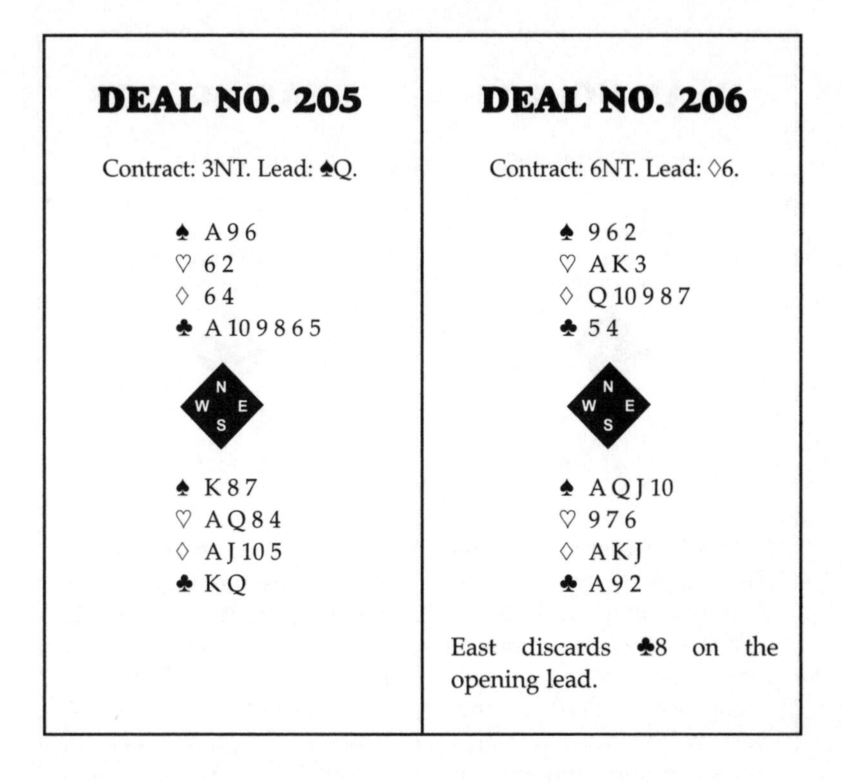

DEAL NO. 205

Contract: 3NT. Lead: ♠Q.

♠ A 9 6
♡ 6 2
♢ 6 4
♣ A 10 9 8 6 5

♠ K 8 7
♡ A Q 8 4
♢ A J 10 5
♣ K Q

DEAL NO. 206

Contract: 6NT. Lead: ♢6.

♠ 9 6 2
♡ A K 3
♢ Q 10 9 8 7
♣ 5 4

♠ A Q J 10
♡ 9 7 6
♢ A K J
♣ A 9 2

East discards ♣8 on the opening lead.

DEAL NO. 205

Contract: 3NT. Lead: ♠Q.

It looks natural to win ♠K (keeping ♠A as an entry to dummy's clubs), cash ♣K-Q, and then cross to dummy to run dummy's long club suit. Unfortunately, East has four clubs to the jack, so dummy's suit doesn't run. You can play ♣10 to knock out ♣J all right but, with ♠A gone, you have no way back to dummy for the rest of the clubs. The answer is to cash ♣K, then overtake ♣Q with dummy's ace, and play ♣10 to drive out East's jack. The clubs are set up, and dummy's ♠A remains intact as an entry to enjoy them.

DEAL NO. 206

Contract: 6NT. Lead: ◇6.

North: ♠ 9 6 2 ♡ A K 3 ◇ Q 10 9 8 7 ♣ 5 4

West: ♠ 8 7 ♡ 8 5 4 2 ◇ 6 5 4 3 2 ♣ K J

East: ♠ K 5 4 3 ♡ Q J 10 ◇ — ♣ Q 10 8 7 6 3

South: ♠ A Q J 10 ♡ 9 7 6 ◇ A K J ♣ A 9 2

You arrive in 6NT after a bidding misunderstanding and start counting tricks. One club, five diamonds, two hearts and hence a required four spades. You have to hope East has ♠K. Cross to ♡A and finesse in spades. This works, so cross to ♡K and finesse again. Now you need to finesse a third time but you can only do so if you won Trick 1 with ◇A (or ◇K)! Then you can cash ◇K (or ◇A), overtake ◇J with ◇Q, cash dummy's good diamonds, and finally take the third spade finesse. Be honest now: did you really notice that you had to avoid automatically winning Trick 1 with ◇J?

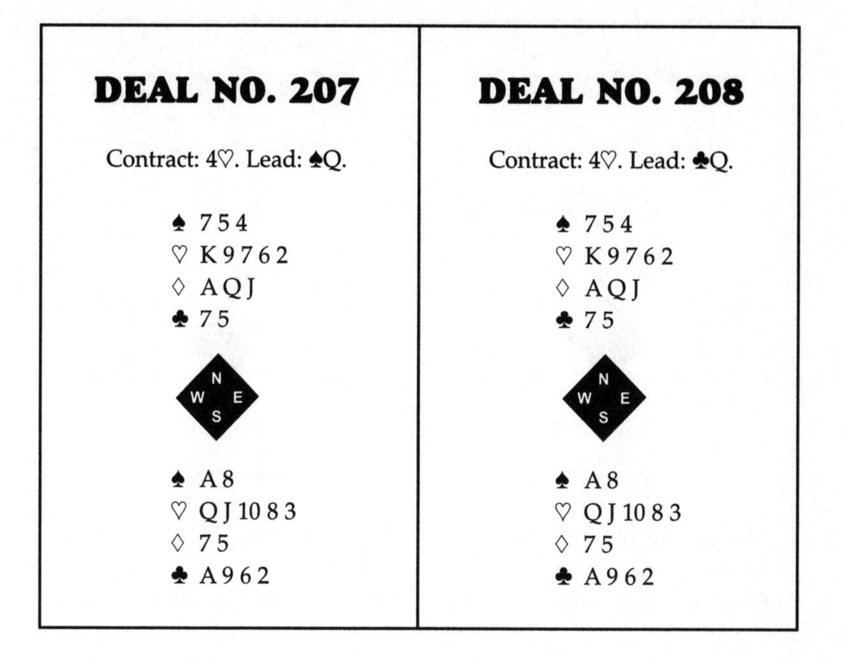
DEAL NO. 207
Contract: 4♡. Lead: ♠Q.
♠ 7 5 4
♡ K 9 7 6 2
◊ A Q J
♣ 7 5
N
W E
S
♠ A 8
♡ Q J 10 8 3
◊ 7 5
♣ A 9 6 2
DEAL NO. 208
Contract: 4♡. Lead: ♣Q.
♠ 7 5 4
♡ K 9 7 6 2
◊ A Q J
♣ 7 5
N
W E
S
♠ A 8
♡ Q J 10 8 3
◊ 7 5
♣ A 9 6 2

DEAL NO. 207

Contract: 4♡. Lead: ♠Q.

The spade lead is the most harmful because it sets up a loser in that suit from the outset. Still, there is nothing you can do but win the trick, knock out ♡A and hope that the diamond finesse works, because you are going to lose a club trick for sure.

DEAL NO. 208

Contract: 4♡. Lead: ♣Q.

North: ♠ 7 5 4 ♡ K 9 7 6 2 ◊ A Q J ♣ 7 5

West: ♠ Q J 9 6 ♡ A ◊ 9 8 6 2 ♣ Q J 10 3

East: ♠ K 10 3 2 ♡ 5 4 ◊ K 10 4 3 ♣ K 8 4

South: ♠ A 8 ♡ Q J 10 8 3 ◊ 7 5 ♣ A 9 6 2

Same deal as *207* but this time the lead is friendlier. Why? Because the defenders have only set up a trick *they were going to make anyway.* But you have to make use of your good fortune. Can you see why it would be a mistake to play on trumps at Trick 2? The defence would win, cash a club and switch to spades and now you are back where you were before – wanting the diamond finesse to work. Instead, take the diamond finesse straight away. Even if it loses and the defence returns a spade, you rise with ♠A, cash the two master diamonds in dummy (pitching your losing spade), and only then lead trumps.

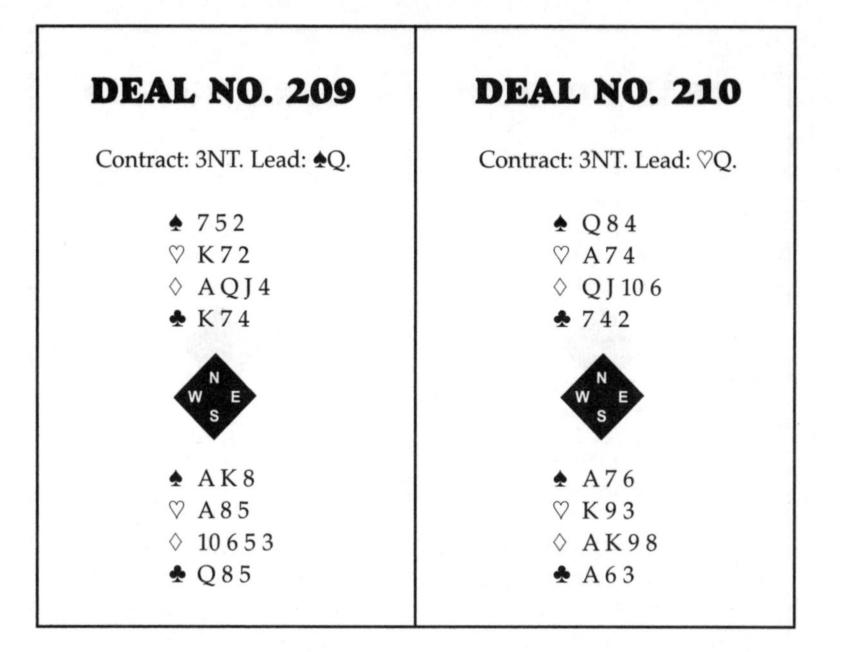

DEAL NO. 209

Contract: 3NT. Lead: ♠Q.

♠ 7 5 2
♡ K 7 2
◇ A Q J 4
♣ K 7 4

♠ A K 8
♡ A 8 5
◇ 10 6 5 3
♣ Q 8 5

DEAL NO. 210

Contract: 3NT. Lead: ♡Q.

♠ Q 8 4
♡ A 7 4
◇ Q J 10 6
♣ 7 4 2

♠ A 7 6
♡ K 9 3
◇ A K 9 8
♣ A 6 3

You plan to make two spades, two hearts, four diamonds and a club. Obviously you are going to take the diamond finesse and, assuming it works, knock out ♣A while you still have the other suits stopped. All well and good, but did you lead ◊10 for the finesse? If you did, West's ◊K forces dummy's ◊A and now East's remaining ◊9-8-7 is good enough to stop you taking the three diamonds you need. You should play a low diamond for the finesse and, when West's ◊K pops up, it causes you no trouble. The moral is to think about the consequences of leading an honour and having it covered by a singleton honour. If – as here – you can't afford for that to happen, lead a low card instead!

This is a horribly flat hand, and you can only make four diamond tricks despite holding the top seven diamonds! As usual, such a 'duplication of honours', as it is called, makes the contract a bit difficult. By now you should see that the only chance is to hope that West has ♠K, and lead towards ♠Q for your ninth trick. We hope you did not even think of leading ♠Q for a 'finesse'!

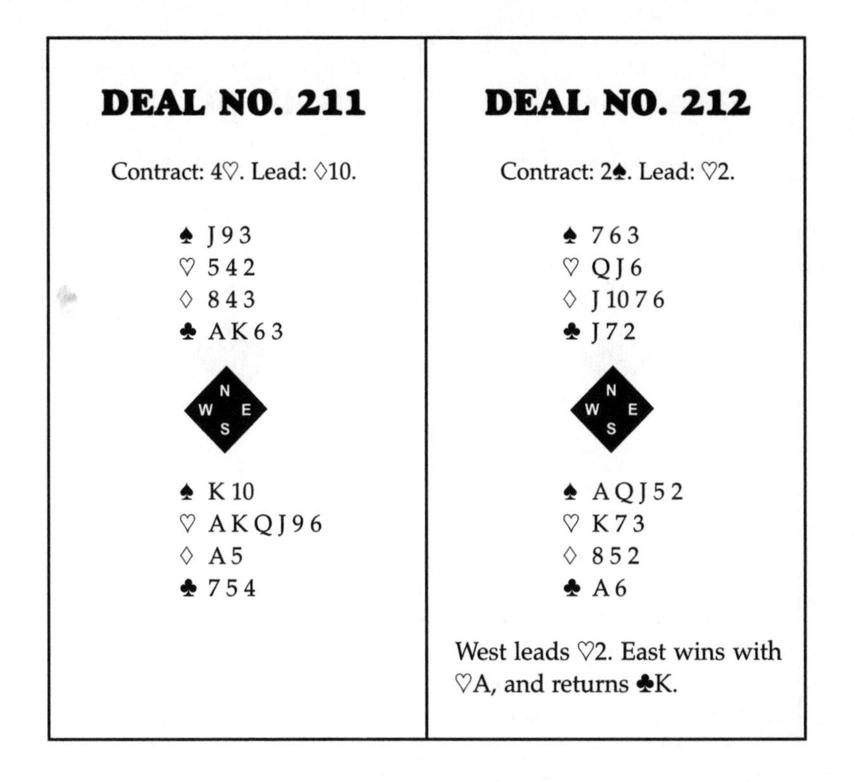

DEAL NO. 211

Contract: 4♡. Lead: ♢10.

♠ J 9 3
♡ 5 4 2
♢ 8 4 3
♣ A K 6 3

♠ K 10
♡ A K Q J 9 6
♢ A 5
♣ 7 5 4

DEAL NO. 212

Contract: 2♠. Lead: ♡2.

♠ 7 6 3
♡ Q J 6
♢ J 10 7 6
♣ J 7 2

♠ A Q J 5 2
♡ K 7 3
♢ 8 5 2
♣ A 6

West leads ♡2. East wins with ♡A, and returns ♣K.

DEAL NO. 211

Contract: 4♡. Lead: ◊10.

Sometimes it is easy to get an *idée fixe* about a hand. Many players would draw trumps and enter dummy with a club in order to lead a spade, hoping to guess right if East plays low. But suppose you guess wrong and West shoots back a club, knocking out your only other stopper. You will find you end up losing two spades, one diamond and one club. You always have a spade trick eventually on which to throw your losing club, but you must preserve those top clubs in dummy. So, after drawing trumps, play ♠K. The defence will win, cash a diamond and lead a club, but you win and play ♠10, setting up ♠J in dummy for a discard.

DEAL NO. 212

Contract: 2♠. Lead: ♡2.

North: ♠ 7 6 3 ♡ Q J 6 ◊ J 10 7 6 ♣ J 7 2

West: ♠ 8 4 ♡ 10 8 5 2 ◊ A Q 4 ♣ 9 8 5 3

East: ♠ K 10 9 ♡ A 9 4 ◊ K 9 3 ♣ K Q 10 4

South: ♠ A Q J 5 2 ♡ K 7 3 ◊ 8 5 2 ♣ A 6

With a heart, three diamonds and a club to lose you have to hope that the trumps break no worse than 3-2 and that East has the king! But to make use of that situation you might need to have two entries to dummy in order to take finesses in trumps. One is ♡Q and the other . . . ? Of course you remembered to throw your ♡K under ♡A at Trick 1! That way, ♡J is also an entry to dummy. Maybe East should have played ♡9 initially but defenders do make mistakes!

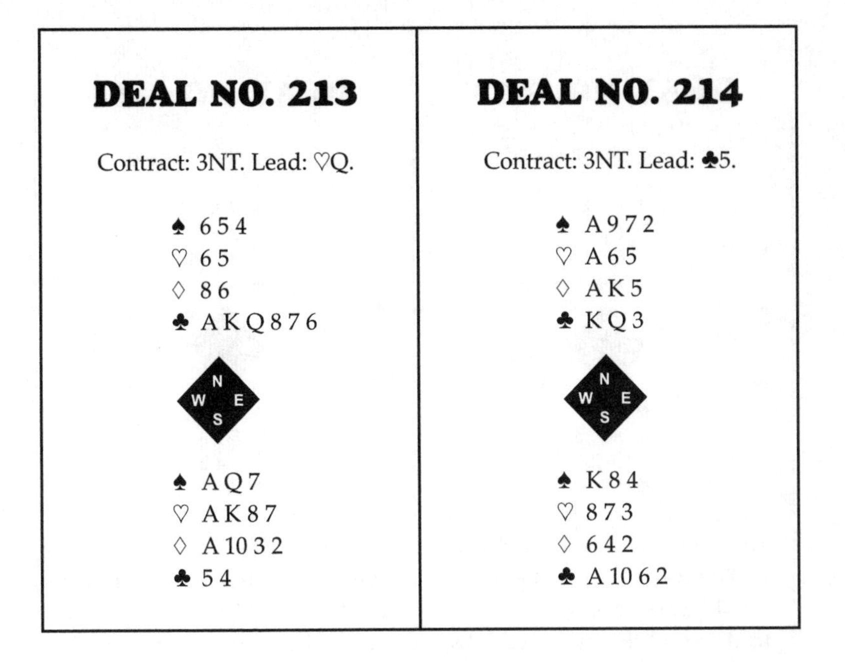
DEAL NO. 213
Contract: 3NT. Lead: ♡Q.
♠ 6 5 4
♡ 6 5
◊ 8 6
♣ A K Q 8 7 6
N
W E
S
♠ A Q 7
♡ A K 8 7
◊ A 10 3 2
♣ 5 4
DEAL NO. 214
Contract: 3NT. Lead: ♣5.
♠ A 9 7 2
♡ A 6 5
◊ A K 5
♣ K Q 3
N
W E
S
♠ K 8 4
♡ 8 7 3
◊ 6 4 2
♣ A 10 6 2

DEAL NO. 213

Contract: 3NT. Lead: ♡Q.

You need six club tricks to make this contract. A beginner would cash ♣A-K-Q, hoping to draw all the missing clubs, and go down when they fail to break 3-2. We hope you are no longer that beginner! Play a low club from both hands at Trick 2, then play out the top clubs when you regain the lead. This manoeuvre enables you to play four rounds of clubs but keep the lead in dummy, so that you can cash ♣8 and ♣7 for your contract.

DEAL NO. 214

Contract: 3NT. Lead: ♣5.

North: ♠ A 9 7 2 ♡ A 6 5 ◊ A K 5 ♣ K Q 3

West: ♠ 10 6 ♡ Q 10 4 2 ◊ J 8 ♣ J 9 7 5 4

East: ♠ Q J 5 3 ♡ K J 9 ◊ Q 10 9 7 3 ♣ 8

South: ♠ K 8 4 ♡ 8 7 3 ◊ 6 4 2 ♣ A 10 6 2

Without the club lead you would have had to search for a ninth trick, but now it is a certainty. Play low from table and win East's ♣8 with ♣10. Then cash dummy's ♣K-Q and use ♠K to get back to hand for ♣A. You have nine top tricks and, provided you play your cards in this order, there is nothing the defence can do to stop you taking them.

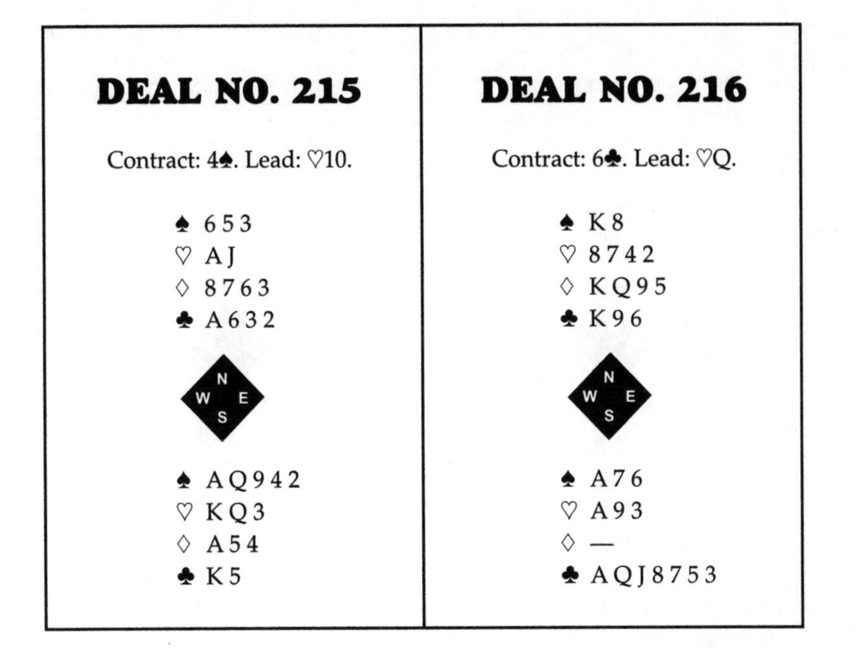
DEAL NO. 215
Contract: 4♠. Lead: ♡10.
♠ 6 5 3
♡ A J
◇ 8 7 6 3
♣ A 6 3 2
N
W E
S
♠ A Q 9 4 2
♡ K Q 3
◇ A 5 4
♣ K 5
DEAL NO. 216
Contract: 6♣. Lead: ♡Q.
♠ K 8
♡ 8 7 4 2
◇ K Q 9 5
♣ K 9 6
N
W E
S
♠ A 7 6
♡ A 9 3
◇ —
♣ A Q J 8 7 5 3

DEAL NO. 215

Contract: 4♠. Lead: ♡10.

North: ♠ 6 5 3 ♡ A J ♢ 8 7 6 3 ♣ A 6 3 2

West: ♠ K 8 ♡ 10 9 8 2 ♢ K J 9 ♣ J 8 7 4

East: ♠ J 10 7 ♡ 7 6 5 4 ♢ Q 10 2 ♣ Q 10 9

South: ♠ A Q 9 4 2 ♡ K Q 3 ♢ A 5 4 ♣ K 5

With two diamonds losers you must hope not to lose two trump tricks. You will need trumps to break 3-2 and at first sight it looks as though you require East to hold the king, but you can improve upon this chance. Win Trick 1 in dummy and play a low trump to the nine. If it loses to the ten or jack you can finesse against the king next time you are in dummy, but once in a while the nine will force the king from West. Note that it doesn't do East any good to play either ♠J or ♠10 early.

DEAL NO. 216

Contract: 6♣. Lead: ♡Q.

North: ♠ K 8 ♡ 8 7 4 2 ♢ K Q 9 5 ♣ K 9 6

West: ♠ J 9 5 3 2 ♡ Q J 10 ♢ J 8 7 6 ♣ 4

East: ♠ Q 10 4 ♡ K 6 5 ♢ A 10 4 3 2 ♣ 10 2

South: ♠ A 7 6 ♡ A 9 3 ♢ — ♣ A Q J 8 7 5 3

Without a heart lead your contract would be safe: you would have time to establish a diamond trick, giving you two spades and a ruff, one heart, one diamond and seven clubs. And it wouldn't matter who held ♢A. But now it does. So win ♡A, cross to ♠K and lead ♢K. If East plays the ace you ruff, draw two rounds of trumps ending in dummy and pitch a heart loser on ♢Q. You must then remember to ruff your losing spade but you will emerge with twelve tricks. And if West has ♢A? Then you will have thrown a heart on ♢K but will still suffer a one trick defeat when the defence cashes a heart.

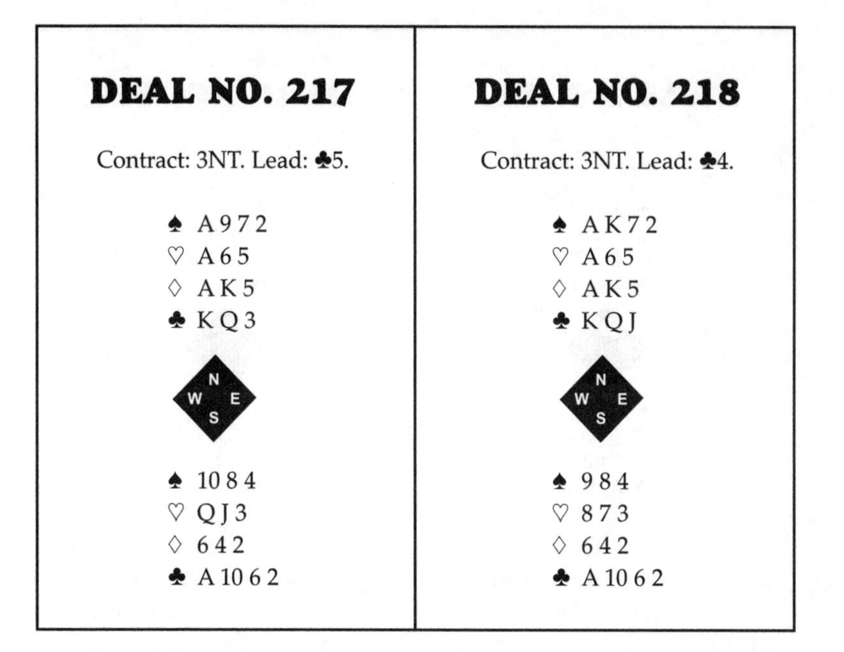
DEAL NO. 217
Contract: 3NT. Lead: ♣5.
♠ A 9 7 2
♡ A 6 5
♢ A K 5
♣ K Q 3
N
W
E
S
♠ 10 8 4
♡ Q J 3
♢ 6 4 2
♣ A 10 6 2
DEAL NO. 218
Contract: 3NT. Lead: ♣4.
♠ A K 7 2
♡ A 6 5
♢ A K 5
♣ K Q J
N
W
E
S
♠ 9 8 4
♡ 8 7 3
♢ 6 4 2
♣ A 10 6 2

DEAL NO. 217

Contract: 3NT. Lead: ♣5.

This is almost the same as *Deal 214*, except that now South has ♡Q-J-3 instead of ♠K. Win ♣10 at Trick 1, cash dummy's ♣K-Q, and then play ace and another heart. It does not matter which defender has ♡K – your ♡Q-J must provide an entry to ♣A in due course. Note that it would be a mistake to take a heart finesse at Trick 2. West will not play ♡K on ♡Q. You can then unblock dummy's ♣K-Q, but your ♡J will never be an entry and ♣A will remain stranded.

DEAL NO. 218

Contract: 3NT. Lead: ♣4.

We hope that this deal now seems ridiculously simple to you. You need four club tricks, but there is no apparent entry to the South hand. Of course, because you have all the top clubs, all you have to do is cash ♣K-Q and then overtake ♣J with ♣A and take ♣10 for your ninth trick. This is just the sort of play a beginner would miss when first playing the cards, when an experienced player would not even notice that there is a problem!

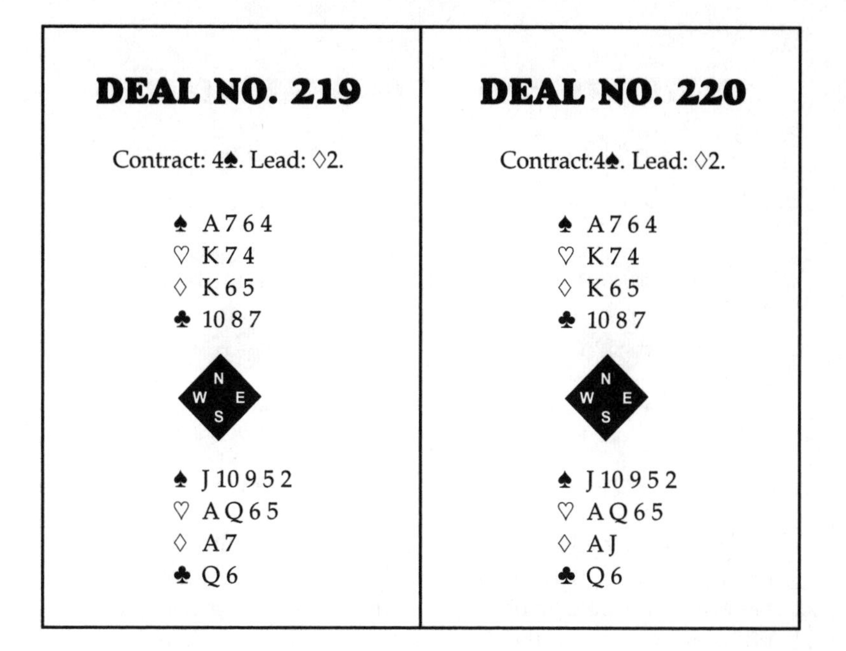
DEAL NO. 219
Contract: 4♠. Lead: ♢2.
♠ A 7 6 4
♡ K 7 4
♢ K 6 5
♣ 10 8 7
N
W
E
S
♠ J 10 9 5 2
♡ A Q 6 5
♢ A 7
♣ Q 6
DEAL NO. 220
Contract:4♠. Lead: ♢2.
♠ A 7 6 4
♡ K 7 4
♢ K 6 5
♣ 10 8 7
N
W
E
S
♠ J 10 9 5 2
♡ A Q 6 5
♢ A J
♣ Q 6

DEAL NO. 219

Contract: 4♠. Lead: ♢2

There is no way you can avoid losing two club tricks, so you have to concentrate on playing the trump suit to the best advantage: that is to take two finesses against the missing honours. Win the diamond in hand and run ♠J. It may well lose to an honour in the East hand but ,as soon as you regain the lead, play ♠10 and let it run if it is not covered. Many people panic and play the ace next, but this is wrong: the chance of East holding the singleton king or queen is much higher than that of holding ♠K-Q doubleton.

DEAL NO. 220

Contract:4♠. Lead: ♢2

Almost the same as *Deal 219* but this time you have ♢J and the lead has given you an extra trick. Win the lead in hand with ♢A or ♢J, depending on which card East plays, and cash ♠A. Return to hand with a diamond (to unblock the suit) and go back to dummy with ♡K. Now cash ♢K, throwing a club from hand. Later you will lose a club and one or two trump tricks, but your long heart can be ruffed in dummy and you will make your contract.

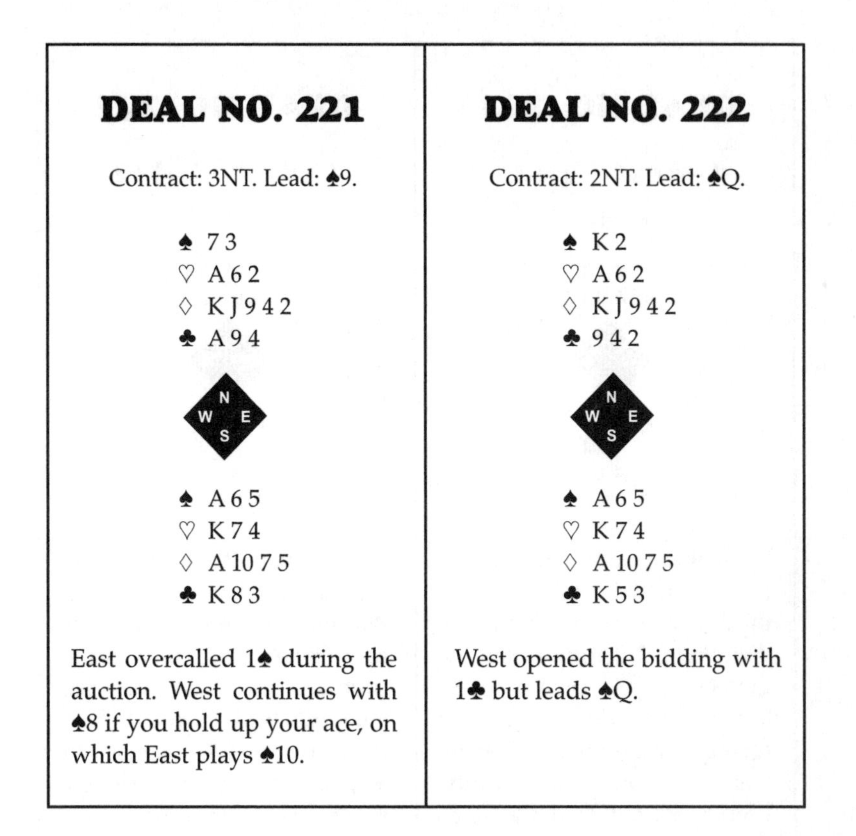

DEAL NO. 221

Contract: 3NT. Lead: ♠9.

♠ 7 3
♡ A 6 2
♢ K J 9 4 2
♣ A 9 4

N / W E / S

♠ A 6 5
♡ K 7 4
♢ A 10 7 5
♣ K 8 3

East overcalled 1♠ during the auction. West continues with ♠8 if you hold up your ace, on which East plays ♠10.

DEAL NO. 222

Contract: 2NT. Lead: ♠Q.

♠ K 2
♡ A 6 2
♢ K J 9 4 2
♣ 9 4 2

N / W E / S

♠ A 6 5
♡ K 7 4
♢ A 10 7 5
♣ K 5 3

West opened the bidding with 1♣ but leads ♠Q.

DEAL NO. 221

Contract: 3NT. Lead: ♠9.

By now it should be routine for you hold up ♠A until the third round. What about the diamonds? Taken in isolation, the best play is to cash ♢A-K because the odds marginally favour a 2-2 break. But here your efforts must go towards keeping East off lead. Cash ♢K and play low towards hand, smiling ruefully when East shows out. West can win ♢Q, but, thanks to your thoughtful hold-up play in spades, can do nothing to prevent you making the contract.

DEAL NO. 222

Contract: 2NT. Lead: ♠Q.

North: ♠ K 2 ♡ A 6 2 ♢ K J 9 4 2 ♣ 9 4 2

West: ♠ Q J 10 7 ♡ Q 10 ♢ Q 6 ♣ A Q J 10 8

East: ♠ 9 8 4 3 ♡ J 9 8 5 3 ♢ 8 3 ♣ 7 6

South: ♠ A 6 5 ♡ K 7 4 ♢ A 10 7 5 ♣ K 5 3

If West had led a club, you would have had to win with ♣K and then guess diamonds correctly. As it is, you are safe provided that East does not gain the lead to fire a club through your ♣K-x-x. Just win ♠K, cash ♢K, and finesse ♢10. No matter if this loses to a doubleton queen (as in fact it does). You make the contract with two spades, two hearts and four diamonds. Note that, if your club holding had been a bit stronger, you would have made the more normal play of finessing ♢J, on the assumption that West was likely to have ♢Q to justify his opening bid.

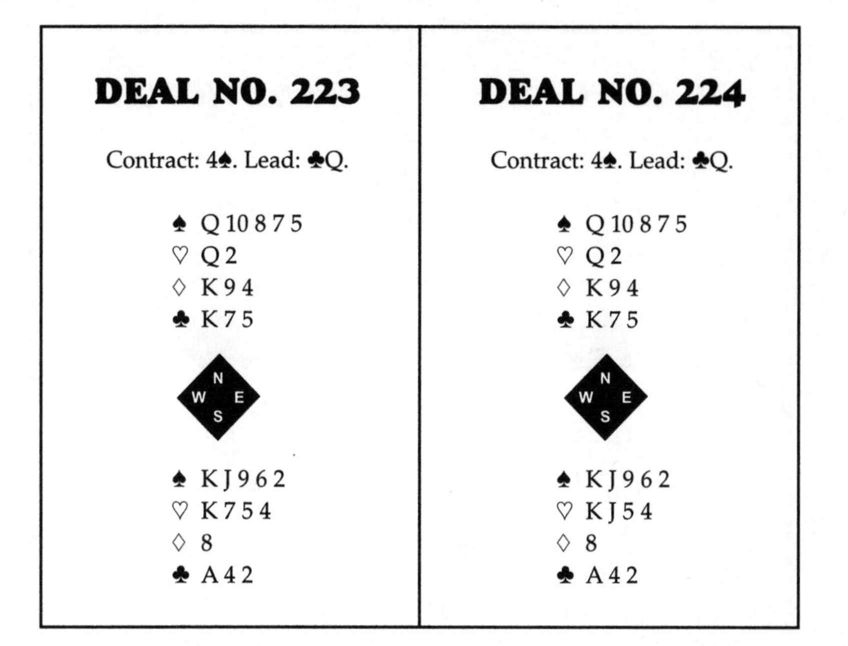

DEAL NO. 223

Contract: 4♠. Lead: ♣Q.

North:
♠ Q 10 8 7 5
♡ Q 2
◊ K 9 4
♣ K 7 5

South:
♠ K J 9 6 2
♡ K 7 5 4
◊ 8
♣ A 4 2

DEAL NO. 224

Contract: 4♠. Lead: ♣Q.

North:
♠ Q 10 8 7 5
♡ Q 2
◊ K 9 4
♣ K 7 5

South:
♠ K J 9 6 2
♡ K J 5 4
◊ 8
♣ A 4 2

DEAL NO. 223

Contract: 4♠. Lead: ♣Q.

What will happen if you lead a trump at Trick 2? Well, the defence will win and play another club and you will find that you eventually lose a trick in every suit. As you have three aces to lose, you must try to eliminate the club loser and to do that you will have to discard a club either from hand or dummy. Clearly the only hope is that West holds ◇A, so win the opening lead in hand and lead a diamond. If West ducks, your diamond loser has flown while if he rises with the ace, you can throw a club from hand on the established ◇K in dummy. Only then will it be safe to tackle trumps.

DEAL NO. 224

Contract: 4♠. Lead: ♣Q.

North: ♠ Q 10 8 7 5 ♡ Q 2 ◇ K 9 4 ♣ K 7 5

West: ♠ A ♡ 8 7 6 3 ◇ J 7 6 2 ♣ Q J 10 8

East: ♠ 4 3 ♡ A 10 9 ◇ A Q 10 5 3 ♣ 9 6 3

South: ♠ K J 9 6 2 ♡ K J 5 4 ◇ 8 ♣ A 4 2

This looks very similar to *Deal 223* but there is a difference. You *could* follow the line of play detailed above, but the presence of the ♡J means you can improve your chances of success. This time win the opening lead *in dummy* and lead ♡Q. The defence will win and lead another club but now you can play ♡K-J, discarding a club from the table. For this plan to succeed, you need the hearts to break 4-3, a 62% chance of success, compared with the 50% chance of finding ◇A with West. There is also the possibility that, if hearts did break 5-2, then the player with the doubleton might have the singleton ♠A. This adds about another 3% to your chance of success!

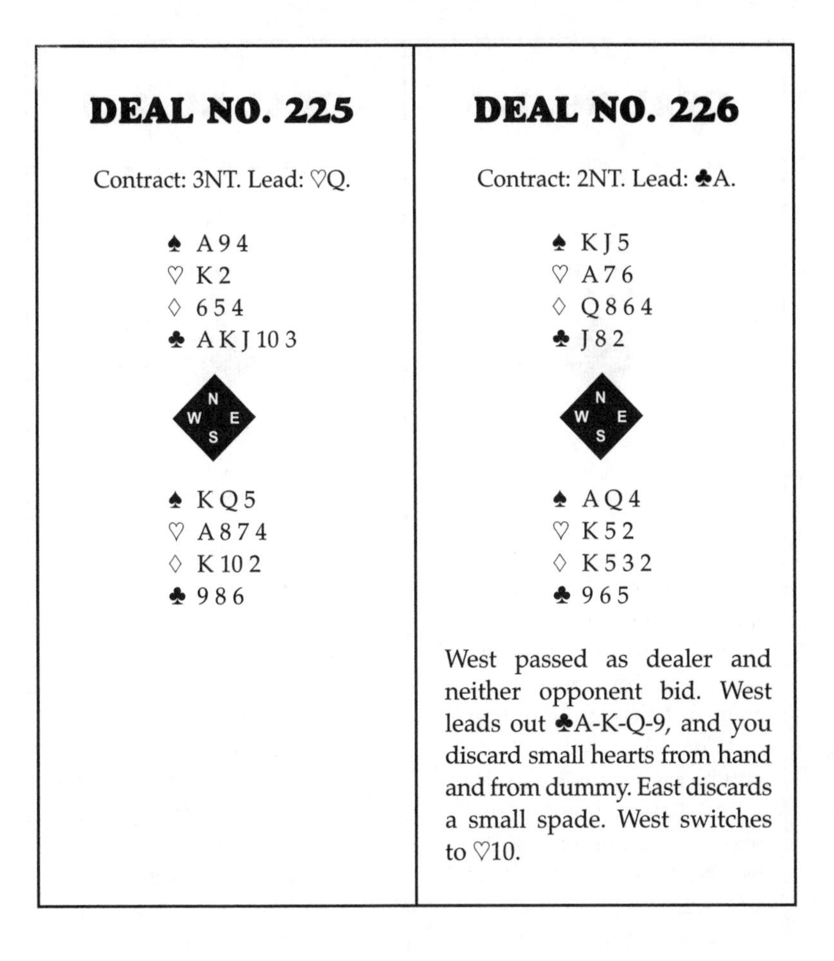

DEAL NO. 225

Contract: 3NT. Lead: ♡Q.

♠ A 9 4
♡ K 2
◊ 6 5 4
♣ A K J 10 3

♠ K Q 5
♡ A 8 7 4
◊ K 10 2
♣ 9 8 6

DEAL NO. 226

Contract: 2NT. Lead: ♣A.

♠ K J 5
♡ A 7 6
◊ Q 8 6 4
♣ J 8 2

♠ A Q 4
♡ K 5 2
◊ K 5 3 2
♣ 9 6 5

West passed as dealer and neither opponent bid. West leads out ♣A-K-Q-9, and you discard small hearts from hand and from dummy. East discards a small spade. West switches to ♡10.

DEAL NO. 225

Contract: 3NT. Lead: ♡Q.

The whole point of this deal is to demonstrate that K-10-x is a surprisingly strong stop. You might think that you should refuse the club finesse to try to prevent East getting in to lead a diamond . . . but in fact the contract is secure. If East leads a low diamond, you play ◊10 and your remaining ◊K-2 acts as a stop with West on lead. If East leads ◊J (or ◊Q), you play ◊K. West will win with ◊A but your remaining ◊10-2 now acts as a stop. So on this deal you can make the normal play of finessing clubs, and make the contract even though it loses. Remember: K-10-x is robust enough to be led through once. Anything weaker – even K-9-x – is not.

DEAL NO. 226

Contract: 2NT. Lead: ♣A.

You can take three spades and two hearts and must therefore make three diamonds. To put it another way, you can afford to lose only one diamond – the ace. First you must work out who is more likely to hold ◊A. Here it is East, since West has already played ♣A-K-Q but passed as opener. Lead a low diamond to your king, which should hold. Then play a low diamond from both hands, hoping that East has to play ◊A. As you can see, your wish comes true and you later cash ◊Q-8 to make the contract.

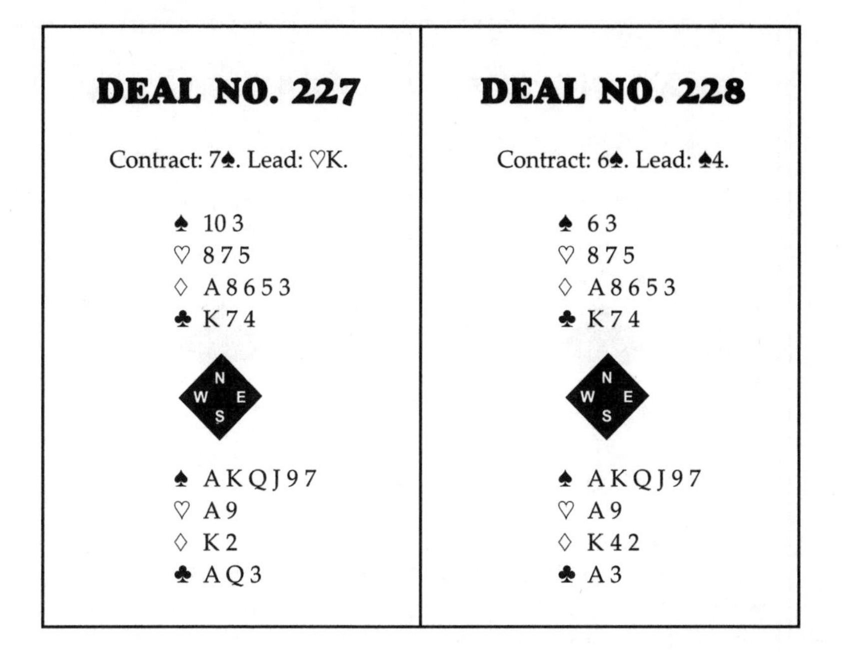
DEAL NO. 227
Contract: 7♠. Lead: ♡K.
♠ 10 3
♡ 8 7 5
◊ A 8 6 5 3
♣ K 7 4
N
W E
S
♠ A K Q J 9 7
♡ A 9
◊ K 2
♣ A Q 3
DEAL NO. 228
Contract: 6♠. Lead: ♠4.
♠ 6 3
♡ 8 7 5
◊ A 8 6 5 3
♣ K 7 4
N
W E
S
♠ A K Q J 9 7
♡ A 9
◊ K 4 2
♣ A 3

DEAL NO. 227

Contract: 7♠. Lead: ♡K.

You have reached an excellent grand slam but there does seem to be a potential heart loser. Can you see how to get rid of it? If you could *discard* your losing heart, that would do the trick and dummy's diamonds look promising. But you have to be careful in case the suit breaks 4-2. Play ◊K-A-3 to the next three tricks, ruffing high in hand. If the suit breaks 3-3 that would make things easy but in reality there is still likely to be a master diamond in one defender's hand. If so re-enter dummy *with ♠10* and ruff another diamond high. Now draw trumps, cross to dummy with a club and then discard your low heart on the last remaining diamond.

DEAL NO. 228

Contract: 6♠. Lead: ♠4.

North: ♠ 6 3 ♡ 8 7 5 ◊ A 8 6 5 3 ♣ K 7 4

West: ♠ 4 2 ♡ K 10 6 2 ◊ Q J 9 7 ♣ Q 10 2

East: ♠ 10 8 5 ♡ Q J 4 3 ◊ 10 ♣ J 9 8 6 5

South: ♠ A K Q J 9 7 ♡ A 9 ◊ K 4 2 ♣ A 3

A heart lead would have proved disastrous but as it is you have been given some breathing space. You need to set up a diamond winner in dummy for a discard but you cannot afford to be casual. Suppose you draw trumps and then play ◊K-A-5. That would be fine if diamonds broke 3-2, but what about a 4-1 split? You can enter dummy with a club and ruff out the last diamond but you will have no route back to table. The answer is to draw trumps *and then duck a diamond from both hand and dummy.* You win the return in hand and now play ◊K-A-6, ruffing if you need to. And you still have that precious club entry to let you enjoy the last remaining diamond.

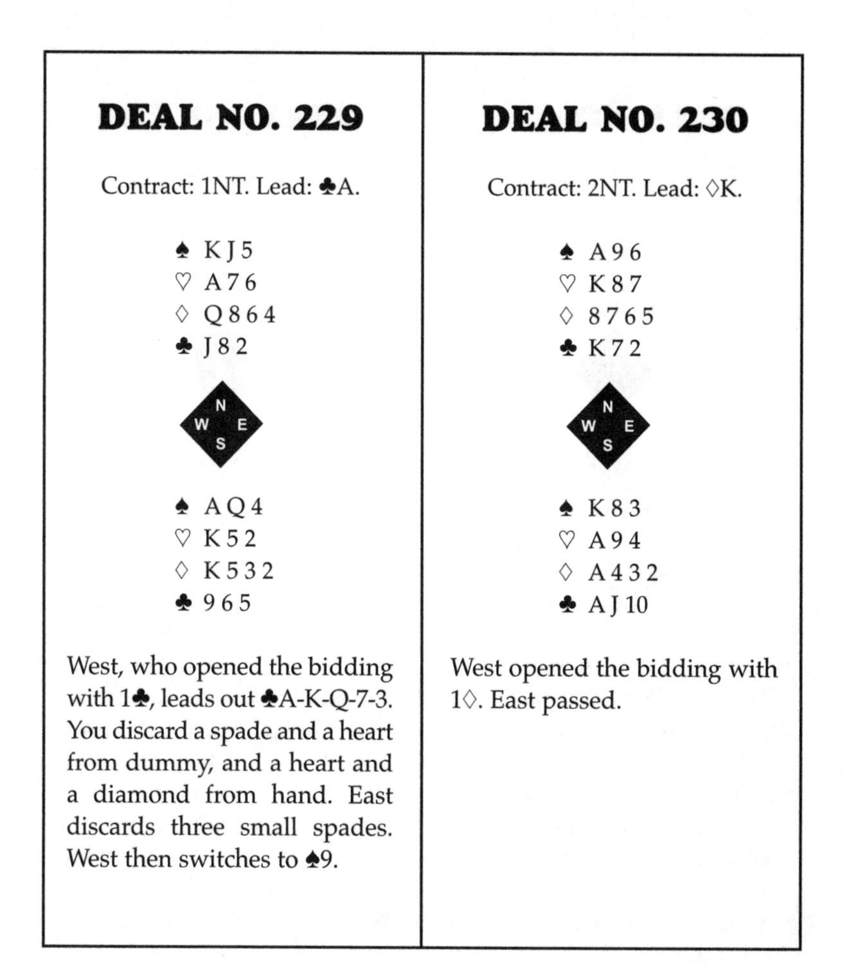

DEAL NO. 229

Contract: 1NT. Lead: ♣A.

♠ K J 5
♡ A 7 6
♢ Q 8 6 4
♣ J 8 2

N / W E / S

♠ A Q 4
♡ K 5 2
♢ K 5 3 2
♣ 9 6 5

West, who opened the bidding with 1♣, leads out ♣A-K-Q-7-3. You discard a spade and a heart from dummy, and a heart and a diamond from hand. East discards three small spades. West then switches to ♠9.

DEAL NO. 230

Contract: 2NT. Lead: ♢K.

♠ A 9 6
♡ K 8 7
♢ 8 7 6 5
♣ K 7 2

N / W E / S

♠ K 8 3
♡ A 9 4
♢ A 4 3 2
♣ A J 10

West opened the bidding with 1♢. East passed.

DEAL NO. 229

Contract: 1NT. Lead: ♣A.

This is similar to *Deal 226*. This time West has cashed five clubs so you can afford to lose only one more trick – to ◊A. Because West opened the bidding, he is far more likely to hold ◊A, so your best play is to lead up to dummy's ◊Q and, assuming this holds, follow up by playing a low diamond from both hands. As the cards lie, West is obliged to waste his ◊A on this trick, so you can duly cash ◊K and ◊8 for your contract.

DEAL NO. 230

Contract: 2NT. Lead: ◊K.

North: ♠ A 9 6 ♡ K 8 7 ◊ 8 7 6 5 ♣ K 7 2

West: ♠ Q J 7 ♡ Q J ◊ K Q J 10 9 ♣ Q 8 5

East: ♠ 10 5 4 2 ♡ 10 6 5 3 2 ◊ — ♣ 9 6 4 3

South: ♠ K 8 3 ♡ A 9 4 ◊ A 4 3 2 ♣ A J 10

You plan to take two spades, two hearts and a diamond – and therefore need three clubs. Normally you might as well flip a coin to decide who holds the missing ♣Q, but on this deal West almost certainly has it to justify his opening bid. Just cash ♣A and play ♣J for a finesse. If West covers with ♣Q you win with dummy's ♣K and your ♣10 is good for a trick. If he doesn't cover, then your ♣J wins instead.

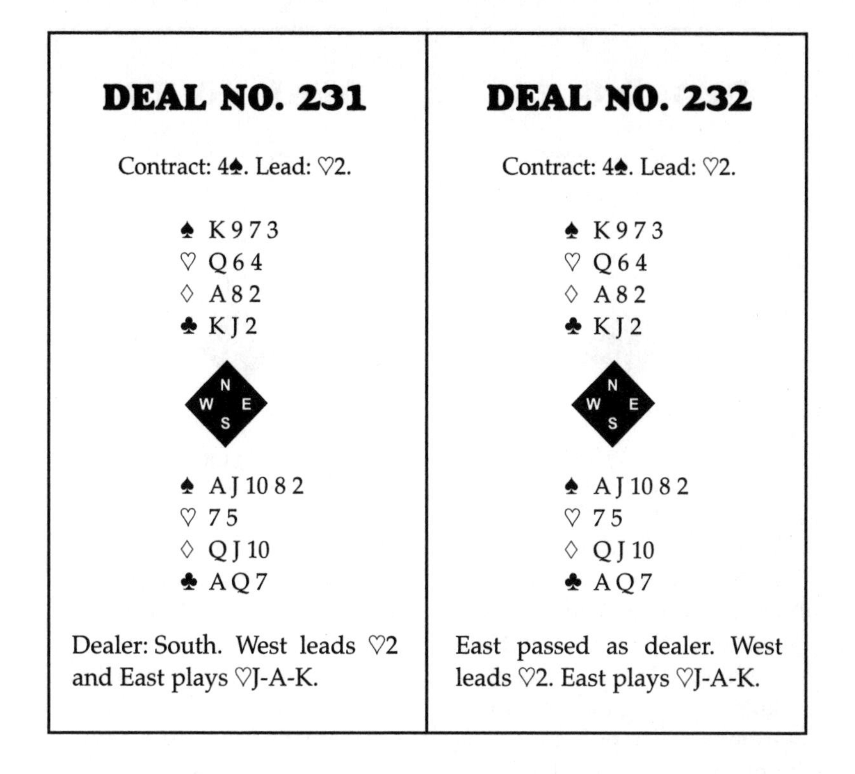

DEAL NO. 231

Contract: 4♠. Lead: ♡2.

♠ K 9 7 3
♡ Q 6 4
♢ A 8 2
♣ K J 2

N / W E / S

♠ A J 10 8 2
♡ 7 5
♢ Q J 10
♣ A Q 7

Dealer: South. West leads ♡2 and East plays ♡J-A-K.

DEAL NO. 232

Contract: 4♠. Lead: ♡2.

♠ K 9 7 3
♡ Q 6 4
♢ A 8 2
♣ K J 2

N / W E / S

♠ A J 10 8 2
♡ 7 5
♢ Q J 10
♣ A Q 7

East passed as dealer. West leads ♡2. East plays ♡J-A-K.

DEAL NO. 231

Contract: 4♠. Lead: ♡2.

This is a straightforward hand in that your objectives are clear – if the diamond finesse fails you have to try to not lose a trump. The odds slightly favour playing for the drop in trumps, i.e. hoping the queen will fall either doubleton or singleton, but even if you find you do have a trump loser you can always hope the diamond finesse is working.

DEAL NO. 232

Contract: 4♠. Lead: ♡2.

North: ♠ K 9 7 3 ♡ Q 6 4 ◇ A 8 2 ♣ K J 2

West: ♠ Q 5 4 ♡ 10 8 3 2 ◇ 9 5 4 ♣ 10 4 3

East: ♠ 6 ♡ A K J 9 ◇ K 7 6 3 ♣ 9 8 6 5

South: ♠ A J 10 8 2 ♡ 7 5 ◇ Q J 10 ♣ A Q 7

What's this? Same deal, same contract and same lead as the preceding hand? Not quite. Here East passed as dealer, which strangely enough makes the contract almost cast-iron! Look at it this way: the contract is only ever in jeopardy if the diamond finesse is losing, but East cannot possibly hold both ◇K and ♠Q because that would give him 13 points – and he passed as dealer. So ruff ♡K, cash ♠A if you like, and then lead ♠J, running it if West plays low. Should it lose to East, you can be confident that the diamond finesse is working.

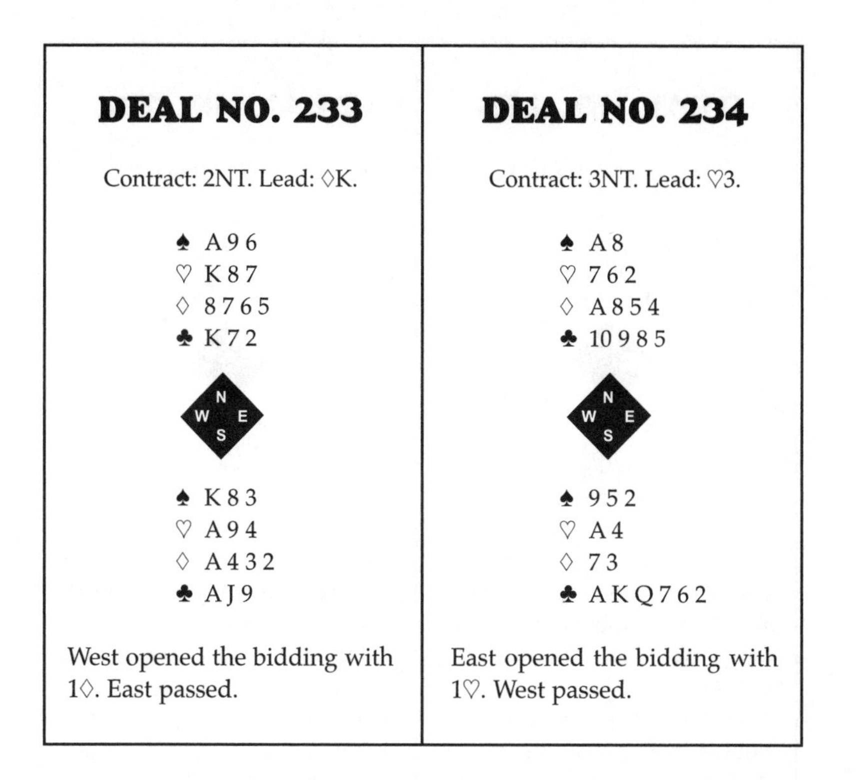

DEAL NO. 233

Contract: 2NT. Lead: ♢K.

♠ A 9 6
♡ K 8 7
♢ 8 7 6 5
♣ K 7 2

♠ K 8 3
♡ A 9 4
♢ A 4 3 2
♣ A J 9

West opened the bidding with 1♢. East passed.

DEAL NO. 234

Contract: 3NT. Lead: ♡3.

♠ A 8
♡ 7 6 2
♢ A 8 5 4
♣ 10 9 8 5

♠ 9 5 2
♡ A 4
♢ 7 3
♣ A K Q 7 6 2

East opened the bidding with 1♡. West passed.

DEAL NO. 233

Contract: 2NT. Lead: ♢K.

This is similar to *Deal 230* except that you no longer hold ♣10 so the club finesse is no longer available. But all is not yet lost. Do you remember *Deal 160?* West must surely hold ♣Q, but East may hold ♣10. So win ♢A, play ♣J to West's ♣Q and dummy's ♣K, then cross your fingers, and finesse ♣9 on the way back. This is a straightforward 50% shot, much better odds than trying to drop ♣Q in two rounds.

DEAL NO. 234

Contract: 3NT. Lead: ♡3.

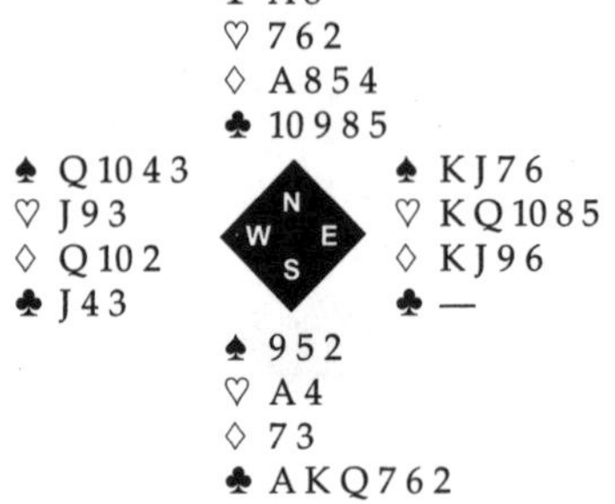

This is a real hand taken from the 2003 Malta Bridge Festival. You appear to have nine top tricks in the shape of six clubs and three outside aces. So you have, but only if you remember to play dummy's ♣10-9-8 on your ♣A-K-Q. Otherwise the fourth club has to be taken in dummy and there is no way back to hand (remember, the defence knocked out ♡A at Trick 1). Fortunately one of the present authors remembered his own words of wisdom and unblocked the clubs to make the contract. That is the point of this deal, and the fact that East opened the bidding is really immaterial.

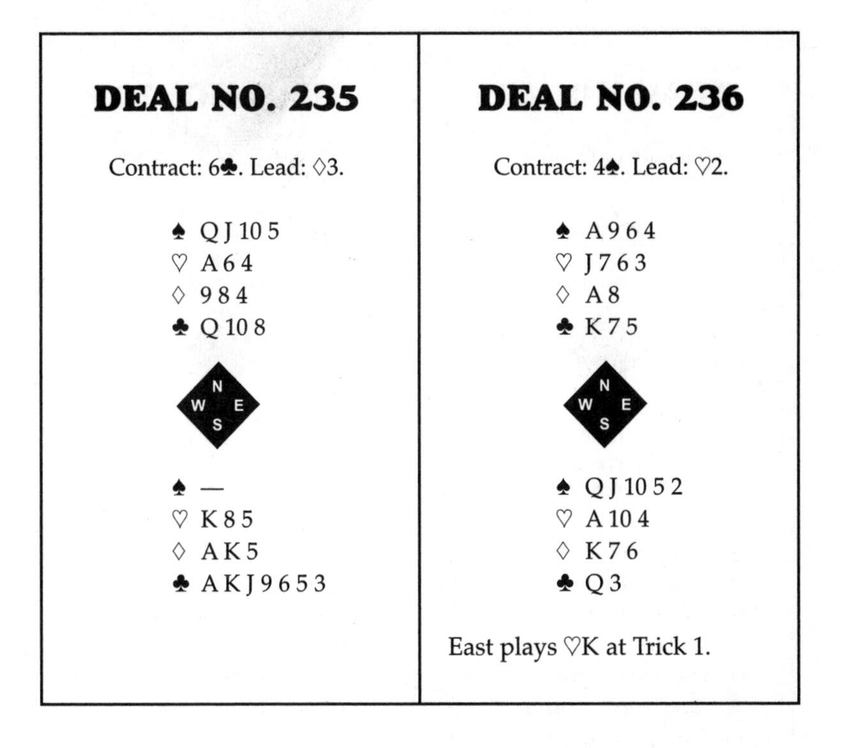

DEAL NO. 235

Contract: 6♣. Lead: ♢3.

♠ Q J 10 5
♡ A 6 4
♢ 9 8 4
♣ Q 10 8

♠ —
♡ K 8 5
♢ A K 5
♣ A K J 9 6 5 3

DEAL NO. 236

Contract: 4♠. Lead: ♡2.

♠ A 9 6 4
♡ J 7 6 3
♢ A 8
♣ K 7 5

♠ Q J 10 5 2
♡ A 10 4
♢ K 7 6
♣ Q 3

East plays ♡K at Trick 1.

DEAL NO. 235

Contract: 6♣. Lead: ◊3.

It looks at first sight as if you must lose a trick in both red suits but dummy's spades can be put to good use. Play ♣A-3, and then lead ♠Q from dummy. If East covers, you ruff, re-enter dummy with a trump and lead ♠J, throwing a low red card if East plays low. You might lose a trick to West but you will have a spade winner in dummy to take care of your other red loser. If East plays low on ♠Q you throw a red loser, win the return and enter dummy to lead ♠J, discarding if East plays low or ruffing if he covers. You will only fail in your contract if West has both ♠A and ♠K.

DEAL NO. 236

Contract: 4♠. Lead: ♡2.

The lead has cut down your heart losers to just one if you play low from dummy, but it does present another sort of threat. From the lead and play it looks as though West started with four hearts headed by the queen, which means that East started with a doubleton. So what will happen if you take the trump finesse and it loses? East will lead his remaining heart, West will win with the queen and give his partner a ruff – and ♣A will prove the setting trick. It must be right to trust your deductions and play ace and another trump after winning ♡A so as to minimise this risk.

WARNING: the last four hands of this book are a little more advanced than anything that has gone previously. We do this deliberately in the hope that you will become inspired to learn more about this wonderfully frustrating game. . . and there are plenty of books, teachers and clubs out there to help you do so.

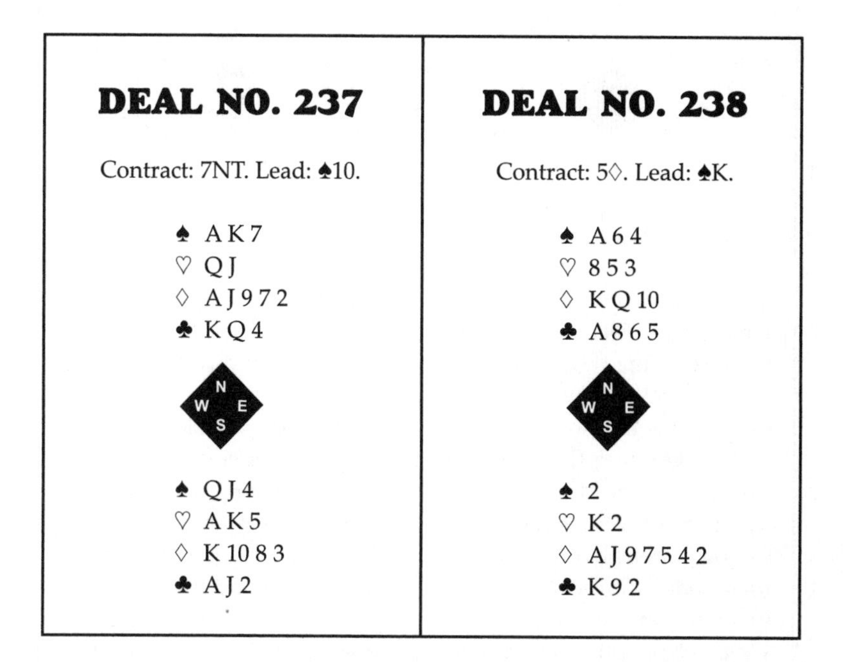

DEAL NO. 237

Contract: 7NT. Lead: ♠10.

You have 38 points in the two hands, but 7NT is not cold because, come what may, you have to guess the whereabouts of ◇Q. Having won Trick 1, you could either finesse ◇J, or finesse ◇10, or cash ◇A-K in the hope that the suit breaks 2-2, or . . . refrain from playing diamonds until you know a bit more about the hand. Cash your other top spades, and learn that the outstanding spades were 5-2. Cash the top hearts – they were 2-6. Cash the top clubs – they were 2-5. Do some arithmetic. West had five spades, two hearts and two clubs – hence four diamonds. Alternatively, East had two spades, six hearts and five clubs – hence no diamonds. Triumphantly cash ◇K and finesse against West's queen to make the contract.

DEAL NO. 238

Contract: 5◇. Lead: ♠K..

With ten tricks available it is not clear where the eleventh will come from. The ♡K will be a winner if East has ♡A but you will have two losers in that suit otherwise. Clubs might break 3-3 giving you one more trick, but the danger is that East might be able to win the third round and fire through a heart. The answer is difficult to see because it goes against what is 'natural'. Simply duck ♠K! Whatever West does now, you can discard a club on ♠A, draw trumps and play ♣K-A and ruff a club. If they break 3-3 you have your extra trick, and if they don't you can still lead up to ♡K. Dummy can be reached via the third diamond.

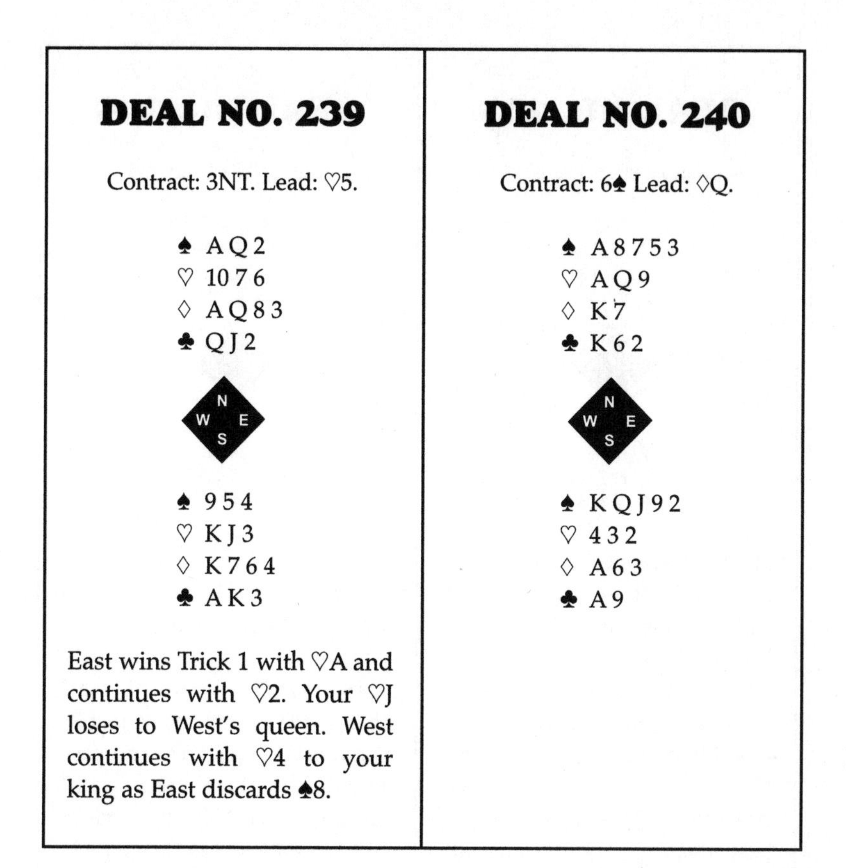

DEAL NO. 239

Contract: 3NT. Lead: ♡5.

♠ A Q 2
♡ 10 7 6
♢ A Q 8 3
♣ Q J 2

N / W E / S

♠ 9 5 4
♡ K J 3
♢ K 7 6 4
♣ A K 3

East wins Trick 1 with ♡A and continues with ♡2. Your ♡J loses to West's queen. West continues with ♡4 to your king as East discards ♠8.

DEAL NO. 240

Contract: 6♠ Lead: ♢Q.

♠ A 8 7 5 3
♡ A Q 9
♢ K 7
♣ K 6 2

N / W E / S

♠ K Q J 9 2
♡ 4 3 2
♢ A 6 3
♣ A 9

DEAL NO. 239

Contract: 3NT. Lead: ♡5.

Hearts have not gone kindly for you, but you will be all right if diamonds break 3-2. Full of hope you cash ◊A-K, but alas West shows out on the second round, which means East has a sure diamond trick. What now? You could try finessing ♠Q but that is only a 50% chance. Try cashing all the top clubs and then playing ◊Q and your last diamond to East's jack. What can East do? He may have a club to cash, but then he will be forced to lead a spade round to dummy's ♠A-Q, allowing you to make the contract wherever ♠K is. Such clever ploys are called 'end-plays', and there have been entire books written about them.

DEAL NO. 240

Contract: 6♠ Lead: ◊Q.

End-plays can occur in suit contracts too! Despite the two possible losers in hearts, this contract is 100% guaranteed. Win ◊K, draw trumps, and then play ◊A and ruff your last diamond. Repeat the process in clubs by playing ♣A-K and ruffing dummy's low club. *Now lead a low heart and simply cover whatever West plays.* A bemused East can win, but what can he do? If he leads a heart, it is up to dummy's tenace, while a minor suit lead allows you to ruff in one hand and throw a losing heart from the other. If you experiment with a pack of cards, you will find that this works however hearts are placed in the East-West hand.